Routledge Revivals

Roman Poetry

Originally published in 1923, this study outlines the aims and methods of Roman poets as well as focussing on technique and subject. Sikes' critique of the subject delves into the general character of Roman poetry with the belief that it provides an insight into Roman life and ideals by commenting on various theories, criticisms and themes found in Roman poetry. This title will be of interest to students of classics.

Roman Poetry

E. E. Sikes

Routledge
Taylor & Francis Group
ROUTLEDGE REVIVALS

First published in 1923
By Methuen & Co. Ltd

This edition first published in 2016 by Routledge
2 Park Square, Milton Park, Abingdon, Oxon, OX14 4RN
and by Routledge
711 Third Avenue, New York, NY 10017

Routledge is an imprint of the Taylor & Francis Group, an informa business

Publisher's Note
The publisher has gone to great lengths to ensure the quality of this reprint but points out that some imperfections in the original copies may be apparent.

Disclaimer
The publisher has made every effort to trace copyright holders and welcomes correspondence from those they have been unable to contact.

A Library of Congress record exists under LC control number: 23018649

ISBN 13: 978-1-138-64324-6 (hbk)
ISBN 13: 978-1-315-62945-2 (ebk)
ISBN 13: 978-1-138-64325-3 (pbk)

ROMAN POETRY

BY

E. E. SIKES, M.A.

FELLOW AND TUTOR OF ST. JOHN'S COLLEGE, CAMBRIDGE

METHUEN & CO. LTD.
36 ESSEX STREET W.C.
LONDON

First Published in 1923

PRINTED IN GREAT BRITAIN

PREFACE

THIS book is intended to supplement rather than to rival the modern histories of Latin literature, although I hope that, within its limits, it may give some idea of the aims and methods of Roman poets to those who have made little or no study of the subject. Sainte-Beuve has taught us to concentrate on a poet's personality, and our scanty knowledge of Virgil and Horace and still scantier conjectures about Lucretius and Catullus are the common property of existing histories. My own object is to emphasize the general character of Latin poetry—to show (without, I trust, falling into the error of Taine's exploded method) the place of the poet as the interpreter of Roman life. I have therefore tried in the first place to indicate the general conception of poetry, as handed down by the Greek critics and modified by the Romans; and, secondly, to illustrate their theories by their actual practice, both in the choice of subjects and in technique. In regard to the subjects, I have chosen two of the greatest—the poetic treatment of Nature and Philosophy; in technique, I have confined myself to the language and ornamental style, as metrical questions are apt to be over-technical for a work of this character.

Some of the statements in the following pages will no doubt seem a little obvious to professional critics; but long experience as a teacher has led me to observe that many students of the Classics are badly equipped with even elementary notions of modern criticism. It may be thought waste of time and ink to warn the reader, for instance, that the Poet is not (primarily) a Teacher; but there are still many, not otherwise ill-educated, who cling to this venerable idea.

The part of the book which has been most pleasant to write is an attempt to bring Latin poetry into direct relation with the English by verse translation. It is useless for a translator to explain his theory, but I may perhaps say that I have no particular or exclusive theory at all. Some Latin poets, like Lucan, belong to the eighteenth century, and must re-appear, if at all, in the dress of that age. Lucretius and Virgil ought to be at home in any century, not least in the twentieth. Horace, too, is dateless, at his best; but he, more than any other, cannot be translated at all; and in venturing to render one of his shortest odes, I must plead the familiar excuse, that the poem is "a very little one."

To my colleague, Mr. T. R. Glover, I owe much, in suggestion, correction, and encouragement.

Two versions (on pp. 83 and 198) have already appeared in the *Spectator* and *Saturday Westminster Gazette*, and I thank the Editors for permission to reprint. I hope no reader will misinterpret the fact that, for convenience, my own versions are printed in larger type than quotations from the poets. Virgil and Wordsworth do not need typographical embellishment.

E. E. S.

ST. JOHN'S COLLEGE, CAMBRIDGE,
March, 1923

CONTENTS

ROMAN POETRY

CHAPTER I

INTRODUCTION

I

IN recent years, the aims and ideals of Poetry have moved so far from the Classical spirit, that, in passing from the study of an ancient poem—an ode of Horace or an eclogue of Virgil—to almost any poem of the twentieth century, we are conscious of a difference not merely of degree but of kind. The present generation has, in fact, to make an effort unknown to its predecessors, if it is to obtain from Roman poetry a satisfaction, equal, or at least comparable, to the enjoyment which it obtains from the imagination of its own age. The eighteenth century found no such difficulty in adjustment. Educated in a Roman rather than a Greek tradition, it regarded Latin literature as its own inheritance. Horace was nearer, more akin, more sympathetic, than Chaucer or even Spenser. His verses were on the lips of every English gentleman, not merely because familiarity with the Classics was the sign of good breeding, but because English culture was in a real sense Horatian. Poetry obeyed the laws of the *Ars Poetica;* society affected the note of ease and simple refinement which pervades the *Epistles* and *Odes;* and Addison had been called not only the interpreter but the re-embodiment of Horace.[1] Even after the Romantic

[1] C. Goad, *Horace in English Lit. of the 18th Cent.* (*Yale Studies in English*), 1916. *Introd.*

movement, the early nineteenth century could pass, backwards and forwards, from Latin to English literature without a sense of discontinuity. Although the splendid poetic outburst from Wordsworth to Tennyson so greatly extended the Roman and even the Greek vision of poetry, yet the classic spirit, in its broadest sense, was still dominant. Landor, Tennyson, and Arnold are largely Græco-Roman; and the impulse which drove poets like Swinburne beyond the Romans to the fountain-head of Greece was itself Roman.

This Græco-Roman mode, strong and vigorous in its own day, is now outworn, and modern poetry has moved away from the fashion which we may conveniently describe as Tennysonian. Although, of course, Victorian poetry is far wider than Tennyson—we have only to think of Browning or Meredith—the Laureate undoubtedly struck the characteristic note of the Victorian age; and (whether rightly or wrongly) the modern criticism of that age is often centred on a single representative. Tennyson—at his best—is too great to be permanently obscured; but he has been at least for a time eclipsed, and our present poets seem resolved to abjure all traces of his influence. But Tennyson, both in form and spirit, was a Virgilian; and, if our sympathy with an English Virgil has declined, we may be even less sympathetic with his master, who, after all, is far more remote in time, and race, and civilization.

As a matter of fact, it is probably true—though a seeming paradox—that the Roman poets are, in certain aspects, nearer to us than the Victorians, who are for the moment suffering the inevitable nemesis of a long and undisputed supremacy. The reaction is no mere matter of fashion, though fashions in literature are as capricious as in dress. Poetry, if it is to be vital, must change, at least in form and presentation, and it changes by a revolt from the immediate past. There is no such revolt against the older tradition of those on whom the secure world has long since passed judgment. We can better appreciate the art of Horace or Virgil than that of their modern followers, because we see the ancients in a clearer light, undimmed by disturbing comparisons.

But this is not all. We have not only a truer perspective of Latin in relation to English, but—which is as important—of Latin in relation to Greek. The most serious hindrance to the study of Virgil and other Roman poets lay in the belief that their art was merely derivative—that they added little or nothing to the poetic legacy of the Greeks. They were not "original". Their metre, their forms, their spirit were all thought to be second-hand. It was forgotten that, judged by this narrow definition of "originality", English poetry itself would be found wanting. In England, as at Rome, an earlier metrical system struggled with a foreign rival and succumbed. Apart from metre, the whole course of poetry, from Chaucer onwards, bears witness to Italian and French influence. Wyatt and Surrey "borrow" from Petrarch, Spenser from Ariosto, Milton and Dryden from the very Roman originals whose originality has so often been denied. There is of course some reason for the charge. As we shall see in more detail, the Latin poets themselves were painfully conscious of their debt to Greece, and gave too little credit to their own genius. They were content—and proud—to "imitate".

The doctrine of "imitation", in its narrow sense, has long ceased to be operative in the theory or practice of letters. A modern poet does not try to "rival" a predecessor, though he may acknowledge a Chaucer or a Keats as his "master". More often, like Keats himself, he seeks to divert his Muse, if she seems to follow too closely some great original. But, in a wider sense, the problem of imitation is still momentous; for the principle underlying it is tradition. And tradition itself, which, since the dawn of literature, has reigned undisputed, is now being assailed.

It is claimed for poetry, as for other arts, that new intuitions require new forms of expression.

Now it is one thing to argue that a poet must not re-echo his predecessors; it is quite a different thing to require that he must entirely cut adrift from all that is traditional, in form or spirit. He is linked with tradition by bonds which cannot be broken without danger to his very existence. Poetry, it may be replied, is emotional, and since our emotions are of the present, it must live in the present. No doubt; but our emotions do not merely reflect the present—they are often evoked by memories of the past or anticipations of the future. The human race is continuous; so that, if poetry is to maintain its place as one of the permanent records of human emotion, instead of being a fugitive and journalistic expression of the passing hour, the poet must be in the succession. He should not, indeed, misconstrue the motto *stare super antiquas vias*, for poetry cannot retrace the tracks of the past; but he must not wholly desert the ancient ways. Human life is the sum-total of the experience slowly gained by the process of the years, and, so far as the poet is an interpreter of life, he cannot dissociate himself from past experience. But—it may be objected—the human race does not move in a smooth and regular progression, being liable, from time to time, to shocks and violent upheavals which—to borrow a metaphor from biology—produce discontinuous variations. The breakdown of the Roman Empire, the French Revolution, the European War, the rise of Bolshevism—these are only a few of the great world-movements which have shaken humanity to its foundations; and it will be said that poetry cannot be forced, like a Galileo, to deny such movements. This argument neglects the fact that poetry is neither history nor politics; its province is emotional and imaginative, and human emotions have not changed since the wrath of Achilles and the sack of Troy. Of course both experience and imagination have widened, so that the modern poet's intuitions cannot be expressed in the manner of the *Iliad*. The process of the years may give poetry its increasing purpose; but the bed-rock of inspiration must always be the same, whatever changes History may work above the surface. Even the changes of History itself may well be exaggerated in their bearing on the subject and treatment of poetry. The French Revolution—to mention the only recent shock whose effects can, as yet, be fully estimated—did not disorganize literature as it certainly disorganized society. There was no real break between Rousseau and Victor Hugo, between the prophet and the recorder of revolution.

But, granted the advantage of literary tradition, it may still be held that its dangers outweigh its use. There is a common argument that tradition stifles originality; and no doubt a lack of originality is most easily detected when there is an obvious model to which the "imitation" adds little or nothing of its own. This sort of imitation, however, is not true *mimesis*; it is *furtum*, plagiarism. On the other hand, there can be no question that real originality is best seen in a traditional setting. It may be difficult *proprie communia dicere*; but herein lies the opportunity for genius.

Again, there is a frequent misunderstanding of tradition, as if it must needs be narrowly continuous. Certainly, if poets, in unbroken succession, work on the same vein, with the same tools, the vein will sooner or later be exhausted. Latin poetry, as a fact, did so perish. But tradition does not actually move in a straight and uninterrupted line. It may skip a generation, or ten generations, or ten centuries. The Renascence is an example on the biggest scale of all, where a whole literature, in several languages, returned, after a great interval, to the Greek and Roman models. To recognize the same process in minuter detail, we have only to look at the history of Chaucer's rhyming decasyllable, which so nearly perished from its own brilliancy in the

Popian couplets, but revived in the hands of Keats and Morris, and has gained new vigour in our own day. Or we might take the pastoral, which, after a long history from Theocritus to Mantuanus and Sannazaro, from Spenser to Phineas Fletcher and Milton, seemed at last to have withered, but yet blossomed with the fresh flowers of *Adonais* and *Thyrsis*.

The question is urgent in a study of Roman poetry, for no people, in literature or political thought, has ever laid more stress on the value of tradition; and it is impossible to sympathize with the aims of Latin poets unless we are prepared to place ourselves at their angle of vision. The Romans themselves had no need to argue the point, which to them was self-evident, since Greek was the only form of literature they knew, and seemed the only possible form. The ancient poetry of India and Babylon and Persia, the Egyptian *Book of the Dead*, were all unknown and unsuspected. By the middle of the first century B.C., there were, indeed, rumours (permeating through Philo from Alexandria) of a people conquered by Pompey, whose writings described the creation of the world by a tribal god not even dignified by a statue; but, until Longinus—here, as so often, in advance of his age—had pointed out that "the legislator of the Jews, no ordinary man," could write sublimely, the Hebrew Scriptures were quite outside the Roman horizon.[1] As late as the Augustans, literature—in any real sense of the word—was identified with Greece. Their former rivals, the Carthaginians, were no less illiterate than their contemporaries—Parthians and Moors, Germans and Gauls and Spaniards, whose highest poetic flight was a war-song, rude and unpolished like the Saturnian verse, which the Romans had rejected in disgust, as Athena had thrown down the pipe of Marsyas. The Romans, therefore, had only the alterna-

[1] Long. *de subl.* 9, 9; see Roberts, p. 231 f. The earliest possible date of "Longinus" is the first century A.D. For Virgil's supposed debt to Isaiah see p. 249.

tive between following barbarians or following Greece. To us, the problem is not so simple, for we know that Greece has now no monopoly, though she may have primacy, and that neither wisdom nor poetry perished with her. We are told that

> There are nine and sixty ways of constructing tribal lays,

and we are quite willing to believe that every single one of them may be right. But, for the Romans, there was only one way—the Hellenic tradition—and here they builded better than they knew. They felt instinctively that tradition was a good thing, but they could only justify their faith by bad arguments. Their greatest poets claimed to be original by the mere fact of imitation (which, in itself, is the negative of originality), whereas they might have justly claimed to have used their models not as an end, but as a means of expressing their own intuitions. Criticism—helped, no doubt, by the analogy of biological science—has now learnt that we must substitute for the mechanic the organic view of poetry, which is a living thing, endowed with the power of absorbing the past and recreating it with the new vitality of its own organism.

It is commonly said that a poet—whether he is to be classed as traditional or not—is "original" for one merit alone: his poems must express his own personality. So far, there is no dispute; only we must be clear about the meaning of personality. A man is individual by reason of very complex characters—to his immediate inheritance, derived from his own ancestors, there must be added the nature of his race, of his environment, and of his society. I shall be told that this argument is quite out of date—that Taine has long been discredited. It is quite true—as I shall have occasion to admit in another place—that Taine's theories were pushed too far: no environment can produce a genius to order. Nevertheless, racial and social influences are all-powerful in directing the flow of genius into particular channels, and it is precisely here that Roman poets pass the test of originality. Borrowing their materials freely and even lavishly, they built a Roman edifice, often less beautiful, perhaps, than its Greek original, but significant of their own character. Lucretius drew his philosophy from Epicurus, the idea of his poem from Empedocles; but the *De Rerum Natura* is a great original work, not only instinct with the fire of the poet's personality, but a real expression of Roman thought and emotion. Catullus, on the mechanical theory a mere Alexandrine, lives his own intense life of passion, as though Callimachus had never been born. Virgil's borrowing—I shall deal with it later—was so patent as to be a stumbling-block even in his own day; and, after his second age of triumph at the Renascence, the charge was revived in the early nineteenth century, when the new impetus of Greek studies led to a depreciation of Roman epic. Coleridge—it will be remembered—the greatest, if not the sanest, of English critics, asked in his *Table Talk*, "If you take away from Virgil his diction and metre, what do you leave him?" It needed half a century before an answer could be given that Virgil is not the imitator or rival of Homer or Hesiod or Theocritus, but the Roman peer of the Italian Dante or the English Milton. If the Latin poets are not original, why do we read Lucretius rather than Epicurus, or Catullus rather than Callimachus? Why do we prefer Virgil to Hesiod or Aratus or even Apollonius?[1]

II

In presenting the case for Latin poetry, it may be well to start with its drawbacks, and especially with those which are least shared by Greek poetry. To a modern reader, perhaps the most serious defect is the weakness of the lyrical impulse. A "lyric" has been variously defined;

[1] On the general question see F. Leo, *Die Originalität der röm. Litt.* (1904), and below, p. 71 f.

but, whether we understand it in its original Greek sense as a poem sung by a single voice or a chorus, to the lyre, or extend the definition to any short poem which gives "perfect expression to a mood of the highest imaginative intensity,"[1] we must admit that Latin poetry does not often satisfy the definition. The Romans realized this weakness and even overstated it, for Quintilian was unduly modest in his remark that "Horace is about the only lyric poet of Rome." It may seem astonishing that he should have said no word, in this connexion, of Catullus, one of the great names in the whole history of lyric; but in Quintilian's formal criticism, Catullus was ranked as a writer of lampoon and epigram, and is therefore technically excluded from the lyrical canon, although his best work is as lyrical in spirit as the love-songs of Sappho or Ronsard or Herrick.[2] Like all Roman poets, Catullus could be witty and reasonable, in an age when wit and reason were —or were soon to become—the hall-marks of poetry; but, unlike most, he was above all things guided by his emotions, either in love or hate; and it is such stuff that lyric dreams are made on. Even in Quintilian's own day, the lyric spirit made a fitful appearance in Latin poetry. Statius felt, at least once, its breath, when he was inspired to write a poem to Sleep, which was quite as much a lyric as anything that Horace ever wrote.[3] But the Romans rarely moved with freedom in lyrical expression—Statius himself disguised his song by using hexameters, the proper vehicle for an epic poem. We are forced, in the end, to agree with Quintilian. Whether we widen or limit our definition of lyric, the fact remains that the Roman poets rarely *sing*. They speak, recite, or even chant; but they do not commonly break out into that ecstasy of emotion which

[1] J. Drinkwater, *Lyric*, p. 20.

[2] Quintilian, 10, 96. His lampoons on Caesar rankled, even if Julius and Augustus ignored them. Tacitus, *Annals*, 4, 34.

[3] Translated on p. 87.

seems to demand music as its medium. Horace himself, though he never lacks the "perfect expression," seldom rises to the "imaginative intensity." He has no burning moments, no absorbing passion, no thrill of rapture when desire is gratified, no spasm of torture in frustrated hopes. His equal Muse is strange alike to the highest joys and the deepest despair.

Is this deficiency of the lyrical impulse due to the Race or the Civilization? If we lay stress on the (real or supposed) character of the Roman as unimaginative, oppressed by the sense of fact, bringing his poetry to answer at the bar of Reason, we may well suppose that such a character is not likely to produce the passionate cry of a Sappho or the melodious ecstasy of a Shelley. But, if the "typical" Roman or Latin is really to be regarded as unlyrical, we must remember that his poetry was largely written for him, by poets who were not Latin at all.[1] Yet there was no second Catullus, nor even a second Horace, among all these Latinized peoples, some of whom—as the Celtic—have been famous for their imagination in other days.

Clearly, therefore, we must look to the environment for at least a partial and negative explanation. Here there is an obvious analogy in the decay of the lyrical spirit during the greater part of the eighteenth century, both in France and in England. The facts are well known and need not be repeated: it is sufficient to recall that there was no great lyrical output from Malherbe to Victor Hugo, or from Dryden to Burns.[2] Malherbe's Consolation of du Perrier ends the lyric of the Renascence no less than Horace's Consolation of Virgil is the last lyric cry of Rome. The causes of this decay have often been discussed, and are, indeed, fairly certain. An urban life, highly artificial

[1] See below, p. 16.

[2] This statement refers to the secular lyric of a century famous for the English hymns of Addison, the Wesleys, and Cowper, among many others.

and conventional, dominated by "good taste", shrinking from any form of eccentricity or excessive self-revelation, could not foster the intensity of personal emotion which overflows in lyrical utterance. The French Court and the English coffee-house were favourable to wit and polish, the give-and-take of a brilliant society; but they had no place for the *cri du coeur*. An individual was bound to suppress such emotions as could not be generalized and so brought within the sphere of the social feeling. He could not unduly parade his private life.

In this reticence, the English "Augustans" were partly following the direct lead of their Roman models, but in the main they were responding to a similar environment, for the age of Augustus—though many of its literary characteristics differed from those of the eighteenth century—was no less intent on repressing "enthusiasm" or self-revelation. This statement may seem in flat opposition to the "subjective" poetry of the elegiac writers, who are chiefly occupied with their own loves or (in Ovid's *Tristia*) their own misfortunes. But Propertius and Ovid were not in the least *lyrical:* they made no song of either their passion or their trouble; they may have felt deeply and truly, but their feeling was restrained by the Rules—the laws of refinement and breeding. The elegy must conform to the character of a Roman gentleman, who might be a profligate, but must never forget to be an artist. And since, for a Roman, art was typical rather than personal, the lover must speak as a typical lover, without emphasizing the individuality of his mistress or himself. Cynthia or Delia or Corinna is any mistress for any lover.

In recent times, there has been a strong current in favour of the Personal in art. If it is meant that the poet must express his own individuality, that he must feel what he sings, that he must inform his poems with his own character, that the style must indicate the man, we may agree that every poet does, and must, express his own personality.

But this obvious truth is often confused by the claim that a poet must be purely "subjective," that he must express his own intuitions, without regard to an audience, that only personal experience counts in the making of poetry. Whether disguised or openly revealed, the poem (it is argued) must be the historic record of a soul.[1] Shakespeare is to unlock his heart in the plays as well as in the sonnets; and the counter-theory—"if so, the less Shakespeare he"—is out of fashion. We are even told that Milton is seen as Man, as Archangel, as the Deity, and as Satan, which, as Sir Henry Newbolt rather naïvely remarks, is "truly a double personality."

The logical result of this theory may be observed in the present trend of poetry, in which the lyric, as the expression of a poet's experience, fills practically the whole field. Poetry tends to become autobiographic. The individual utterance (which of course is the one essential of poetry) has been interpreted to mean the revelation of the artist's personal and immediate experience. Horace is often "subjective," but he does not perhaps fully satisfy the modern demand, as he satisfied our grandfathers; and he has been (I think) displaced, at least for the moment, in favour of Sappho and Catullus. The mention of these two names is a proof—if proof were needed—that the Greeks and Romans could be individual enough; but it is certain that, at any rate for Rome, the Aristotelian theory of the Universal narrowed the expression of lyric. "What happened to Alcibiades" was a matter for the historian—the poet had a message for the state. Literature must be typical: the self-revelation of an individual must not run counter to the claims of society.

But we have not yet reached the conclusion of the whole matter. The classical preference for the type does not

[1] See e.g. Sir H. Newbolt, *New Study of English Poetry*, ch. 3. I do not of course deny that the theory is often true—Don Juan *is* Byron; but Mr. Pickwick is not Dickens: there is need of discrimination.

entirely explain the absence of the lyric. Great lyrics have often been purely typical—we think of *Sigh no more, ladies*, or *Take, O, take those lips away*, or of hundreds of other Elizabethan songs which cannot be confined to the particular. The chief cause of the difference is, surely, that Shakespeare (who could use Reason when it suited his poetry) could also subordinate Reason to pure feeling. But, whereas the true lyric demands that the emotions must be supreme, the Latin scheme of poetry required that all feeling must be tested by the intellect. It is significant that the theme of Love—the most emotional of all subjects—should have been most fully handled by a Roman in a poem, sensuous and sensual indeed, but schooling and directing the senses by the intellect. Ovid's *Ars Amoris* is eloquent, not only as positive evidence of the decay in Roman morals, but negatively, as a proof that Love was not a lyric impulse but material for didactic treatment. We may think of reasonable love (unless we happen to be in love) as a contradiction in terms. But the Roman attitude towards Love (after the time of Catullus) might be expressed by a parody of the famous lines:

> I could not love thee, Dear, so much,
> Loved I not Reason more.

Ovid's heroines are—or at least try to be—logical, even in passion, and Ovid himself applies the same logic to his own love. Like most Romans, he has little humour; but he has much wit; and—since feeling may be restrained by either wit or humour—he checks his passion, when it threatens to escape from the Reasonable, by the curb of wit. Thus, invoking Dawn to delay her unwelcome return, he will not end his poem on a *crescendo* note: the tension of

> *lente currite, noctis equi*

—words which, on the lips of Marlowe's Faustus have so terrible a poignancy—must be slackened.[1] So the poet

[1] *Amores*, I, 13.

laughs at his own infatuation, reducing it to the level of good society by a jibe, nominally at Aurora, really at himself:

> *iurgia finieram; scires audisse: rubebat;*
> *nec tamen adsueto tardius orta dies—*
>
> She heard my protest, since, for very shame,
> She blushed; but, none the slower, Morning came.

Wit is often the safest solvent of extravagant emotion; but there are times when its test may be too acid. There is a place for good sense, but (as even Horace knew) there is also a place for unreason—*desipere in loco.* And sometimes the wit may sacrifice the poetry. Martial made no pretence to lyric love; but once or twice, at least, he was touched by true emotion. His epitaphs on the little girl Erotion show both his true feeling and (unfortunately) the danger of satire misapplied.[1] The first of these poems is pathetic to the end—an elegy in form, it has a lyrical spirit, as we may see from Herrick's fine imitation:

> Here she lies, a pretty Bud.

The second also begins delightfully

> *puella senibus dulcior mihi cycnis—*

with its tender description of Erotion's charm and winning way: Martial's affection and his sorrow are obviously sincere. But the pathos and the sincerity are spoiled by a witty application, which turns a lyrical threnody into a rather feeble epigram. It is a clear case of the maxim *pas trop de zèle.* The poet knows that it is his business to amuse, even although, like Queen Victoria, "we are not amused".

Such instances must not of course be confused with the "falling close," when a poem of high and tense emotion ends on a note of calm. This, too, has its perils—the note may be not merely calm, but flat. We remember the unhappy close of *Enoch Arden,* where Horace would surely have dismissed the costly funeral with *bonus dormitat;* and

[1] *Ep.* 5, 34 and 37.

he would have been privileged to criticize, since his own falling closes are, I think, uniformly successful. After his stirring eulogy on Regulus, the sober end

—tendens Venafranos in agros
aut Lacedaemonium Tarentum—

is real art, in which emotion is not only recollected, but ended in tranquillity.[1] But the witty close of a Martial is the deadly foe of lyric. It discounts emotion altogether.

There seems no doubt, then, that both the civilization and the literary fashion (which is largely the reflex of the civilization) were responsible for the sudden death of the true emotional lyric, after its brief flash of brilliancy in Catullus. The Augustan age, with its strong hold on corporate life, expected the singer to mix with his fellow-men on equal terms, and to voice the common feelings of humanity. The social lyric was completely expressed—and exhausted—by Horace, who had himself crushed the individual lyric of Catullus.

III

The defect of personal expression in the lyric was the gain of poetry as a social instrument. The noblest odes of Horace are those in which the poet lays aside his Greek manner and becomes *Romanae fidicen lyrae*, a singer of Rome —the city of Romulus and Cato and Regulus in the past, and now the city of Augustus, the mistress of the world. From Ennius to Claudian and Rutilius, the whole content and spirit of Latin poetry, at its highest, is centred in the symbol of the Eternal City. It is true—as has often been pointed out—that Rome or Latium counted for little as the birthplace of the poets; even before the Augustan age, and still more in the Empire, the greatest names are provincial

[1] *Od.* 3, 5, 55. The close of 2, 17 and 4, 2 is a calculated *diminuendo*, not only to relieve the preceding tension, but to contrast Horace's humble part with that of Maecenas or Augustus.

—first Italian, then Spanish, Gaulish, African. Virgil himself was a Transpadane, and (though possibly of Latin descent) a provincial.[1] But a Spanish Seneca or Lucan, was as much a Roman as a Cato or Scipio. In literature as in politics, the nerve-centres of the Empire were gathered in Rome, as they have never been gathered in London, or even Paris. Claudian, the Egyptian, said no more than the truth when he apostrophized the City through which *gens una sumus*—a mother who makes the conquered her citizens and gives security to the traveller on the Rhone or the Orontes.[2] Provincials might live their own social life, little influenced by the central government; but, in literature, all paths led from Rome—and returned thereto.

The absence of a provincial note is not surprising. Latin Literature—prose or verse—was essentially aristocratic, and a member of the governing class did not renounce or modify his tastes when he became a proconsul in Spain or Gaul. As for the provincials themselves, their ambition as well as their interest was plainly to do credit to their Roman education. In the most remote part of the Empire, our own island, the task begun by Agricola had been completed in the very next generation, when Martial boasted that even Britain sang his verses, and, according to Tacitus, those Britons who had lately rejected the Latin language were now clamouring for *eloquentia.*[3] Rhetoric served to train not only the lawyer and the politician, but the poet; and it is here that the *gravamen* against Latin poetry is most serious. To the Roman, the art of speaking was the staple of education (*humanitas*), quite apart from its practical use —*instruit etiam quos non sibi exercet*,[4] as its defenders claimed;

[1] G. E. K. Braunholtz (*Class. Rev.*, June, 1915) thinks that he may have had Etruscan and Celtic ancestors; but see T. Frank, *Vergil*, p. 4 f.

[2] *de laud. Stilich.* 3, 150 f. Cf. Prudentius, *c. Symm.* 2, 602 f.; Rutilius, *Poet. Lat. Min.* 5, p. 6. Hence there could be no dialect poems—there was no room for a Latin Sappho or Burns or Mistral.

[3] Mart. 11, 3, 5; Juv. 15, 111; Tac. *Agr.* 21.

[4] Seneca, *Contr.* 2, *pref.* 3.

and the marks of this training are apparent in every form of the literature. Except Martial, no Augustan or post-Augustan poet was wholly free from the influence of rhetoric, whether—like Virgil—he might try to escape, or—like Lucan—gloried in his "eloquence."

The very word "Rhetoric" is now invidious, even when applied to its proper sphere of formal oratory, and it is at least justly suspected as a basis of poetic art. Possibly the French and other Latin races are less contemptuous of a study which still counts in their education; but Englishmen, at least, are apt to pride themselves on their "plain-speaking"—or their silence; and (as one of their own poets has said) they "arrive at their conclusions—largely inarticulate."[1] Even those who feel that the pose of the "strong, silent man" may be overdone, and that any education should include the power of self-expression, may well object that rhetoric has no place in the equipment of a poet, whose function is not to persuade but to entrance. Here, however, we must distinguish. A poet is not—or should not be—exempt from the duty of making himself intelligible; and, as far as Latin rhetoric served that end, it served a good purpose. As a fact, it was eminently successful: no poetry, I think, has ever been more lucidly and logically expressed; nowhere has the affectation of obscurity been so little admired. This statement may seem questionable to those who have grappled with Lucretius, and who find him—as Quintilian complained—to be "difficult." But difficulty need not be obscurity. Lucretius makes hard reading because his subject-matter is often unfamiliar—*obscura de re;* yet, he adds, *tam lucida pango carmina*, and the boast is well justified. He had scanty patience with those who

magis admirantur amantque
inversis quae sub verbis latitantia cernunt.

Obscurity is a broad term—we have only to remember that

[1] Kipling, *Actions and Reactions.*

(to exclude prose-writers) it has been charged against such different poets as Aeschylus and Pindar, Lycophron and Persius, Browning and Meredith. This list proves, at all events, three things: firstly that any kind of subject-matter *may* be treated obscurely, since the ground covered by the six poets is very wide; secondly, that obscurity must be assigned to various causes, since no single formula can possibly cover the art of (say) Pindar and Meredith; and thirdly, that to be obscure is not necessarily a poetic fault, since—although it may prevent our enjoyment of Lycophron or Persius—many of us can enjoy the other four poets, even when they are most obscure. Coleridge thought that "poetry gives most pleasure when only generally and not perfectly understood";[1] and it may be conceded that many modern poets give ample opportunity for this pleasure. Some people may even enjoy obscurity *per se*, just as there is a class of person that likes puzzles or acrostics. On the whole, however, I suspect that most readers of poetry will agree with Milton that a poem should not only be sensuous and passionate, but also simple—it will be noticed that simplicity stands first in Milton's order; and this is no accident, for the great Epic poet knew that simplicity is the first essential of a classic style. Here, of course, as always, we must define our terms: simplicity is too often confused with obviousness of ideas and baldness of expression, whereas its true meaning, in classical art, is rather lucidity of thinking expressed in the most natural and appropriate words. It does not mean that a simple statement should not encourage thought; it means that it should not baffle thought. When Virgil wrote

sunt lacrimae rerum et mentem mortalia tangunt

the bare idea—there are tears in mortal things—is the simplest possible; the line is a direct recognition of universal experience. Yet the line has haunted the minds of many

[1] *Anima Poetae.*

generations; its pathos, its strange beauty, is not merely due to verbal felicity, but to its elusiveness. It cannot be called ambiguous—much less, obscure—for the general meaning is perfectly clear; but it is an expression of subtle *nuance*, infinitely suggestive, and giving scope to the most delicate shades of interpretation.

But Virgil, dealing with the universal, was not exposed to the temptation, to which modern poets so often succumb, of trying to express the rarer and more complex emotions that seem to defy analysis, and are therefore incapable of direct expression. Like Euripides, he can touch things common, and lift them to the spheres, but he is not concerned with abnormal states of consciousness, or semi-consciousness—with the moods that shift and vanish before they can be fixed by language, if, indeed, any language can adequately represent feelings so far removed from the limitations of the intellect. Such attempts are bound to be obscure; but from this kind of obscurity the more concrete, sculpturesque nature of classical poetry was free. There are, however, other phases of the obscure to which both Greek and Roman poets were exposed. There is the "oracular" style, natural to a poet who—like many ancient poets—claimed to be a prophet or a priest. Heraclitus (ὁ σκοτεινός, the Dark) was famous for mysterious sayings, and it is interesting to find that Lucretius, at least, had little sympathy with one whom he dismisses as *clarus ob obscuram linguam*. Pindar, too, prided himself on his enigmas, φωνάεντα ξυνετοῖσι—not understanded of the people.

Finally, there is the pedantic phase of the obscure, recurring in every literature at a time when all simple and straightforward expression seems to have been exhausted, so that only the involved or allusive speech is thought to be novel or original. Greek poetry itself fell under this affectation in Lycophron; and the Romans did not entirely escape. Alexandria—if sometimes a real inspiration—was always a danger to Rome, and it was inevitable that there should be a Propertius, who, if not obscure in an ordinary sense, was at all events affected and allusive. But most of the Augustans, in shaking off the more galling bonds of Alexandria and returning to purer models, were determined, above all things, to be clear. And it is certain that the study of rhetoric, even more than the purity of their models, enabled them to avoid the pitfalls of obscurity. From their boyhood they had been taught to persuade; and you cannot persuade if you are not intelligible. Once, in later times, the temptation was too strong. Persius found that Horace had been before him; and, having nothing very new to say, he tried to attain a fictitious novelty by making Horace more difficult. Quintilian may have thought of Persius, when he told his story of a master who criticized his pupil's exercise with the comment "Make it harder." The pupil tried again, and the master was delighted: "Much better," he said—"now I don't understand it myself." [1] But this merit did not really appeal to the Romans, either in pure rhetoric or in poetry. Persius, here, as in other and better ways, is a solitary figure, and his great successor, Juvenal, whatever his faults, is free—sometimes painfully free—from ambiguity.[2]

A poet, whose chief form of education had been purely rhetorical, was predisposed to recite his own poetry, and to regard it as a species of the controversial or persuasive art. The practice of recitation did not begin until the age of Augustus, but from that time forward its influence was enormous, both for good and for evil.[3] On the credit side, we may allow that Pollio, the originator of recitation, intended it to be an opportunity for criticism; and this theory survived till at least the age of Domitian, although the practice soon became really a form of publication. In either

[1] Quint. 8, 2. The story was borrowed from Livy, so that, as Quintilian remarks, "the fault was not new".

[2] For classical references to obscurity, see Roberts, *Dionys. de comp. verb.* App. A. As causes, the ancients noted (1) brevity—Horace's *brevis esse laboro, obscurus fio*, (2) prolixity, (3) faulty arrangement of words.

[3] See W. C. Summers, *Silver Age of Latin Literature*, p. 3 f.

case, poetry gained directness by the immediate appeal to an audience who must grasp the meaning at once; and here, surely, we may look for the cause of those sharp, staccato sentences, piercing with one quick and final thrust, of which Ovid is the acknowledged master:

annuerat: promissa fides; posuere labores;
nomina mutarunt: hic deus, illa dea est.

This is rhetoric, if you will; but it is also the perfection of narrative.

On the other hand, if the meaning is more complex, or if the poet wishes to drive home his point, there is always a danger that an audience may lag behind the speaker; and so rhetorical poetry leads from the one extreme of terseness to its opposite, repetition. The famous pronouncement "What I tell you three times is true" might have been made in all seriousness by Ovid himself, in such lines as

os homini sublime dedit, caelumque tueri
iussit, et erectos ad sidera tollere voltus.

Since Dr. Henry wrote the *Aeneidea*, we have all realized that this use of "theme and variation" is the most striking characteristic of Virgilian art—"the reader or hearer must have time to dwell a moment or two on the thought just presented before he is hurried off to another."[1] Henry admitted that this "poetic artifice" was common in prose; he might have gone further, and have pointed out that it was actually borrowed from prose, for Virgil is really adopting the method of the orator.[2] Of course he wrote to be read and pondered, as well as heard; but his method is for the audience and not for the study.

In the hands of a master, the practice of theme and variation may be as artistic in poetry as in music. An

[1] Henry on *Aen.* 1, 550 f.
[2] See Quint. 8, 3, on expansion—*minus est totum dicere quam omnia.*

instance, chosen at random, will show its possibilities. When Virgil wrote

> *quem si fata virum servant, si vescitur aura*
> *aetheria, nec adhuc crudelibus occubat umbris,*

formal criticism will say that the last two clauses add nothing to the first. Logically, this is true; poetically, it is sheer falsehood. The whole point is whether the theme and the variations are worthy of each other. Can the theme be better grasped by expansion, so that it may be observed from different points of view? Do the succeeding strokes of the brush fill in the beauty of the outline? In this and countless other passages of Virgil, we can answer with confidence that theme and variation have been perfectly combined. But the device had its dangers: with Lucan, it became an intolerable trick. The opening of the *Pharsalia*, intended to be a forcible illustration of the theme *bella plus quam civilia*, sinks into complete bathos. With tiresome iteration, Lucan hammers on the nail, long after it has been driven home—the people fought itself with standards and eagles and javelins of the same pattern. The last word of criticism was said by the Romans themselves, in Fronto's protest, "Why end here? Why not go further and throw in horns and pipes, cuirasses and helmets, swords and belts, and the whole kit—*omnem armorum supellectilem?*"[1] Lucan could do better than the promise of his first lines suggested, and Virgil was far better than the best of Lucan; but, good or bad, such passages show that, to appreciate any Latin poetry, we must divest ourselves of modern preconceptions. No Roman would have agreed with Mill's distinction that oratory is to be heard, poetry, overheard. Their scope, their art, their subject were different; but both rested equally on that *eloquentia* which was required from all forms of literature. Rhetoric became an established abuse,

[1] Fronto, *de orat. ad. M. Ant.*, Naber, p. 157 f.

although there were some who protested against a one-sided system of education. Petronius says some bitter things about it; but by his time the evil was incurable. It is more to our purpose to recognise that a greater than Petronius had already raised his voice against rhetorical training, at a time when the warning might have been heeded: Virgil himself, in one of his early poems, condemns the system, in the person of its teachers—it could hardly have been congenial to the shy, poetic temperament of a youth who, a little later, pleaded in a single law-case, and found that experience enough. The poem (which is almost certainly authentic) was no doubt written when Virgil was leaving Milan for Rome, and was contemplating the study of philosophy in the capital.[1]

Off with you!
Bombast-throats that vainly bawl
Your tricks and tropes rhetorical,
Pedant tongues that never knew
A sip of pure Athenian dew!
Selius, Tarquitius, Varro—all
Whose brazen cymbals fill the schools
With the empty din of pompous fools!
And Sextus—ah, 'tis time to part,
Charmer of those who charm my heart!

For now my ship leaves on her quest
To find the harbours of the blest,
Seeking, in Siro's learned lore,
Peace, for evermore.
So, my Muses dear, good-bye,
Dear in truth—I'll not deny—
Muses, once ye were . . . and yet
Do not utterly forget,
Nor leave my paper wholly bare,
Visitants, but shy and rare.

[1] He seems to have moved from Cremona to Milan at the age of 15 (55 B.C.), and from Milan to Rome two years later. Of his youthful poems see R. S. Conway, *The Youth of Virgil* (1915); E. K. Rand in *Harvard Studies Class. Phil.* xxx. (1919), p. 102; T. Frank, *Vergil.*

Yet Virgil—perhaps in part unconsciously—did more than any other Roman to bring poetry within the sphere of oratory. It was not merely that the speeches of the *Aeneid* conform to the rules—that was to be expected—but his rhetoric went far deeper, when he set himself to construct a verse-period corresponding with the prose-period of Cicero, and entirely breaking from the older type of hexameter, in which the sense tended to coincide with the unit of a single line.[1] Those to whom rhetoric is *anathema* will resent the statement that—on the formal side—it was the basis of a Virgil's art. It is disconcerting to be told that the eulogy of Rome, the last speech of Dido, the lament for Marcellus, were written after the rules of the rhetorician, and conformed to the models for the panegyric or the funeral oration. But a poet takes his good where he finds it; and the only point of importance is to recognize the genius by which Virgil lifted these commonplaces into the heights of poetry.

Not the least of Virgil's claims to greatness is the consummate skill with which he dominated the rhetoric that overpowered Lucan The true defect of poetry in the Silver Age was not so much that it was rhetorical as that the rhetoric was unreal, being only used to bolster up the lack of poetic feeling which followed the Augustan age. Second-rate poets, in default of imagination, could only have recourse to those *colores*—purple patches and exaggerations—which Lucan inherited from the *controversia* and *suasoria* of Roman education. Virgil had described a storm in simple language; the later poet could only embroider the same theme with ludicrous turgidity, making the waves rise so high that the bottom of the sea is visible. Yet it is only fair to add that even Lucan has gained his fame by rhetoric, which taught him to say a fine thing finely, so that no Latin

[1] See Norden on *Aen.* 6, *Introd.*, who thinks that Virgil adopted definite rhetorical rules. This has been doubted, but in any case he was certainly influenced by rhetoric.

poet, perhaps, has expressed so many striking thoughts in terse and monumental speech. What is sometimes true for Lucan is always true for Virgil. He found in rhetoric the training to become the spokesman of the Latin race, which, now as then, has always demanded from its writers, whether in poetry or prose, the logic and the lucidity that can be best given by the art of speaking.

But here, again, there lurks a danger. We may concede that poetry is good speaking; but the converse—that good speaking is poetry—is plainly false; and it is sometimes argued that the Romans, in practice, failed to notice this obvious fallacy, assuming that almost any statement could be made poetic by metre: the statement must be logical, but it need not be emotional. Modern poetry, on the other hand, exactly reverses the formula: it must be emotional, though it need not be logical. As a result, the poets of the present day have almost entirely confined their art to the expression of lyric, and fight shy of the "long poem" with more than Callimachean mistrust, on the ground that inspiration is short-lived, and that, even if it could be sustained by the poet, the reader could not breathe, for long, the rarified air of the highest emotion. Indeed, a prominent critic has suggested that if a narrative poem, comparable in bulk to the *Aeneid* or *Paradise Lost*, is ever to be written again, a large part of it might well be written in prose, metre being reserved for passages of "pure poetry".[1] We are apparently to discard Virgil and Milton in favour of Menippus and Boethius, if we are not contented with Alexandria. But the prevailing demand for "inspiration" can surely be carried too far, unless we are prepared to relegate poetry to the compass of the primitive Song, neglecting its splendid evolution in the hands of Homer and

[1] Coleridge, however, seems conclusive: "A poem of any length neither can be, nor ought to be, all poetry. Yet, if a harmonious whole is to be produced, the remaining parts must be preserved in keeping with the poetry" (*Biogr. Lit.*).

Dante, of Chaucer and Keats. Is *Hyperion* to be barred, and only the *Ode to Autumn* allowed? Are we to resign *Paradise Lost*, because Milton—in Dryden's phrase—has some flats among his elevations? Those who argue (in effect) for this conclusion seem to neglect one very important feature of the poetic art—the pleasure of metre in itself. No doubt this pleasure may be minimized by the practitioners or admirers of free verse; but the experience of many ages and peoples has proved the reality of the pleasure in the past, and free verse—though it has gained a deserved place as one form of poetry—has yet to prove that it can offer an equal satisfaction in the present or future.

If the pleasure of metre is conceded, it follows that the modern pendulum of poetry has swung too far, and that we may well return—at least some part of the way—to Classical practice.[1] The Greeks and Romans may have gone too far in poeticizing what is essentially prosaic. They tried to conquer too many poetic worlds, and some of these—like Philosophy—were recalcitrant; but their greatest poets showed the falsity of the complacent *dictum* that nothing which can be said in prose is better said in verse. The *Aeneid*, between its peaks of high imagination, has many tracts of lower level, which the ardent mountaineers of poetry may affect to despise. But, if most people read Virgil with more delight than an equal bulk of Livy, the "prose-poet" of the Roman Empire, we can hardly deny that the charm of verse is its own justification, quite apart from the relief which purely narrative verse can give between moments of high tension. We have much to learn from the Roman poets, and not least, perhaps, the truth that Poetry has many mansions, some of which are now dusty from long neglect.

[1] Mr. Masefield has, in fact, returned, if not to the Epic, at least to the "Epic idyll"; and Mr. Doughty's *Mansoul* is in the true succession of Lucretius.

CHAPTER II

ROMAN CRITICISM—I. FROM CICERO TO HORACE

I

IT is the veriest commonplace to call the Romans a "practical" race; and no one who knows their achievements in arms and law, in politics and architecture, would disagree. But this unimpeachable truth is often taken to imply that a genius for the practical must be opposed to poetry—an implication which Shakespeare's countrymen might well mistrust. There is, however, this much excuse for the antithesis (as far as Latin poetry is concerned), that Virgil's countrymen themselves felt the difficulty, and they have too often been taken at their own valuation. "Others might win fame in bronze or breathing marble; it was Rome's mission to impose peace, to spare the conquered, to crush the proud"—Virgil's disclaimer of art has contributed to obscure the real merits of Roman sculpture, which, though of course derived from Greece, was a complete expression of the Latin character; and, in the same way, the modesty of Latin poets, in the face of their Greek "originals", has done them a real disservice. Few races, after all (except perhaps the Greeks and the English), have actually produced three poets who can rank before Catullus, Lucretius, and Virgil. No race, certainly, has shewn a greater will for poetry, whatever its achievement; and though we may not be Stoic enough to value the Will above the Issue, we must allow that the will was at least sometimes successful, as the three (or, if we add Horace, the four) great Roman poets surely prove. My present aim, however, is not to estimate the number of poets, but to point out that, whether there were few or many, the *need* of poetry was so widely recognized that it may be called the universal feeling of cultured Romans. The enormous reputation of the Poet, during the great period of Roman civilization, shows that, however exceptional the genius of a Lucretius or a Virgil, the appreciation of genius was not confined to a few. Virgil was not a voice crying in the wilderness: he was *Romanus*, the spokesman of his race.

The need of poetry, it may be objected, is not merely Roman, but human—an instinct common to all mankind. This may be true (within degrees), but it fails to explain why the Romans did not regard poetry as an inessential luxury or harmless amusement, but as something more important than any art, except the art of the orator. And here, perhaps, the true explanation lies. Oratory—at least in Republican times—was a necessity for public and private life, and the poet, like the orator, justified his calling by his usefulness. He was *utilis urbi;* and so the antithesis between the practical and the poetic disappeared.[1] The modern conception of the poet as a star which dwells apart —an individualist, and often in revolt—was quite alien to Augustan thought. Horace might take refuge in the woods and valleys from the smoke and riches and din of Rome; but his flight was from the Dog-star, not from society. Even if his subject was not Rome—or, what was the same thing, Augustus—the chief business and glory of a poet was to be a good citizen. He had an organic place in the community; and, to prove it, he was a member of a guild—the *collegium poetarum*—so ranging himself with the other trades and

[1] In Tac. *Dial.* 9 the poet's utility is minimized, in contrast with that of the orator; but this is in a debating speech.

professions of the city-state.[1] He was as much a civil servant as the priest, or the undertaker. To this rule of public service there was one seeming exception: Lucretius —possibly in his life, certainly in his poem—stood apart from the State. But the Rome of Lucretius had ceased, for a time, to be an ordered community; and, even so, there is nothing of the recluse in a poet who has a message for every individual, if not for the State—*orbi*, if not *urbi*. With this partial exception, all Roman poets—since the time when Ennius had imagined Rome as Greece, and Carthage as Troy—were faithful to the conception of a communal office. Even the erotic poets, who appear to be self-centred, if not selfish—more concerned with their Delias and Corinnas than with Rome—are yet Roman citizens to the core. If it would be true to say that, to Propertius, Rome was nothing without Cynthia, the converse would be as true. He claims to be honoured no less, perhaps, than an Epic poet, for his service to the State, being the first to introduce the Greek mysteries of Love, and so to win that fame for Italy which Callimachus and Philetas had won for Greece.

It was precisely because the Poet was a servant of the State that he won more recognition than has commonly fallen to the lot of his class. Roman poetry, of course, was aristocratic, in the sense that it was written either by, or for, the rich; and it was at least secure from material want. But absence of poverty does not in itself confer dignity, and will not account for the fact that, when Virgil was recognized in the theatre, the whole audience rose in his honour, giving him the welcome that was usually reserved for the Emperor.[2] Virgil was only of the middle classes; Horace, not even that. Yet Horace, the son of a freedman,

[1] On this *collegium* see E. G. Sihler in *A.J.P.* 26 (1905), p. 1 f. It may be doubted whether Virgil or the other great poets belonged to the College, and Horace speaks disrespectfully of its president Tarpa; but its activities survived at least to the time of Martial (3, 30, 8; 4, 61, 3).

[2] Tac. *Dial.* 13. Virgil's father must have been a landowner of some position (see Frank, *Vergil*, p. 8 f.), but he was "provincial."

rose to the friendship of Augustus, and could afford to refuse the Emperor's offer of an appointment as his own secretary—the post would have given him no higher rank than his poetry had already gained. At a later date, Martial complained of poverty; but this must have been very relative—in contrast, no doubt, with the wealth of the consuls and plutocrats who admitted him to their palaces. Even in his early days his house in the Subura was far removed from Grub Street. Of course the poetic ease of a Horace or a Martial was due to patronage; but this fact is in itself a mark of honour: Maecenas and Augustus would not have given estates to a despised profession. As we shall see in more detail, this profession was twofold; Horace is both Teacher and Priest: in his own words:

The poet moulds the tender, lisping tongue,
Wrests childhood's ear from obscene talk; anon
He forms young hearts with friendly counselling
And purges the stain of cruelty and spite
And passionate wrath. Singing of famous deeds,
He sets the pattern of nobility
Before the growing youth. The poor, the sad,
Listening, take courage. And how should innocent maids
Or modest boys learn to entreat the gods,
If the Muse gave no poet? Taught by him,
The choir implores high Heaven, and the gods hear
Presently, sending seasonable rain,
Or staying the plague and ruinous disaster,
Or bringing peace and plenteousness. By song
Are won the Powers above us, and below.[1]

The social function of poetry must be borne in mind, if we are to understand Roman criticism, which so often seems to appraise literature by the sole canon of utility. To some extent, this outlook was a direct legacy from Greek criticism, which had so largely fallen into Stoic hands; but the

[1] *Ep.* 2. 1, 126 f.

Romans were even more anxious than Greek Stoics to emphasize the social duty of literature, and of poetry in particular.

The Romans, then, started with the axiom that poetry is not mere self-expression, more or less independent of an audience, but that it bears on the life and well-being of the community. But this definition does not go very far, since all other branches of literature—oratory, for example, and history—made an equal demand. What quality, therefore, differentiated the poet from the orator or the historian? How was the Roman critic to decide whether a "poem" was good or bad?

Since the time of Plato and Aristotle, the Greeks had been debating on the origin and function of poetry, its relation to metre, its impulses from art or inspiration—in a word, on the preliminaries of criticism. They had already settled some principles, though others remained (and still remain) a subject of dispute; and it was left for the Romans to accept what was undisputed, and to thrash out, according to their own lights, the uncertainties. It would be wrong to suppose that they had merely to follow their Greek masters. Aristotle or Dionysius could not help them in settling a problem with which they were at once confronted—the relation of Latin to Greek poetry—and contemporary Greek critics were very chary of discussing Latin literature, which, they said, was best left to the Romans themselves.[1] But the solution of this all-important problem depended on more fundamental conceptions of poetry, and here Greek criticism at least pointed the way.

II. The Preliminaries

Roman literary criticism may be said to start with the period of Varro and Cicero, when Latin poetry had reached a respectable age and had made a considerable output.

[1] Cf. Plut. *vit. Dem.* 3; Longinus 2, 5; see Roberts on *Dion. Letters*, p. 36.

Ennius was already a classic; Lucretius and the neoteric school of Catullus were producing works which were a direct challenge to the older poetry. At a time of great creative activity, there were both the material and the stimulus for criticism. Latin literature was now effectively in being, as something distinct from its Greek originals, and was regarded with mixed feelings. It had become a "rival" of the Greek, and this was a matter of legitimate pride; but there was often a certain uneasiness—a suspicion that the rival could not justify its existence. Varro—the first Roman who can be called a critic—seems to have started the fatal habit of pairing Greek and Roman authors, which so seriously obstructed a clear view of sound criticism.[1] But we know scarcely anything of Varro's lost works *de poetis* and *de poematis*, so that the real history of Latin criticism begins, for us, with his contemporary, Cicero.

At first sight no critic of poetry could well be more suspect. It is no great matter, perhaps, that Cicero's own poetic talent was slender—great critics have often been poor poets; and if we agree with John Dennis that "there never was an admirable Poet, but he was a great Critick," we must also allow that "there have been Criticks, who have been approved of by all the World, who never meddled with Poetry".[2] We may set off Aristotle and Sainte-Beuve against Coleridge and Arnold, though indeed both the Greek and the French critic meddled with poetry, and not without success. As a matter of fact, Cicero's verse has been unduly belittled, since the time when the wits of the Empire fastened on his least felicitous line. For a short time—between Accius and Lucretius—he was even acknowledged as the chief poet of Rome; and, in any case, his high position as an orator and prose-writer entitled his views on poetry to be heard with deference. Unfortunately, it was just his

[1] See Nettleship, *Journal of Philology*, xviii. p. 251 f.

[2] *Reflections upon a Late Rhapsody*, 1711.

oratorical fame that warped his poetic judgment. Engrossed in his own profession, Cicero could hardly fail to regard poetry as a species of rhetoric. It is true that no real injustice was done to the bulk of Latin poetry by this definition; for—as we have seen—no Roman poet is entirely free from rhetoric, and some—in particular, Lucan—are little more than rhetoricians in verse. We cannot therefore complain that (speaking for the poetry which he knew) Cicero noted the fact that "the poet is akin to the orator".[1] Still, it is regrettable that he was more anxious to shew the likeness between the two arts than to point out their essential difference. Roman criticism was thus started on unsound lines, and never entirely recovered from its initial mistake. No Roman, even after Longinus, could fully grasp the truth of that great critic's distinction between the art of Persuasion and the art of moving to ecstasy.

No doubt Cicero was dealing rather with the letter than with the spirit of poetry—he was anxious to shew that the language and rhythm of the two arts are similar, though not identical. But what *is* Poetry? Cicero himself nowhere attempts to define what so many have thought indefinable—but his reticence is not due to any doubt; on the contrary, the ancients were here unanimous, and Aristotle held the field.

The theory of Imitation has often been misunderstood, and not least by the Romans. Whatever Aristotle meant, he certainly did not mean a slavish or mechanical copy of Nature. He would not have said that his favourite play—the *Oedipus*—was a copy of life, any more than that the Aphrodite of Praxiteles was the duplicate of a human model. Indeed, he makes his meaning perfectly clear by his comparison between poetry and other representative arts: tragic poets must follow the example of portrait-painters who make men handsomer without losing the likeness. He allows

[1] *de orat.* 1, 70; 3, 27; *Orator* 67.

for realism—the poet or painter may represent things as they were or are; but he also allows for the ideal, "as things ought to be". And it is clear that the true mission of art was to represent the ideal—τὸ γὰρ παράδειγμα δεῖ ὑπερέχειν, the model must be improved.[1] Thus, for Aristotle, μίμησις is a creative revelation of the ideal, and not a mere transcription of Nature. It is important to observe that the essence of *mimesis* lies precisely in this creative faculty. As Professor Murray has remarked, mimesis is a form of *poiesis*, "making". The poet is said to imitate, because, in making a Sack of Troy, he does not make a real Sack, but an imitation Sack. Poetry, according to Aristotle, makes an imitation world, which is ideal, because it is concerned with "what might happen", but also real, because it must at least be based on the world which we know.[2]

None the less, the doctrine of *mimesis* was peculiarly open to misconstruction, as is evident enough in the long history of criticism. There was always the risk that the creation should be merged in the imitation. It was this danger, perhaps, that led Philostratus to throw over *mimesis*—which "will only fashion what she sees"—and to substitute φαντασία, Imagination, which can fashion "what she has not seen, supposing it is on the analogy of the rest".[3] The gain was enormous, for henceforward all theories of creative art were based on the imagination instead of a mechanical formula. Yet, except for convenience of terminology, it may be doubted whether Philostratus saw deeper into the root of the matter than Aristotle, or even Plato. For the Platonic view (which Aristotle only developed) was wide enough to include even music as "imitative", since it represents human feelings and mental qualities.[4]

[1] *Poet.* 1454b, 10; 1460b, 8 f.

[2] G. Murray, *Essays and Addresses*, p. 107 f.

[3] Philostr., *vit. Apoll.* 6, 19. See Saintsbury, *Hist. of Crit.*, 1, p. 118 f.

[4] *Laws*, 668b. Cf. *Politicus*, 306c. See W. C. Greene, *Plato's View of Poetry* (*Harvard Studies in Class. Phil.* xix. (1918), p. 72.

But Philostratus, a Greek of the second century A.D., came too late to remind the Romans that Imagination—however we name it—is the fountain of Poetry. As it was, Imitation could only too easily be degraded into mere transcription, and we shall find that its chief use in Latin criticism was to justify the Roman "rivalry" with Greek models.

THE FUNCTION OF POETRY

Accepting the theory of Imitation as a fixed principle, sufficient to explain the nature of poetry, the Romans were now concerned with its Function. This problem, though logically second, would perhaps be first to occur, in an age almost totally ignorant of elementary aesthetics; for, even now, few people trouble themselves about the essence of poetry, whereas anyone would probably feel competent to say what poetry is "for." Stated in a popular way, the question obviously admits one of two answers: the function of the poet is to give either pleasure alone, or pleasure with instruction. In the latter alternative, it may still be doubted whether the pleasure is secondary to the instruction, or conversely, or whether the two are equal co-partners.

The early Greeks had no hesitation in coming to a conclusion. Their Sacred Books were poems, and poetry must therefore be instructive. It is true that Homer and Hesiod are not "the Bible of the Greeks", in the traditional sense of that word; for the Greek Epic was always regarded as a purely human work, which could be criticized, and—as we see from Xenophanes and Heraclitus and Plato—condemned.[1] But on one point all early criticism was agreed, that Homer and Hesiod were teachers. Homer's teaching was not, as we now realize it, indirect—the influence of a great mind communicating noble thoughts in noble language—but was that of a conscious moralist, and indeed of an encyclopædist, since he was regarded as the final authority in

[1] See p. 158.

every branch of learning. Hence the whole of Greek literary criticism was long subordinate to ethics. This was inevitable, since, apart from the natural reverence paid to the founders of Greek poetry, the epic was actually used as the basis of all education, and Hesiod, at least, was professedly didactic. The prophetic mantle of the epic was inherited by the tragedy; and, although there is some sort of literary criticism in the *Frogs*, where the styles of Aeschylus and Euripides are contrasted, it is clear that Aristophanes is mainly concerned with their moral teaching. "Boys have a schoolmaster, men have the poet," and Euripides is indicted for the misuse of his proper vocation.

This narrow view of the poetic aim persisted to the last, partly owing to a revival of didactic verse in the Alexandrine age, but chiefly through the influence of the Stoics, who were determined to annex art to the province of morality. The poet could not be altogether identified with the philosopher, but, if their methods were different, their ends might be the same; and so the Stoic Strabo regards poetry as a philosophic primer—a pleasant form of education suited to the young—and Plutarch, though not himself a Stoic, loses all sense of literature in his eagerness to point a moral.[1] But, from Aristotle onwards, the ethical view was seriously challenged. The stubbornness of facts was not to be denied, and, after all, the chief fact about Greek poetry lies in the pleasure which it gave and continues to give. Aristotle was probably not the first to distinguish the æsthetic and moral spheres of poetry, but we owe to him the first clear statement that the poet's function is to give pleasure (*πρὸς ἡδονήν*) or refined enjoyment (*πρὸς διαγωγήν*). He assumed, rather than explicitly stated, that each kind of poetry has its special pleasure for the cultivated man, who is the standard of taste. Pleasure, for Aristotle, is no Cyrenaic self-gratification: it perfects the activity of a natural state, "like the bloom of

[1] Strabo 1, 2, 3; Plut. *de audiendis poetis.*

youth," and therefore, as it perfects human life, it is at least an object of reasonable desire, even if it is not the supreme good. This view of Pleasure as a biological function does not of course imply that, in the sphere of Art, it is the only or the ultimate end. Aristotle would have warmly resented any suggestion of " Art for Art's sake", although this modern Parnassian theory may often be warranted by the actual practice of classical poets. Clearly, he never tries to divorce art from ethics. Tragedy—with which species of poetry the *Poetic*, as we have it, is mainly concerned—has a moral power, purging the emotions of pity and terror by means of pleasure. Man is a social animal, and his pleasure must be social or "political"; and, since the state is held together by morality, it follows that poetry must not be unmoral, far less immoral. But Aristotle never allows the moral purpose of his art to take the place of the artistic end.[1] Ultimately, art is a means to a good life; but this means has its own artistic end. His position is accurately stated by Timocles, one of the comic poets who so often reflect the current philosophical views of the time: the spectator forgets his own troubles in seeing tragic examples, and so "goes home with pleasure and instruction"—ψυχαγωγηθείς—"transported".

So far, Pleasure is still only the efficient cause, the final end being (in some sense) Instruction. But as soon as Pleasure was allowed to be at least *one* proper end of poetry, the way was paved for claiming it as the sole end. This decisive step was apparently taken by Eratosthenes, the famous Alexandrine scholar, who boldly asserts that the poet's function is not to teach but only to move.[2]

It was just here that poetry differed from oratory. From the time of Plato the power of stirring the emotions (ψυχαγωγία) had been demanded of the orator, who must

[1] Butcher, Arist. *Poet.* p. 198. See Bywater on *Poet.* 1460b, 14.

[2] Eratosth. in Strab. 1, 15, 3, ποιητὴν στοχάζεσθαι ψυχαγωγίας οὐ διδασκαλίας.

move as well as convince;[1] but, whereas the orator's end was to persuade (whether by sheer argument or an appeal to the emotions), the poet's sole business was now clearly stated as emotional.[2]

We may here trace an Epicurean influence. If Pleasure is the end of all human endeavour, must not Poetry be included as one of these activities? Epicurus, himself, it is true, was little interested in literary speculations, but writers in the New Comedy could hardly fail to apply them to their own profession. At a much later time Longinus was to insist on "ecstasy" or "transport" as the sole poetic end; but though the Greek critic deserves all Mr. Saintsbury's praise, the credit of priority must here be given to the Alexandrines.[3]

Thus Greek criticism had fairly covered the ground, giving two broad alternative answers to the question of the poetic end—the Stoic answer of Instruction (with Pleasure more or less tolerated), and the answer of Eratosthenes, exactly reversing these two constituents, if indeed he allowed Instruction a place at all; while Aristotle—here, as always, the champion of the Mean—stands between the two extremes. It remained for Cicero and the Augustans to draw a Roman application; and the result is very characteristic. Roman gravity, from the first, was unwilling to acquiesce whole-heartedly in the doctrine of Eratosthenes, which must have seemed to degrade the poet into a mere minister of Voluptas—to the Roman moralist an inauspicious word. Cicero was certainly drawn to Eratosthenes—his own excursions into poetry gave him (if not perhaps his readers), a real delight—but he was not prepared to renounce the doctrine of Instruction. So he compromised; poetry, if

[1] Cic. *Orator* 69, where see other reff. in Sandys' Ed.

[2] Plat. *Phædr.* 271d. See G. L. Hendrickson in *A.J.P.* xxvi. (1905), p. 249 f.

[3] Saintsbury, *Hist. of Crit.* 2, p. 9 f. On *ἔκπληξις* or *ἔκστασις* as an aesthetic term see Heinze, *Virgil*, p. 455.

impeached at the bar of public opinion, might be defended by more than one argument. If it could be proved "useful", so much the better; if not, it might be justified "alternatively", as a means of innocent delight. This defence was not merely metaphorical—it was actually Cicero's pleading before a jury in defence of the poet Archias. The orator argues that the study of letters is useful as an education, and poetry, in particular, has the function of commemorating great nations and illustrious men. Here Cicero was not speaking beyond his literary brief. Greek poetry had always claimed a close alliance with History, since the time when the Homeric muse had inspired the bard to sing of the *κλέα ἀνδρῶν*—the glorious deeds of men. The tales of Troy and Thebes were history even to Thucydides, for all his suspicion of the mythical. As for Rome, Cicero himself deplores the loss of the old Saturnian songs, whose subject was the noble deeds of early Rome—songs which suggested Niebuhr's theory of an Italian epic, and Macaulay's *Lays*.[1] These songs—for they certainly existed, though not as an epic—were swept away by the Hellenism of Ennius; but that poet at least preserved the subject of history in his *Annals*. Cicero's favourite Muse was Clio, though he showed a strong desire to identify history with his own consulship. To the very end of the classical period—in Claudian no less than in Virgil—history remained the keenest stimulus for the poet, the justification of his high calling. Quintilian speaks of historical composition as an art akin to the poets, a kind of *carmen solutum*, free poetry.[2] Historical subjects might be treated in prose or verse, and the treatment naturally differed;[3] but in either case the function was the same—to

[1] Cic. *Tusc.* 4, 2, 3; *de orat.* 3, 51, 197; *Brutus* 75; see also Varro *ap.* Non. 77; Val. Max. 2, 1; 10.

[2] Quint. 10, 1, 31; cf. *Lucian de hist. conscr.* 45.

[3] See p. 203, on Lucan's conception of a historical poem.

present the deeds of great men (*exempla maiorum*) for imitation, and thereby to perpetuate their fame.[1]

By this very Roman argument of "utility", Cicero vindicates the place of poetry as a national service and not merely an ornament of life. But such pleading is perhaps *ad captandam benevolentiam*, to prove that his Greek client was not a parasite of Roman society. Cicero was no Stoic, but a cultivated scholar who read Greek and Latin literature for "delight", without stopping to estimate its instructive value. His own verse was not only historical, and didactic (his translation of Aratus might be reckoned as instructive), but included various renderings of passages from Greek tragedy, which, if "purgative", were not directly educational. Even to the jurors, he enters the *caveat* that poetry must not be judged as purely utilitarian—pleasure, he adds, would be a sufficient excuse for studies which pass the night in our company, go with us on our travels, and share our holidays—*pernoctant nobiscum*, *peregrinantur*, *rusticantur.*[2]

A few years after this speech, the *de Rerum Natura* was published; and it is interesting to examine how far a great poet allowed his philosophy to colour his views on literature. At first sight it would appear that Lucretius accepts the theory of Delight with its fullest implications. His poem is inspired "by the sweet love of the Muses"; it is a labour he delights in—*dulcis labor* - just as the actual discovery of Nature's secret is a "divine pleasure". He does not discuss the point directly; but, if he wished to be consistent, he would have argued that poetry is a natural activity prompted by pleasure alone,[3] and, as an orthodox Epicurean, he would have added that a poet aims at his own pleasure, even though he may produce it for others, by "sweetening his verse" to make the philosophy more palatable.[4] But it is here that our suspicions are aroused. Is

[1] This aspect is prominent in Horace; cf. *Od.* 4, 8; *Ep.* 2, 1, 248.
[2] Cic. *Arch.* 7.
[3] See 5, 1377-1402.
[4] 1, 924 f.; 2, 730; 3, 28, 419.

Lucretius really consistent? Is it not the philosophy, rather than the pleasure that counts? Lucretius seems to give his case away by clearly implying that he pleases only in order to convert. No doubt, by converting his friend Memmius, he looks for an increase of pleasure in his more intimate and sympathetic society, so that we may allow Lucretius the satisfaction of a successful missionary—a rarefied form of hedonism, which the most rigid Stoic might allow.

From Lucretius we naturally turn to Horace, who, as a professed Epicurean in youth, and a practical hedonist to the end of his life, might have been expected to support the theory of poetic Pleasure in its most undiluted form. Yet even he could not accept it without reserve, and—strange as it may seem—the hindrance lay in Epicureanism itself. That school—as I have argued elsewhere[1]—made a special study of anthropology; and Horace, following the lead of Lucretius (who had traced the rise of civilization from a savage state) applied the anthropological method to a particular case—the development of poetry. Lucretius, in his general sketch, had not dealt with this problem at any length. He had been content to show that poetry, like other arts, was evolved by nature, being (he thought) a species of singing which man imitated from the birds. His main point was to exclude the religious hypothesis—the rustic Muse was purely secular.[2] Horace, writing at a time when he had become a free-lance in philosophy, adopted the method of Lucretius, but disagreed with this conclusion. He saw, quite rightly, that religion could not be excluded from the early evolution of poetry, whose origin he attributed to Orpheus, the first teacher of civilization. Greek comedy—he noted—was bound up with ritual; and the future author of the *carmen saeculare* knew that the most primitive Roman songs, such as the *carmina Saliaria*,

[1] *Anthropology of the Greeks.*
[2] Hor. *Ep.* 2, 1, 16; Livy, 27, 27, and 31, 12.

were religious, and that hymns of intercession or thanksgiving were the very essence of the ancient Italian cults.

It is clear that Horace, in spite of his modest disclaimer, aspired to be the Roman Pindar—a priestly poet.[1] Many of his Odes are oracular, enigmatical, and moralizing; and, whereas Lucretius had sharply cut the link between religion and ethics, Horace is determined to bind them anew. Primarily, he is only *Musarum sacerdos*, but the Muses are daughters of Jupiter, who represents the moral government of man. Homer and Tyrtaeus had "showed the path of life," and Horace applies the theory of instruction, not merely to the *Ars Poetica*, which is professedly didactic, but to the *Odes* where Virtue is often no less conspicuous than Pleasure. He is quite ready, in fact, to accept the Stoic view of poetry as the education of the young;[2] but he is not prepared to relegate Pleasure to the background, as the Stoics demanded. Like Cicero, therefore, he hedges: the poetic end may be either Delight or Instruction; or—since the two were not incompatible—the palm is his who has mingled the useful with the pleasant.[3]

This is very far from a recognition of Pleasure as the *only* poetic end; but it is probably as much as Roman criticism could admit. Quintilian, it is true, seems to go much further—indeed, the whole way—in his uncompromising definition of poetry as "seeking Pleasure alone"—*solam petit voluptatem*.[4] Clearly he regarded Pleasure as the only efficient cause, but it need not therefore be the final cause; and no one who has read Quintilian will credit him with any pandering to *l'art pour l'art*. A serious teacher—and Quintilian is the most serious of Romans and professors—would not have paid so much attention to poetry, had he held it to be a mere amusement. To Quintilian, poetry is not only the groundwork of early education—as he shows in the First book—but invaluable as a later training for the orator.

[1] See Jebb, *Growth and Influence of Class. Greek Poetry*, p. 144 f.
[2] *A.P.* 391 f.; *Ep.* 2, 1, 126. [3] *A.P.* 333 f. [4] 10, 1, 29.

The famous opening chapter of the Tenth book is a better explanation of his real attitude towards poetry than his loosely-worded and superficial definition. Quintilian, in fact, was a thorough Aristotelian—not, like the Stoic Manilius, despising *dulcia carmina*, nor claiming that a "poetic theme refuses to be adorned, content to be taught",[1] but very ready to recognize that poetry, however instructive, must also please.

It seems, therefore, that Horace's line

omne tulit punctum qui miscuit utile dulci

is the last word in the criticism of a nation that demanded at least some respect for morality or utility in all spheres of public life. But, though Horace gave the palm to the combination of Delight and Instruction, he had left at least a loop-hole for the theory of Delight as the final cause; and so the problem remained for the critics of the Renascence to handle afresh. Nevertheless, the Horatian stress on utility seems to have stifled the claims of Pleasure—for Horace was the critical dictator to Vida and other early Renascence scholars—until his undisputed authority was shaken by the new interest in Aristotle. Castelvetro, who published a commentary on the *Poetic* in 1570, boldly declared that the sole function of poetry was delight, and that utility was, at most, accidental.[2] This was a counterblast to the orthodox view of the time—championed by Scaliger and Minturno—that the mission of the poet was to "teach delightfully";[3] and, for the next two centuries, the question was still argued—or, more often, the answer was assumed without argument.

This is not the place to follow a controversy which has often been described, and nowhere more fully than in

[1] Manil. 3, 38 f.

[2] See J. E. Spingarn, *Hist. of Lit. Crit.* (1899), p. 55; Saintsbury, *op. cit.* ii. p. 89, and H. B. Charlton, *Castelvetro's Theory of Poetry* (1913), p. 60 f.

[3] Scaliger's *Poetices libri septem* was published in 1561, Minturno's *L'Arte Poetica* in 1564.

Saintsbury's *History of Criticism.*[1] Readers of that notable book will find that the problem of the poetic function—if not finally settled—has been viewed in a clearer light, since the time when Sidney looked to the poet to win the mind from wickedness "with a tale which holdeth children from play and old men from the chimney corner". The debate lasted for more than two centuries, and most of the literary leaders had their say. We need only glance at Dryden, whose ringing battle-cry—"Delight is the chief it not the only end of Poesie"—was afterwards qualified by the concession that "to instruct delightfully is the general end of all Poetry".[2] His contemporary, Rymer, felt no less insecure; for, though he admitted that "some sorts of poetry please without profiting", he hankered, like any Timocles, for the profit of tragedy.[3] In the eighteenth century, the prevailing opinion may be summed up in Dr. Johnson's view that the poet (Milton) should "teach the most important truths by the most pleasing precepts"—a venerable doctrine which is almost pure Stoicism, with a slight lip-service to Epicurus.[4]

The real gain of modern criticism has been to insist on the cardinal point that the *immediate* aim of poetry is not instruction but enjoyment. Here Wordsworth must have due credit; for, although in practice he may sometimes deserve Keats' censure—"we hate poetry that has a palpable design upon us"—his theory and his better practice are sound. He wished, it is true, to be regarded as "a teacher or nothing"; but he laid stress on "the necessity of giving immediate pleasure—the moral effect

[1] See also R. P. Cowl, *Theory of Poetry in England*, p. 303.

[2] *Defence of an Essay of Dramatick Poesy* (1668), and Pref. to *Troilus and Cressida* (1679).

[3] T. Rymer, *Tragedies of the Last Age* (1678).

[4] So, e.g. Dennis, *Grounds of Criticism in Poetry* (1704), ch. 3. "Poetry, unless it is transporting, is abominable," but its end is "to reform the manners".

is not to be confused with a moral purpose".[1] Coleridge, too, was firm: "A poem is a species of composition opposed to science as having intellectual pleasure for its object or end".

Since Wordsworth and Coleridge, there have been some (and no doubt will be others) to demand more from poetry than this—notably Shairp, in his Oxford Lectures, where the Stoic position is restated in Christian terms.[2] The view has at least a noble lineage, but those who hold it must eliminate poetry from the list of the arts—a conclusion which modern aesthetics (and common sense) will not tolerate. Poetry is—in this respect—akin to music, and, though we rightly expect music to refine and elevate, we demand, in the first place, that it shall delight—pleasure is not a secondary object, but the law of its being. Modern critics, no doubt, are inclined to beware of the word "pleasure" in this context, preferring the vaguer term "aesthetic satisfaction." But this satisfaction is allowed to be a pleasurable emotion, so that—if we are not professional psychologists—we may perhaps be content with the intelligible, if somewhat old-fashioned, term of Pleasure, or, better, of Delight.

The whole question has been worn a little threadbare, and phrases like the "moral indifference of art," recalling heated memories of the later nineteenth century, have now only an historical interest. The whole trouble arose, not from the formula itself, if reasonably interpreted, but from the exaggerations alike of its Parnassian defenders and Philistine opponents. It is an abomination, if it means that art is to offend the wholesome instincts of humanity; it is true—or even a truism—if it means that art should not be bound by any laws except those peculiar to itself. The end of art is to create or reveal beauty.

[1] *Of Peter Bell* (Grosart, 2, p. 183), *Letter to a Friend of Robert Burns*, and Preface to Lyrical Ballads.

[2] *Aspects of Poetry*, ch. 1.

We need not here enter into the question whether beauty is absolute or relative, nor discuss whether it is adequate to hold that beauty is simply successful expression, or significant form. The thing that matters is to recognize that the aesthetic fact gives *aesthetic* pleasure. It is true, as Croce allows, that pure aesthetic pleasure is not the only satisfaction to be derived from a work of art—there may be concomitant pleasures, as when an artist reflects that his finished work may have ethical value or even bring him money or repute; or, again, when the spectator of a play obtains rest and relaxation after fatiguing work. But these pleasures have strictly nothing to do with the aesthetic satisfaction which results in the artist's own mind, and is communicated to the minds of others, by the work of art.[1]

The Romans themselves (true to their doctrine of utility) were perhaps more anxious to insist on the pleasure given to others than on that which the artist himself experiences, though, as we have seen, Lucretius held the true Epicurean view of the *dulcis labor.* Even Wordsworth, who must have felt to the full an artist's satisfaction, seems to have thought it morally proper to emphasize the *giving* of immediate pleasure. There was by no means a self-evident truism in Matthew Arnold's "caution":

> What poets feel not, when they make,
> A pleasure in creating,
> The world, in *its* turn, will not take
> Pleasure in contemplating.[2]

At the present day the caution would seem needless, or rather meaningless. A work of art must give aesthetic pleasure to its creator, by the mere fact of expression; and surely no expression can be perfect unless it is communicable to others.[3]

[1] Croce, *Aesthetic* (E.T.), by D. Ainslie, p. 131 f.

[2] Compare Eur. *Suppl.* 182 f., who anticipated Arnold.

[3] Expressionists deny the need of communicating their expression—an artist can "liberate his soul" without an audience. On the other side it is

Such a claim is not to demand that Art should either pander to vitiated tastes, or should run counter to the deepest sentiments of humanity. The poet, like any other artist, claims freedom, but not licence to offend. He may choose any subject, only—as one of the least puritanical of poets has said—the subject must be handled aright.[1] We may go further, and hold with Pater that, while good art may result from *any* subject, the greatest art requires a great subject, and that literature, at its highest and best, depends ultimately not so much on its form as on its matter.[2] If this is so, we may agree with a living poet that, as pure Ethics is man's highest beauty, it has even the first right to artistic recognition.[3] The argument—as Mr. Bridges goes on to say—can only be evaded by the theory that Art is nothing but competent expression, in which case the ugly can be expressed as competently as the beautiful. But even expressionists, while contending that art is distinct from morality, allow that art should not needlessly offend. In the words of their leader, the artist is under the dominion of morals, and must regard his art as a mission.[4]

The Romans, in defining utility as the function of poetry, were no doubt misled by psychological ignorance; none the less, the definition has a pragmatic value—it is itself "useful". From time to time the world needs the warning that poetry cannot be divorced from social life, and that it is not the preserve of a few writers or readers. At no time, perhaps, has the warning been so necessary as in modern days, when the poet is apt to be detached from the full life of the community, wrapping himself, not indeed in his own virtue, but in the contemplation of his own mental processes.

argued that "an artist fails in so far as he keeps his matter to himself"—there can be no art without external expression, i.e. publication. See L. Abercrombie, *An Essay Towards a Theory of Art* (1922), p. 49.

[1] A. C. Swinburne, *Studies in Prose and Poetry*, p. 138.

[2] W. Pater, *Appreciations*, p. 38.

[3] R. Bridges, *The Necessity of Poetry* (1918).

[4] See Croce, *Breviario*, 23-26.

This introspective self-communing may be a transitory phase; but it is not without reason that a brilliant writer and teacher of English reminds us that "we cannot separate art, and specially the literary art, from life—from daily life—even from this passing hour—and get the best out of either".[1] Poetry is something much more than a criticism of life; but Arnold's definition is so far true that if poetry ceases to "criticize"—that is, to reflect the poet's judgment on human affairs, it must itself cease to be vital. The great Roman poets never lost this power of criticizing life, even when their subject was most remote from the ordinary course of a workaday world. Lucretius, in spite of his nominal individualism, and his concentration on the vastness and sublimity of the Universe, never long forgets to interpret it in terms of human society. Indeed, the danger to the Roman poets was not that they should fail in this humanism, but that they should become *mere* critics of life, and so miss its poetry. The poet sinks to the satirist. From its beginnings in the second century B.C. to its end in the second century A.D., satire was the most characteristic *genre* in which Roman Society was reviewed, and the famous remark—*satira quidem tota nostra est*—has even more truth than Quintilian conceived. That critic thought only of formal satire from Lucilius to Persius, and rightly saw that—in spite of analogies, more or less close, in Archilochus or the Old Comedy—Roman satire was essentially of native origin. But Quintilian, if he had been less a formalist, might have gone further, and have pointed out how deeply other forms of Latin verse are infused with the satiric spirit. Lucretius paints his wonderful pictures of the bored aristocrat rushing from town to country, from country to town, in the equivalent of a motor car, or of the mistress concealing "the life behind the scenes" from her lover, in colours which Juvenal could hardly match.[2] Even Virgil,

[1] Sir A. Quiller-Couch, *Studies in Literature* (2nd Series), p. 142.
[2] Lucr. 3, 1060 f.; 4, 1186.

whose gentler soul is more rarely touched by the vanity of Roman life, is moved to indignation by the luxury and avarice and ambition of his day, turning with relief from the Forum to the country fields.[1] Ovid's *Art of Love* is not less a satire because it is unintentional, since the real object of his criticism is—or should be—the poet himself. Later, when the springs of poetry were almost dry, Claudian found inspiration from Juvenal, rather than from Virgil, and lashed his enemy Eutropius with a vigour which he seldom showed in praise of his patrons.

The satirist, like the "legitimate" poet, was a teacher. His teaching might be largely negative—how *not* to live —but Horace had learnt from his excellent father that *exempla vitiorum* are at least as instructive as *exempla virtutis*. And so the satire fell into line with other and higher forms; for, though Horace, as a satirist, modestly disclaims poetic rank, he would perhaps have been a little hurt to be taken at his word. There may have been some Romans who denied Lucilius the title of poet, just as there are some English who refuse it to Pope; but neither the critics, such as Quintilian or Macrobius, nor the plain men who knew that satire was the characteristic note of Roman expression would have agreed with the heresy.[2] Satire was always spoken of as *carmen* or *poema*;[3] and perhaps its highest claim to the rank was not the metrical form (which, we shall see, was discounted by Horace) but the didactic function, by which the satirist became the censor of morals and the poetic voice of public opinion.

METRE

There remains the question of metre. Is it essential to poetry, or merely an additional ornament? The answer depends, of course, on whether, in defining poetry, we lay

[1] *Georg*. 2, 458-512.
[2] Cf. Quint. 16, 1. 93; Macrob. *Sat*. 3, 16, 17.
[3] E.g. by Horace himself, *Serm*. 1, 10, 64; 2, 1, 62.

more stress on the spirit or the form. Aristotle took account of both, though his ultimate criterion of poetry is concerned with the spirit—the poet must imitate *Universal* life. The definition excludes Empedocles, whom Aristotle must have regarded as purely didactic; "he is more of a physicist than a poet." It also excludes historical poetry; for "the work of Herodotus, if versified, would still remain a species of (prose) history".[1]

The first and most famous of all attempts to define poetry must be treated with respect: Aristotle proved, once for all, that the poet is not the historian of Fact but its interpreter in terms of the Ideal. He has been criticized for insisting on the Universal—poetry, it is often said, is really concerned with the Particular; it is the expression of the poet's unique intuition. Yes; but the poet's intuition is of no value unless and until he can express the general application of his own individual feeling. We should not respond to his own emotions on love or life or death if they failed to strike a universal chord of sympathy. Where Aristotle falls short is rather in underrating the force of emotion itself. The "Master of those who know" paid too little attention to those who feel, despite his recognition of Pity and Terror. He neglected the basic truth that any subject—history included—can be touched with the poetic imagination. His own followers here refused to follow him. Dionysius, commenting on Herodotus and Thucydides, is explicit: "I would not hesitate to call their works poetry (ποιήσεις).[2]

It is plain therefore, that, in theory, at all events, the Greeks were free from what Shelley called the "vulgar error" of opposing poetry and prose. Many, before and after Shelley, have protested against the error, and we need

[1] *Poet.* 1447b, 18.

[2] Dion. *Ep. ad Pomp.* 3; cf. Demetrius, *On Style* (of Ctesias), Marcell. *vit. Thuc.* 41. See Quintilian's remark on history, p. 39. In general cf. Norden, *Kunstprosa*, p. 91.

only recall Sidney's warning that verse is only "an ornament and no cause to Poetry; sith there have been many and most excellent poets, that never versified, and now swarme many versifiers that neede never answere to the name of Poets."[1] But, for our present purpose, the interesting point is that neither Aristotle nor his Greek successors define poetry in terms of form—the antithesis between poetry and prose is recognized as unsound. Dionysius, after shewing that prose can resemble verse, by the presence of a marked rhythm, proceeds to the complementary statement that certain types of verse may be read as prose, if the natural division of the sense is followed rather than the metrical break. His illustration is the *Danae* of Simonides—certainly one of the most "poetic" odes in Greek or any other language.[2] All the critics, in fact, were searching for "elevation" (*ὕψος*), which is, at least mainly, the vehicle of emotion, and they found it equally in Homer and Demosthenes; and so, although Dionysius would not have classed Demosthenes as a technical poet, he boldly affirms that the orator's speeches are "like" poetry.

But "likeness" is not identity; and the line which the Greeks drew was real, though not always distinct. A man might be a poet, whether he wrote in verse or rhythmical prose; but he could not be a singer (*ἀοιδός*), unless he was metrical. Aristotle was convinced that the instinct for melody and rhythm was a "cause" of poetry; and as he saw that metre is an organized species of rhythm, he must have held metrical composition to be the effect of natural poetic impulse.[3] To the Greeks, as to some modern critics, poetry is melic[4]—a definition the more easy for the Greeks to formulate, since their own poetry was so largely sung, or at least recited to a musical accompaniment. As a vehicle

[1] *An Apologie for Poetry* (Arber, p. 28).
[2] Dionys. *de verb. comp.* 26.
[3] *Poet.* 1448b, 21.
[4] Dionys. *de verb. comp.* 11; Longinus 1, p. 305.

for song, poetry admitted a certain distinction of language, and it differed from rhythmical prose in being accurately metrical, even if the metre, unless analyzed, could not readily be distinguished from prose. The two arts were cognate, but not to be confused; it is certain that Aristotle would have held a "prose poem" to be a contradiction in terms.[1] His successors, as we have just seen, were less sure of the distinction, mainly, perhaps, on the formal ground that no clear line could be drawn between rhythm and metre. That poetry must be expressed in language rhythmical, if not metrical, the Greeks of course never doubted. They knew by instinct (what modern physics has confirmed) that the order of the Universe is a harmony, that the music of the spheres is no empty metaphor, that the sun is kept on his course by an appointed rhythm; they knew, too, that Life is not less rhythmical than the forces of Nature; that birds sing "because they must," and that man when stirred by emotion, is impelled to express it in the measured dance or the measured language of song. A race accustomed to associate dance and song, whether in the village chorus or the city Dionysia, would have welcomed a modern view, that poetry is something more than akin to dancing—it may be even derived from that vital emotion, which is first expressed in the simple dance, and is then heightened by language in harmony with the rhythm.[2] And, if emotion may often be adequately expressed by rhythm, it finds its fullest satisfaction in metre, which is at once the outlet and the curb for the utterance of human passions.

The Greek poets, with their strict attention to form, would have resented any attempt to regard metre as a mere ornament, to be retained or discarded at will. Aristotle would not have agreed with Wordsworth that "metre is but ad-

[1] So Bywater on Arist. *Poet.* 1447a, 28. For passages dealing with the distinction cf. Isocrat. περὶ ἀντιδ. 46 f., Arist. *Rhet.* 3, 3; and see Norden, *Kunstprosa*, p. 52 f.

[2] See Newbolt, *New Study of English Poetry*, p. 26 f.

ventitious to composition"[1] (though "early superadded"); and if he might have accepted Coleridge's definition that poetry is the best words in the best order, he would have been careful to explain that the best, and only, poetical order is not merely logical but metrical. It was perhaps unfortunate for Greek critics that they were entirely ignorant (at all events before Longinus) of Hebrew poetry. The Psalms or the Book of Job would have shown them a form of ancient poetry based on accentual rhythm instead of syllabic metre; and neither Aristotle nor Dionysius would have regarded the rhythmical English version as other than "poetic". But they would hardly have allowed this version, or the original, to be *technically* a poem. To them, spirit and form were inseparable; and "free verse" would lack the form which is necessary for full poetic expression. Perhaps this opinion would have been modified, if they could have compared the English metrical version of the Psalms with their rhythmic original.

The danger of viewing metre as *an* essential is that it may easily come to be regarded as *the* essential. No sane man, of course, would hold metrical composition to be *per se* poetical; but, as soon as attention is fastened on the technique, the spiritual content may fall into the background. Poetry, after all, is an emotional state; it is certainly not completely realized without adequate expression, and some form of rhythm is no doubt proper, or even necessary, to communicate it. But poetry is not rhythm in itself. We must not confuse the emotional activity with the means of expression. The besetting sin of the Classical theory lay in this confusion. From the earliest times there was a tendency to identify verse with poetry. No doubt this is often due to mere looseness of language. When Plato speaks of writing "in metre as a poet, or without metre, as a layman," or when Aristotle says that, if a

[1] *Lectures* (1818). See generally Wordsworth, *Of Poetic Diction* and Pref. to *Lyrical Ballads*; Coleridge, *Biogr. Lit.*

sentence has metre, it will be poetry,[1] we can pardon a momentary lapse, remembering that both Plato and Aristotle were of all men the most careful to hold by the spirit. But, for the Romans, the danger was very real. With far less than Greek imagination, they possessed at least an equal sense of verbal music, and they favoured, very naturally, the aspect of poetry that best suited their genius. A single instance may illustrate. Cicero (followed by Quintilian) makes the interesting observation that (oratorical) prose is more difficult than verse, as metre is fixed and ready-made, whereas prose must show variety in its structure.[2] From one point of view, the remark is perfectly just, for other languages than Latin,[3] and it might well give pause to the opponents of Verse Composition as a training in schools. If verse is a pattern, we must agree with R. L. Stevenson that "it is much easier for men of equal facility to write fairly pleasing verse than reasonably interesting prose; for in prose the pattern itself has to be invented and the difficulties first created before they can be solved."[4] Cicero himself no doubt spoke from experience—he must certainly have found it easier to write his own respectable verse than to perfect his elaborate prose. Quintilian, however, has less excuse for following Cicero, since Virgil had come between the two writers, to change the whole character of the hexameter, by substituting subtle elisions and skilful variations of pauses for the simple and monotonous regularity of the Ciceronian verse. In Virgil's hands, the old verse-unit (with the sense largely coinciding with the line) had been superseded by the verse-period, the structure of which required at least as much skill as the prose-period of Cicero.

But the point is, that whether we agree with Cicero and Quintilian, or not, their outlook on poetry is wrong. The

[1] Plat. *Phædr.* 258d; *Gorg.* 502c; *Laws* 810b; Arist. *Rhet.* 3, 8.
[2] *Orator* 58; Quint. 9, 4, 60 f.
[3] Leopardi held this view for Italian.
[4] *Essays in the Art of Writing*, p. 9 f.

handling of metre by any poet is a very interesting and important branch of the study of that poet; but to approach poetry in general by way of metre—as if the two were synonyms—is ridiculous. The Romans, it need scarcely be said, were better critics than might be expected from this starting point; but the fact remains that much of their criticism was vitiated by their reverence for the Form. After this practical—if not theoretical—insistence on metre, in all Greek authorities, it is not surprising that the Roman line of cleavage was strictly drawn. To Horace—puzzled by Pindar's difficult metres—that poet seemed clearly to be *lege solutus*, rhythmical rather than metrical; and Quintilian, as we have noticed, allowed in theory for free verse; but the Romans, with their strict adherence to Form, could have had little sympathy with critics who over-stepped the proper boundaries of verse and prose. Horace knew, of course, that verse need not be poetry—

neque enim concludere versum
dixeris esse satis;[1]

but the converse—that poetry might be independent of metre—was unthinkable. For him, much more than for Aristotle, a prose-poem would have been a confusion of *genres*, a monster which—like the human face on a horse's neck, or the fair woman ending in a fish—would have moved him to cry with scorn:

risum teneatis, amici?

Genius and Art

If later Greek and Roman critics had no doubt as to the nature of poetry, there was room for discussion on a cognate problem: Is poetry the product of genius or art? The question may now seem unprofitable, when we are all agreed that a poet is both born and made—as Tennyson once remarked, *poeta nascitur et fit*—but the history of the debate

[1] *Sat.* I, 4, 40.

has an interest in throwing light on classical thought. In the traditional Greek view, from Hesiod to Plato, the poet was regarded as the mouthpiece of the Muses, a prophet inspired or "mad." Pindar, with his strong aristocratic bent, decided that Nature was superior to art or training, though his own poetry might well have demanded an equality of partnership. A serious discussion of the problem began at the end of the fifth century, when sophists maintained that anything—including Virtue—could be taught, and if Virtue, why not Poetry? Not the least of Plato's services to mankind was his protest against this position. He had his own reasons for banishing the poets, but he had not read Homer and Aeschylus to no purpose. Genius could call to Genius even if their ways lay apart.[1]

Democritus, his bitter opponent, agreed with Plato at least in this respect; and even Aristotle, the champion of Reason, admitted that poetry was a thing inspired, "a happy gift of nature or of madness."[2]

But a nation of artists was not likely to undervalue the counter-claim of art. If a poet were mad, there must be a method in his madness. Aristotle, in spite of his passing tribute to tradition, is only concerned with the sane. His aim in the *Poetic* is to show that poetry is an art as much as rhetoric or sculpture—a conclusion not only founded on experience and common sense, but the natural outcome of even Platonic speculation; for Plato had laid equal stress on breeding and training, which act and re-act on one another; and Aristotle only applied Plato's general conclusions to the special province of poetry.[3] In the same generation, the last word was said by the poet Simylus: "Neither nature without art, nor art without nature suffices for anyone for any accomplishment."[4]

[1] Plato's attitude towards poetry is discussed on p. 155.

[2] Democr. *ap.* Dio. Chrys. 53; cf. Cic. *de div.* 1, 38, 80; Arist. *Rhet.* 3, 7; *Poet.* 17, 2.

[3] *Rep.* 424a; *Laws* 766a.

[4] Stobaeus (Meineke i, p. 352), cf. Long. 36, 4.

Henceforward, it was no longer possible to exclude either partner from a share in Helicon; but it does not follow that the two should be admitted on equal terms. On the one hand, there have always been those who, like Boileau and Pope, incline the scales in favour of Art; and, on the other hand, there will always be a reaction towards "native wood-notes wild," and the "unpremeditated song." It is to the credit of the later Greek critics, that they held the scales so evenly. Dionysius thought Homer to be not only the most inspired, but the most artistic of poets—a criticism infinitely more sound than the one-sided view of a past generation who forgot the real art of the Epic in their enthusiasm for its genius.[1]

But, as not every poet is a Homer, the terms Genius and Art tended to become mutually exclusive instead of complementary. Roman criticism is full of the antithesis,[2] and we may here find a clue to Cicero's puzzling estimate of the *de Rerum Natura: Lucretii poemata ut scribis ita sunt, multis luminibus ingenii, multae tamen artis.*[3] It was once the fashion to insert *non*, either before *multis* or *multae*, thus making Cicero deny Lucretius either genius or art. But it is now recognized that the text is sound, and the only difficulty lies in the force of the *tamen*. Cicero can hardly refer to the poet's insanity—it is at least doubtful whether Lucretius was ever insane—by allowing that Lucretius showed art, as well as genius, *in spite of* his affliction, as has been curiously suggested.[4] The alternative is to explain the *tamen* as marking the orator's surprise at the presence of two qualities which—at least in Roman poetry—seemed almost incompatible. Nor is the view confined to the

[1] See Roberts on Dionys. *de verb. comp.* p. ix.

[2] Cic. *de orat.* 1, 25, 72, and 113; Ovid, *Amor.* 1, 15, 14; *Trist.* 2, 424; Quint. 1 *proem.* 26; 1, 7, 8.

[3] *ad Q.F.* 2, 9, 3.

[4] H. W. Litchfield in *Harvard Studies in Class. Phil.* xxiv. (1913), p. 147 f. The explanation which I follow is now generally accepted; see Norden, *Kunstprosa*, p. 182 n. 1; Plessis, *Poés. lat.* p. 123; Merrill, *Lucr.* p. 18.

Roman: as a modern critic remarks, "Nature has always been loath, except in cases of her very choicest favourites, to combine true artistic instincts with great poetic energy."[1]

Cicero's own taste in poetry led him to prefer the old school of Ennius

ingenio maximus, arte rudis

to the neoterics—the *graecissantes*, whose chief aim was to replace the uncouthness of early Latin verse by the artifices of Alexandria. In that school, Catullus alone shews (to our judgment) equal genius and art: for while no one can dispute his *ingenium*, his mastery of Greek metres—sometimes, as in the *Attis*, rare and difficult—has placed him foremost among pre-Augustan poets. In Roman judgment Catullus, above all others, was *doctus*—an epithet which (whatever its precise connotation) was certainly the hall-mark of an artist rather than of a native genius.[2] Here, indeed, the Romans were perhaps better judges than those modern admirers of the poet, who are too apt to extol the fire and passion of Catullus at the expense of the very strict technique that kept this emotion under control.

But, artist though he was, Catullus had by no means explored all the secrets of art, as defined by Augustan canons. His hexameters are monotonous, and it was left to Virgil to invent a more flexible and musical rhythm; his elegiac metre, rough, and often a little uncouth, was completely remodelled by his successors; and his rare experiments in Horatian metres are equally deficient in the polish of the Augustan lyrist. No side of his art, indeed, could have fully satisfied the taste of the next generation, and it is this fact, I think, that may throw light on the question of his repute in the age of Virgil and Horace. Were the Augustans, as a whole, unfriendly to the aims and

[1] T. Watts-Dunton, *Poetry and the Renascence of Wonder*, p. 4. We may remember that Shakespeare was denied *l'art* by the French in general from Voltaire to Chateaubriand.

[2] On *doctus* see p. 86.

art of the neoterics? Only a few years ago, it was assumed that Catullus was out of favour with his immediate successors. This view—championed by Lucian Müller, Robinson Ellis, and others—was an undisputed article of belief until it was attacked by Riese, as a phantom unworthy to appear in any future discussion of Latin poetry. But the phantom was not laid at rest, and more recently, Riese's position has been reaffirmed, with fresh argument, by E. K. Rand, in an able and scholarly article.[1]

Mr. Rand argues, with much force, that, though the poetic tendencies of the Augustans differed widely from those of their precursors, yet the younger poets looked for inspiration from both Lucretius and Catullus: Virgil aimed at generous rivalry, not depreciation, and himself passed through a Catullan and a Lucretian period, the former in his youthful works,[2] the latter in the *Georgics*. In fact it seems clear from many parallels in the *Aeneid*, that he remained a constant student of Catullus, as well as of Lucretius, to the very end. Of the elegiac writers, Propertius and Ovid mention Catullus in terms of admiration.[3] Tibullus alone is silent; but an argument *ex silentio* cannot be pressed. There remains Horace, in a single allusion to his predecessor:

nil praeter Calvum et doctus cantare Catullum.[4]

The line is obviously a sneer; but, as Mr. Rand points out, it is not necessarily a sneer at Catullus. It is possible to condemn the ape of a great master without condemning the master himself. Horace *may* have disliked neoteric poetry; but this line is no proof. To this we may add that the reasons commonly given for his alleged contempt of Catullus are not conclusive. Was he jealous of a rival in his own sphere? If he could have anticipated modern judgment, he might have had cause for jealousy—or humility; but, in his

[1] *Harvard Studies in Class. Phil.* xvii. (1906), p. 15 f.

[2] The *Ciris*, which is almost certainly Virgilian, betrays the influence of Catullus, in tone, in verse-structure, and in the use of diminutives.

[3] Prop. 3, 34, 87; Ovid *Am.* 3, 15, 7; 3, 9, 62.

[4] *Sat.* 1, 10, 9.

own day, Horace had no rival, for the simple reason that Catullus was not regarded as a lyric poet at all.[1] Horace could fairly claim that he was *primus* in Latin lyric, for Catullus had anticipated him only by a couple of Sapphic odes. Again, it has sometimes been suggested that Horace may have been ill-disposed to Catullus on political grounds as an anti-Caesarian. But why should a poet, who had himself fought against Caesarians at Philippi, blame one whom Ovid and Propertius praised? After all, Catullus had only lampooned Caesar; and Horace finds admiration for Cato, who fought against the dictator's heir.

If these arguments have weight, there would be a good case for expelling the phantom. It would appear that the so-called unpopularity of Catullus rests on a single passage of disputed application; and further, that even if Horace sneered, his censure is more than balanced by the approval of his contemporaries. Nevertheless I cannot think that this is the last word. If Catullus was really popular with the Augustans, how came it that they gave up all Catullan characteristics in their own work? Maecenas, perhaps, may be said to have lingered as a belated neoteric; but one does not judge Augustan poetry by Maecenas. No fact is more obvious than that the poets of the Empire formed a school entirely opposed to their immediate predecessors. It is true that there was no violent break—as we have just seen, Virgil wrote like Catullus, until he found himself, while Propertius always remained an Alexandrine, and—to that extent—a neoteric. But more and more, as Octavian became Augustus, the circle of his poets passed from Alexandria, not so much to earlier Greece as to Rome. For the preference of earlier and purer models, which is often said to mark the age of Augustus, may easily be exaggerated—Virgil "borrowed" from Apollonius at least as much as he borrowed from Homer. His real poetic discovery was Rome. There was

[1] See p. 9.

thus a complete change affecting both the style and the subject of poetry; and such changes are not found to occur without some corresponding readjustment of old values. When Victorian poetry passed into Georgian, the older gods, if not dethroned, at least became mortal. These fashions, no doubt, are fleeting; and just as there are signs that Tennyson—after a few years of unpopularity—is now being more fairly appraised, so Lucretius and Catullus were restored to favour, after the great Augustan impetus was spent. But under the first Emperor, at all events, the new imperial movement must have carried all before it, brushing aside the neoterics, who themselves had swept away, for a time, the old veneration for Ennius and Lucilius: Ovid might have said for the poet, as for the priest,

et perit exemplo postmodo quisque suo.

Of course taste had to reckon with tradition—the chief factor in Roman poetry as in Roman life. Virgil "imitated" Catullus and Lucretius, just as they (or at least Lucretius) had imitated Ennius. So far we may agree with those who deny that Catullus was ever out of fashion. But Horace and probably the rest of his fellows had good cause, according to their lights, for criticism. It was precisely those features of Catullus which the moderns most admire—his self-revelation, his burning passion, his complete absorption in love or hatred—that are most foreign to the severe Classicism of which Horace is the prophet. Good taste, orderly arrangement, conformity to the type, an unsparing use of the file—all these are the virtues of Augustan poetic theory, and Catullus had, or seemed to have, a slender part in them. Above all, the ideal poet must be sane, for he is a teacher of Reason, and Catullus had only the unreason of an overpowering love. The spirited horse of the *Ion* and *Phaedrus* and *Symposium* must be restrained by sharing the harness with a more disciplined and sober yoke-fellow.

Such is the creed of the *Ars Poetica* and its companion,

the *Letter to Augustus;* and it marks the final triumph of the new school. Henceforward no poetry could pass muster if it neglected the Rules, which are summed up in the word Form or Art.

The Rules, in themselves, were no new thing. Aristotle had already sanctioned the doctrine of the literary Form, which is itself derived from the Platonic Idea. All that Aristotle did was to substitute the Species for the Platonic Form, as a constant and immutable subdivision of his reality, the Universal. As each species in the vegetable and animal world is fixed, eternal, and sharply differentiated, so each literary Form is rigid and ultimate: epic and lyric, tragedy and elegiac, cannot be blended or contaminated; and—since Aristotle knew no specific evolution—a new literary form cannot strictly be invented, though the Romans, in claiming Satire as their own, may have here forgotten to be logical.[1]

In Horace—both as critic and writer—we find the full flower of this Classicism. Genius—a "diviner mind"—is essential, and is a sworn ally of Art.[2] After Simylus, he could say no less; but he certainly seems to regard Art as the predominant partner. And, although he sometimes assumes a dithyrambic vein in his Odes, and claims to be "full of Bacchus," his definition of genius would probably have been satisfied by an infinite capacity for taking pains. A toiling bee rather than a Pindaric swan, he knew and confessed that his songs were laborious;[3] and his "careful felicity" sums up his reputation in ancient Rome. At the present time there are many who admit the carefulness but deny the felicity. His appeal to the moderns has waned since the days when to quote him was the sign of a gentleman. His sentiments are reckoned as commonplace, his attitude towards life, as mère hedonism; and, above all, the critics who look for personal expression find Horace—in

[1] See generally R. K. Hack, *The Doctrine of Literary Forms* in *Harvard Studies in Class. Lit.* xxvii. (1916).

[2] *Sat.* 1, 4, 43; *A.P.* 408 f.

[3] *Od.* 4, 2, 31.

spite of some frank revelations—too "objective" for a lyric poet. Yet here again, we must remind ourselves that a change of taste is rarely final; the poet who pleased Ronsard and Herrick, Milton and Pope, Prior and R. L. Stevenson—to mention no other names—is not lightly to be despised. If these poets had all belonged to the eighteenth century, their testimony might perhaps be suspected; but they represent the judgment of four centuries, and the six were themselves so diverse, that their most binding link might perhaps be called a love of Horace. And the latest of the six, at least, cannot be accused of showing any great favour to classical poetry simply because it is classical. Horace has therefore certainly appealed to his fellows, but this is not his strongest claim. As Mr. Mackail observes, he is not (exclusively) a poet's poet;[1] his popularity, in the past, has rather been with the average man of education.

Horace's present reputation is a matter of some concern, precisely because he is not only the chief critic, but the chief writer of his native poetry in its most characteristic form. Catullus, Lucretius, and Virgil are more than typical classicists—they are too great. But Horace stands or falls by virtue of classicism, pure and unadulterated. If it is allowed that his thought rarely rises beyond the level of commonplace, it is fair to add that much of his thought has become commonplace merely by reason of its perfect expression in Horace himself. The cry *pereant qui ante nos nostra dixerint* is human, as every scholar knows; but the complaint that Shakespeare wrote little except hackneyed quotations is not helpful to criticism. There are, of course, other charges against Horace, and it may be partly to the credit of the present age that he is a little out of fashion. Life is taken so seriously to-day that, if there is a modern Epicureanism, it is the Lucretian rather than the Horatian sort that is rightly admired, if not always followed. Poetry

[1] *Latin Lit.* p. 113.

too, is taken very seriously, and—though the Parnassian theory of Beauty for Beauty's sake is happily not dead—a generation, that is intensely introspective, is not satisfied with the mere singer of love and wine, unless both these stimulants are more fiery than Horace, with his studied *mediocritas*, was wont to countenance.[1] Even when the poet passes from the love and wine to the higher theme of patriotism he may fail to move the modern reader, who is apt to regard Songs of Empire as thinly disguised propaganda. At a time when Imperialism is being tempered, if not wholly changed, by new political ideals, the Horatian model of government may seem less commendable to us than it possibly seemed to the first readers of *Barrack Room Ballads*. Although the Roman Empire (like the British) is one of the greatest facts in human history, the fact—it may be argued—is a matter for the historian or the politician alone.

There is perhaps a still more deeply rooted objection, not so much based on any special characteristic of Horace as on his whole attitude to life and art. He has been called the most perfect example of that spirit of "acceptance" which may be contrasted with the spirit of wonder or even of revolt. To define acceptance as a mark common to all classical poetry would be absurd—it is certainly no mark of Lucretius or Catullus, but it is true for Horace, who, if not satisfied with the best of all possible worlds, seems at least to have believed that Rome was the best of all possible States.

To many minds—and not least in the twentieth century—there is more satisfaction to be drawn from the poetry of revolt, from the divine discontent of a Shelley, the indignant protest of a Burns. Horace was no doubt justified in hailing Rome as saved through Augustus; but the modern world has certainly no faith in Kaisers, and does not feel so

[1] *Od.* 3, 14, 21-28 is instructive.

sure of its own salvation—although, after a violent upheaval, it cannot but recognize that this salvation must depend on that order and discipline which Horace found in the political life of imperial Rome, and which he reflected in his own poetry.

Whatever drawbacks may explain Horace's temporary eclipse, they cannot for long affect the reputation of a poet whose "place" is really beyond the danger of fluctuating fashion. Horace is a perfect artist, and artistic perfection is not so common that it can be permanently neglected. His art, it is true, is that of a gem rather than of a statue; but art is not measured by bulk.[1] His poetry, if not "passionate," is at least "simple and sensuous"—poetry which must be written once in the history of man, and which cannot be written again, because Horace has written it once for all.

[1] It was a sound instinct that led C. W. King to illustrate Horace by reproductions of gems.

CHAPTER III

ROMAN CRITICISM—II. POST-AUGUSTAN CRITICISM

BY the time of Horace, the preliminaries had been settled—or were settled by Horace himself. As we have seen, the Roman poets followed their Greek originals with just so much modification or selection as was due to the difference of language and nationality. They would no doubt have been content to follow the Greeks to the end, if a new phase in literature had not suddenly arisen. The outburst of Augustan poetry, in which Horace himself played no small part, but which later critics chiefly identified with Virgil, had no Greek analogy, and could not therefore be explained on purely Greek lines. Post-Augustan criticism was faced with an unprecedented phenomenon.

When Horace wrote the *Ars Poetica* the work of Augustan literature was practically finished. Horace himself had gained fame as a great lyric poet; Propertius and Tibullus had opened a new field for Latin song; and Virgil—alread popular as the author of the *Bucolics* and *Georgics*—was known to be engaged on his masterpiece, for which the Roman world was waiting, confident that "something greater than the *Iliad* was about to be born."[1] So far, the models of Latin poetry had been Greek, at first hand. Virgil and Horace had no doubt borrowed freely from their older compatriots; but their real and avowed aim was to go back to the fountain-head, and the imitation of Ennius or

[1] It is probable that the *Art* was actually written a year or two after the publication of the *Aeneid*.

Lucretius was only a stepping-stone on the way. Horace, as a critic, only set the seal to his own practice in his advice

vos exemplaria Graeca
nocturna versate manu, versate diurna.

To thumb the Greeks by night and day was advice the easier to follow because, hitherto, no Roman poet was sufficiently famous to interrupt a clear vision of the Greek *exemplaria.* Henceforward, there was no need to apologize—as Afranius had done—for borrowing "*even* from a Latin,"[1] since Roman poetry had now produced its own models in Augustan literature, and above all in Virgil. During his lifetime, Virgil had already attained something of the glory which was afterwards to place him upon a pinnacle above the rest. But, if he was then the first of Roman poets, he was still only *primus inter pares.* Horace—in spite of his warm affection—makes no special claim on his friend's behalf, bracketing Virgil with Varius, whose poems have not even survived. As an innovator, both in subject and style, Virgil encountered opposition from a critical public, bred in the traditions of Ennius. Before, or shortly after, his death, hostile and friendly critics seem to have quarrelled over the new movement; and, though the names of his *obtrectatores* are scarcely worth preserving, it is of interest to discover the grounds of offence.[2]

In the first place, it was quite an easy matter to accuse the poem of plagiarism, and we are not surprised that a certain Perellius Faustus collected these *furta.* But, apart from this main charge (the justice of which will be discussed below), there were other indictments. In especial, the poet was blamed for *κακοζηλία,* affectation, preciosity, or bad taste.[3] This literary sin might take various forms, as in extreme "Atticism," or its opposite, extreme "Asianism."

[1] Macrob. *Sat.* 6, 1, 4.

[2] Donat. *vit. Verg.* 180. See generally Nettleship in Conington's *Virgil* 1, p. xxix f.

[3] See Quint. 8, 3, 56.

Virgil certainly could not be charged with either a bald or a florid style; but Agrippa accused him of being "put up" (*suppositum*) by Maecenas to use ordinary words in an unusual manner. To suggest that Virgil's style was moulded by Maecenas—if Agrippa really meant this—is of course absurd. None the less, the criticism is illuminating; it shows the sort of opposition which, in an intensely conservative public, was bound to be directed against a newer school. Agrippa and Maecenas stood for very different ideals of art. The former is conspicuous as perhaps the only leading man of the day (not excepting Augustus himself, even if his Ajax "fell on his sponge") who seems never to have written in verse. He was an author, but his recorded writings bore the practical title of *commentarii*, and dealt with r ad-surveys and aqueducts—the natural interests of a great aedile; and his other work, an autobiography, appears to have been no less severely prosaic. According to Pliny, he made no pretensions to taste—*vir rusticitati propior quam deliciis*[1]—though he could speak on occasion with dignity. Agrippa, in fact, was a Roman of Cato's type. Maecenas, on the other hand, though proverbially a patron, was also at least an amateur poet, with a style notoriously Asian and affected. Augustus laughed at his literary "curling-tongs" (*calamistri*),[2] and his prose-rhythm seemed inebriated to Seneca, who chose him as a proof of the theory that a bad style reflects a luxurious life.[3] In verse, his choice of metres (galliambics and glyconics) reflects the influence of the Catullan school on their least pleasing side, while the worthless sentiment of his longest extant fragment —"Life at Any Price"—does not increase our respect for him either as artist or man. Virgil, of course, owed nothing to Maecenas, except for patronage, but it is quite likely that he had to bear some of the blame for his patron's curling-

[1] *N.H.* 35, 26. [2] Suet. *Aug.* 86; Tac. *Dial.* 26.

[3] Seneca, *Ep.* 114, 4; 101, 11; cf. Quint. 9, 4, 28. See generally Norden, *Kunstprosa*, p. 263 f.

tongs. However, Virgil's "innovations," when we examine them, appear harmless enough. He was criticised for introducing "new figures," like *ater odor, caeso sanguine* (for *caesorum*) *recens caede, per mille coloribus arcum, tela exit*—all (except the first) uncommon usages of cases, adjectives, and verbs, which offended the grammatical purist of the day.[1] Again, the classical dread of metaphors—the most striking difference between Roman and modern poetry—is illustrated by the objection to such simple instances as *aquae mons, ferreus imber* and *telorum seges*—metaphors which have now become so familiar that they have almost ceased to be felt as metaphorical. Besides these *vitia*, Virgil coined several words; and this was probably the crown of his transgressing, since Horace found it necessary to defend him (with Varius) on this count.[2]

It is possible that some of these criticisms belong to a later age—Macrobius does not give names or dates—but, taken as a whole, they undoubtedly reflect a certain dissatisfaction, or even active hostility, hardly silenced by the chorus of admiration that celebrated the birth of the *Aeneid.* At more than one later period this note of censure was heard again. In the early Empire, contemporaries of Tacitus and Quintilian protested against the excessive homage offered to the Augustans, and there were critics who preferred Lucilius or Lucretius to Horace and Virgil.[3] Later, there was an outbreak of archaism which lasted from Hadrian to M. Aurelius and Lucius Verus. Hadrian himself preferred Ennius to Virgil; and the triumph of the old school appears in Fronto, the tutor of the two Antonine emperors. His letters to Marcus show the complete swing of the pendulum: quoting freely from the ancients, he never mentions the name of Virgil. It was not till the end of the fourth century that

[1] Macrob. *Sat.* 6, 6.

[2] On *ater odor* (*Aen.* 12, 591) see Warde Fowler, *Death of Turnus*, pp. 92 and 111. The adjective implies terror or ghastliness.

[3] Tac. *Dial.* 33; Quint. 10, 1, 98 and 43; Plin. *Ep.* 6, 21.

Ennius was finally dethroned, the quotations from Servius and Macrobius proving that he was then chiefly regarded as a "source" for Virgil.[1]

In general, such variations of taste need no explanation: or rather, perhaps, they cannot be explained, but can only be noted as coming under that mysterious law of Change which operates in literary as in other human fashions. But it is worth while to point out that, in Rome, there were special causes for these several attempts to shake off the Virgilian yoke. From time to time the natural conservatism of the Roman people asserted itself in an attempt to recapture the ancient spirit, and to return to the simple Italian life, uncorrupted, as yet, by the luxury of imperial Rome. These attacks, however, were powerless to dislodge Virgil from his place as the supreme poet of Rome, during the four centuries in which Latin literature and its attendant criticism were to maintain a vital existence. With the further growth of his supremacy in the medieval age we are not concerned; although of course his fame was based on the real criticism of the past, it was swollen beyond the bounds of literary recognition by all kinds of superstitious accretions. But, from Horace to Servius and Macrobius, the critics were competent to judge, and it is not too much to say that, throughout these four centuries, Roman criticism was in effect monopolized by the study of a single poet. Even when a temporary wave of fashion set against him, Virgil seems to have triumphed with ease. About the very time in which Tacitus commented on the preference of "certain people" for Lucretius, Statius was confessing his debt to the *Aeneid:*

> *nec tu divinam Aeneida tempta,*
> *sed longe sequere et vestigia semper adora,*

while his contemporary Quintilian—not to speak of Martial

[1] Gellius, *N.A.* 18, 5. See Comparetti, *Virgil in the Middle Ages* (E.T.), p. 39; Friedländer, *Roman Life and Manners* (E.T.), iii. p. 6.

and others—acknowledged Virgil as undisputed master of Roman poetry. Gellius, a pronounced archaist in the time of Fronto, excepted the national poet from his general neglect of the Augustans. But here we come to the *crux* of the situation. Granted that Virgil was supreme among his own countrymen, how did he stand in relation to the Greeks? Hence, the ultimate problem, which in one form or another exercised all post-Augustan critics, was the ethics of imitation.

In itself, the practice of borrowing did not trouble the Roman conscience. Latin literature had started with actual translation, in the rude version of the *Odyssey* by Andronicus; and, after the Romans had passed this stage, it was sufficient praise for anyone of their poets, if he was the "first" to adapt Greek forms or sentiments to his own language. Lucretius and Virgil, Horace and Propertius are all satisfied with this claim to originality—if, indeed, the use of *primus* can fairly be said to connote the term "original" in any modern sense. For it must be remembered that the classic spirit cares—or understands—very little about priority of invention. In the earliest age of poetry, no question of originality can arise at all.[1] There can be little, if any, sense of literary ownership in oral poetry, and therefore no sense of borrowing. This statement has nothing to do with the theory of the "communal ballad"—the idea that a poem could be the work of a syndicate. Such a theory, though it has been seriously advanced, need not be seriously discussed. But it is true, I think, that in an early social stage, when transmission of poetry is oral, the authorship must be largely anonymous, just as, at the present day, there is a floating mass of "poems," constructed on the model of Edward Lear, but of strict and sometimes desirable anonymity. Even when the author of a primitive poem was known, there could be no

[1] See R. G. Moulton, *The Modern Study of Literature*, p. 22 f.

rights reserved. Ideas and forms of art at once become common property, and the individual author is lost in a group. Imitation (or at least reminiscence), in Greek literature, seems to be a kind of survival from this earlier stratum of communism. Rhapsodists, or Homeridae, are in the succession, and sing impartially their own songs or those of Homer himself. But Greece had no need, and—one may almost say—no time for mere imitation. In the short efflorescence of Greek literature, new forms followed each other so rapidly that tradition counted for little. It was not until Alexandrine times, when the creative impulse of Hellenism had been almost exhausted, that poets returned to the old forms—and to the Epic in particular—as Models. Plato and Aristotle had now formulated the theory of Mimesis, which of course was the imitation of nature, at first hand.[1] But now Nature was to be rivalled, if not displaced, by the Book. The change—though it might well have astonished Aristotle himself—was really implicit in his doctrine; for if the epic of Homer is the perfect form, it is inevitable that, in the epic sphere, we must follow Homer. The logic seemed flawless, not only to the Romans, but to the Humanists, who merely transferred to Virgil the homage which he had paid to Homer. We must follow the ancients—said Scaliger—because they created a nature more perfect than reality—a strong statement slightly tempered by Boileau, who was content to claim that, by imitating the classics, we imitate the real truth of Nature. Their poetry, in the words of his disciple,

> Is Nature still, but Nature methodized.

Even Wordsworth could not wholly cut himself adrift from the venerable doctrine of

> The great Nature that exists in works
> Of mighty poets.

[1] See p. 33.

But, although those poets gave Wordsworth "knowledge and enduring joy," no one knew better than he that they can never be a substitute for Nature herself. The doctrine, after all, has been fatal only to the lesser breed of poets, who alone have rigidly observed it. Lucretius and Virgil were "mighty poets," who could use the Models as Longinus held they should be used: "Proper imitation and emulation of great writers leads to the attainment of the sublime; for the great natures inspire by their effluences (*ἀπόρροιαι*), just as the divine afflatus impregnates the Pythian priestess. This is not plagiarism (*κλοπή*), but like taking an impression from beautiful forms or works of art." [1]

The passage is a splendid defence of the classical spirit; but it shows the dangers, as well as the strength, of the traditional method. If Longinus may have assured himself that imitation is not plagiarism, others were not so easily satisfied. Indeed, to take an "impression" is not, in itself, a very good proof of originality. The ancient critics had, therefore, to remove the odium so often attached to "imitation," before they could vindicate an author's claim to be original. In the first place, a poet must be above-board—the debt must be open and acknowledged; and here Virgil, according to Seneca, amply fulfils the ethical code of mimesis.[2] But something more than frank avowal was needed to refute the charge of "theft," and Virgil's own apology is more to the point: it was easier to steal the club of Hercules than a single verse of Homer. He did not, in fact, deny the charge, but pleaded the difficulty of the feat as its own justification.[3] In one sense, of course, Virgil's claim holds good—his borrowings made Homer Virgilian; but on formal grounds, his plea must have seemed inadequate, for a burglar cannot hope for

[1] *de subl.* 13.

[2] *Suas.* 3, *non surripiendi causa, sed palam imitandi hoc animo ut vellet agnosci.*

[3] Donat. *vit. Verg.* 186 f.

acquittal on the ground that he is not an amateur but an expert cracksman. Ultimately, therefore, the poets and critics were thrown back on another line of defence: Imitation is a form of rivalry. As we have just seen, Longinus uses the two words (μίμησις and ζήλωσις) as synonyms, and the Romans make no distinction between *imitor* and *aemulor.*[1] A poet must not masquerade in borrowed plumes —he should "avoid the literature of the Palatine Apollo," unless he can do better.[2] Virgil's admirers are never tired of pointing out his improvements, especially on earlier Latin verse.[3] Their position, in fact, is exactly that of Dryden's apology for Ben Jonson who "invades authors like a monarch, and what would be theft in other poets is only victory in him". But this vindication, though it served its immediate purpose, laid bare the vulnerable spot in the armour of Roman criticism. A Latin author could no longer be judged on his own merits; he must needs be pitted against a Greek antagonist, and patriotism demanded that, if he could not win, he should at least put up a good fight. The competition was merely extended, when in post-Augustan times the Romans imitated their own compatriots. But the main point was always to make out a good case in competition with the Greeks. It was an easy matter to prove Virgil, as an artist, superior to Ennius or Lucretius; but, after all, Virgil had challenged the greatest of the Greeks, and unless he could maintain his rights to the title of a Roman Homer, the whole case for Latin poetry collapsed.

Unfortunately, the sole weapons in this literary duel were "parallel passages". The method was as old as the

[1] So Cicero (*Ac. post.* 1, 8) uses *imitor*, Gellius (2, 18, 7), *aemulor*, both referring to the same work—Varro's Menippean satire.

[2] Cic. *Brut.* 19, 75; Hor. *Ep.* 1, 3, 15 f.

[3] E.g. Macrob. *Sat.* 6, 1, 6, *indicio transferendi et modo imitandi consecutus est ut quod apud illum legerimus alienum melius hic quam ubi natum est sonare miremur.* Cf. Gellius 1, 21, 7 on his debt to Lucretius; Serv. on *Aen.* 9, 511 and often. See Norden on *Aen.* 6, p. 359.

Frogs of Aristophanes, in which Aeschylus and Euripides had each been armed with his line or "passage," to be weighed in the balance; but the Romans failed to recognize that a weapon, sharp and serviceable for comic purposes, was useless in the real arena of literature. The duel was not only demanded from combatants who could not be matched, but was fought with dummy arms. It is true that the parallel passage has still a place in the critic's equipment; and, in view of the contempt into which the old method has not undeservedly fallen, there is the more reason to acknowledge its real service. To the scholar and editor parallel passages (from the same or a different author) are often essential, whether to emend a corrupt text or to explain an obscurity of meaning. A rare construction, a striking phase, or a particular sentiment is best illustrated by a quoted parallel. Again, no author can be completely detached from his predecessors or his contemporaries: and Roman poets, in particular, cannot be completely understood—though they may be enjoyed—in isolation. Indeed, it may be fairly claimed that the method can give enjoyment as well as understanding—to some minds, at least, it is a pleasant task to trace back a sentiment or expression from one poet to another, just as the classical poets themselves found pleasure in rehandling the work of their predecessors—*adamat poeta ea quae legit diverso modo proferre* [1] —by "comparing" such a passage as the Homeric description of Olympus with its reminiscences in Lucretius and Tennyson and Swinburne. But the only *critical* value of the comparison is to provide material for an estimate of personality—to show, not how one poet has imitated another, but how far he has stamped his own impress on common metal.

The inadequacy of the Roman comparative method may best be judged if we apply it to such a poem as Milton's

[1] Serv. (*Don.*) on *Aen.* 2, 797.

Lycidas. That masterpiece is not only "borrowed" in theme and general conception, but has been proved to be a cento of classical and neo-classical allusions.[1] Confronted with the *Lycidas*, a Roman critic would have praised its art or learning, and might perhaps have claimed that in some passages Milton had improved on Theocritus or some other "original." Beyond this a Macrobius could not go. Intent on explaining—or explaining away—the significance of the passage, he would have missed the meaning of the whole poem. He would not have emphasized—though he might have dimly felt—the fact that formal imitation is a small thing in itself, counting but little either for or against the imitator; that what really matters, is whether a new spirit has been infused into the old matter; whether Milton, in gathering up alien threads, has made of them a pattern of his own, to express his personal experience and reflect his his true individuality.[2] Criticism by parallel passages can never show this, because it starts from the hopeless assumption that the "borrowed" element might be separated from the original, and that the residuum, after all deductions are made, is the sole contribution of a poet which deserves to be considered. Milton, in his turn, furnished Keats with a famous line

> To one who has been long in city pent:

but what should we think of a critic who denied originality to Keats, or deducted the line from the great sonnet, of which it strikes the keynote?

The misuse of comparison has had the unfortunate result that all comparisons are now reckoned as odious by the fashionable school who demand that every work of art must be appraised entirely by itself. It is often said that you cannot compare Homer and Virgil at all—both being poets

[1] See Sir J. E. Sandys in *Trans. R. Soc. Lit.* xxxii.

[2] For criticism by parallel passages see also Saintsbury, *Hist. of Crit.* i. p. 331 f.

whose work is individual, unique. To this it may surely be answered that a relation of Virgil to Homer is a very patent and acknowledged fact. Its meaning may be, and indeed has been, misunderstood; but that is no reason for denying the relation; we should rather make a new effort to understand it. Modern criticism is seriously menaced by the catchword of "uniqueness." Logically, such a position is itself the denial of all criticism, since there can be no standard by which to judge the unique. But, as a matter of fact, no poet is independent of his forerunners; he cannot work *in vacuo;* and if he could, the result would be only bombination. Whether nearly or more remotely, he carries on a tradition, and we cannot estimate his work unless we are more or less familiar with the tradition. It may be contended that one can enjoy Shakespeare without knowledge of earlier English dramatists, of his sources, or of his dramatic tradition. Croce, representing this view, argues that "disputes and doctrines as to the three unities, as to the characters of tragedy, as to the manner of obtaining the catharsis or purgation, have considerable importance for anyone investigating the history of aesthetic and critical ideas . . . but they have no importance whatever as an element in the judgment of a poem . . . We care nothing for the canvas, but only for what of embroidery in the shape of poetry there is upon it".[1]

In fairness to the great Italian critic, it should be added that he points a way of escape from purely subjective criticism. Although he holds that every work of art, being personal and new, is unique, and therefore not to be classified or compared, he is careful to lay stress on the importance of history: all works of art are part of an organic whole, each marking a stage in spiritual development.[2]

[1] Croce, *Ariosto*, etc. (E.T.), p. 405.

[2] See p. 107. Croce's view may be recommended to those who "have grave doubts if there is such a thing" as a history of poetry. I quote from Mr. Robert Graves' interesting book *On English Poetry* (p. 86), where the section

The admission is significant; it implies that even if a poem is to be judged by itself, it can only be judged aright by the critic who knows the history of poetry—who can, in fact, "compare". And this is surely the sole position of common sense, unless we are altogether to abolish criticism, whose function is to point out the beauty which may escape the uninitiate. It may be right (in theory) to aim at pure aesthetic enjoyment of an author without the disturbing factor of intrusive analogies or differences; we must always remind ourselves, in reading *Hamlet*, that Shakespeare is not Marlowe or Jonson, but Shakespeare, and—as Mr. Clutton Brock somewhere says—we must beware of judging his Cleopatra on the ground that her behaviour was "so unlike the home-life of our beloved Queen". We should look for what a poet gives us, not for what he might (or might not) have given. Virgil must not be turned into a later Homer or an earlier Milton.

These warnings are salutary, and a welcome revulsion from the old pedantry of criticism. But they do not relieve the critic from the duty of knowing all, if he is to judge one. We cannot appreciate Virgil or Shakespeare without knowing the conventions of their art, and these conventions are historical and traditional. It is not disputed that good music may be enjoyed without any technical knowledge; but it is equally certain that some acquaintance with the technique will heighten the enjoyment. Feeling cannot be wholly divorced from knowledge, just as the artist himself works not only by emotion but by reason. We have all met the person who is proud of his ignorance of art, but knows "what he likes," and we know the sort of thing that he is apt to like.

The mistake of classical critics, then, was not in comparing the two great poets, but in mis-comparing them. With their inadequate apparatus of parallel passages there is small

"Histories of Poetry" bears a suspicious resemblance to a famous chapter on snakes in Iceland.

wonder that the Romans, in spite of their patriotic affection for Virgil, did scanty justice to his real merit. Weighed in such a balance with Homer, he was certain to be found wanting. In fact, during the first two centuries, his admirers are more apologetic than laudatory. Valerius Probus, a Virgilian scholar and the chief critic of the early Empire, was forced to belittle his favourite author, on the evidence of the parallel passage. He contrasted the Homeric description of Nausicaa with Virgil's imitation, and preferred the Greek original: Nausicaa, playing with her maidens by the seashore might well suggest the huntress Diana and her train; but such a simile was inappropriate to Dido, a queen making a royal progress with her courtiers through her rising city.[1] Even in details he thought that Virgil came off second-best, with a 'hesitating' translation, in which the "flower of the whole passage" was omitted: *ῥεῖα δ' ἀριγνώτη πέλεται, καλαὶ δέ τε πᾶσαι*, (where, it may be remarked in passing, Matthew Arnold comes to the rescue of Virgil:

> The leader is fairest,
> But all are divine).

The criticism—as far as it goes—is interesting; it shows, at least, that Probus had literary taste, and most people will agree with his conclusion, though an acute student of Virgil has retorted that compared objects need not resemble each other in all respects, and thinks that the queenly Dido need not yield to Nausicaa in her likeness to Diana.[2] In the next century, another distinguished critic—Favorinus, the contemporary of Fronto and Plutarch—depreciated Virgil's account of Etna in eruption, as inferior to the Pindaric original; and to explain the inferiority, he recalled the poet's own remark that he produced some verses like a bear and had not "licked them into shape".[3]

[1] *Od.* 6, 102 f.; *Aen.* 1, 498 f.; Gellius, *N.A.* 9, 9, 12 f.
[2] Henry, *Aeneidea*, p. 724 f.
[3] Gellius, *N.A.* 17, 10; Macrob. *Sat.* 5, 17, 7; Donat. *vit. Verg.* 81.

Defeated by the scales of the poetic weighing-machine, the Romans must have found it difficult to justify a poem like the *Aeneid*, which, on the face of it, was an imitation. The best that could be done was to lay stress on Virgil's art; and the criticism of the first century may be summed up in the verdict of Quintilian, that Virgil is a good second, and his superior art makes amends for the lack of Homer's "heavenly and immortal genius".[1] Quintilian knew that Virgil was *Romanus*—that his poetry expressed the sum of the achievement and aspirations of a great people, proud of a destiny which was something wholly different from the mission of the Greeks. But his critical method could not communicate his knowledge. Having had the opportunity, denied to Aristotle, of studying two literatures, he might have profitably "compared" the *Odyssey* and the *Aeneid*, and have done fuller justice to the younger poet. He might—to take a single example—have shown that, although the idea of a descent to Hades is borrowed by Virgil from the Greek, the Sixth *Aeneid* owes but little to the *Odyssey*—that the personal adventure of Odysseus, eager only for his safe return, has become the great quest of Aeneas, anxious not so much for his own sake as to learn the future of the Trojan destiny, which was to be fulfilled in the Roman Empire. To talk of imitation, here, is to misconceive the first principles of poetry; but, with the ancient lack of historical perspective, the use of the parallel passage was a mere trap, diverting criticism from the spirit to the form.

This false method persisted to the end. Servius and Macrobius, in the fourth century, still continue to rely on the doctrine of rivalry, and "weigh" Homer and Virgil. But a change has now come in the estimate of the Roman poet. The moderation of a Probus or Favorinus has disappeared, replaced by a Virgil-worship as extravagant as that of Vida

[1] Quint. 10, 1, 86.

or Scaliger. It is true that Servius (born about the middle of the century) is fairly restrained; while yielding to none in enthusiasm for his author, he generally avoids superlatives. But with his later contemporary, Macrobius, criticism is almost entirely lost in panegyric. In the *Saturnalia* Virgil is the chief subject of discussion by a symposium, in which the chorus of admiration is only broken by the voice of a single dissentient—a certain Evangelus, who is obviously a man of straw, introduced to make the debate possible, and to increase the poet's triumph by feeble opposition.[1] The outcome of the debate is that Virgil—if sometimes inferior to Homer—is often his equal or superior, "improving" on his great original almost as much as he improved on his own countrymen.

The mere fact that, between Quintilian and Macrobius, the fame of Virgil had so greatly increased, is not wonderful. The perspective was now clearer; other competitors, like Varius, had dropped out of the running, and surrendered to Virgil the undisputed place as the representative of Roman ideals. What is more surprising, is in the reasons assigned by his admirers, which are strangely different from the grounds of modern appreciation. Servius and Macrobius agree with Quintilian (and with the moderns) in emphasizing Virgil's art; but they have been blamed for laying undue stress on two aspects of that art which, to a modern critic, seem no very striking, nor even necessary, equipment for a poet: his Eloquence and his Learning. Yet it is precisely these two qualities that were bound to impress the ancient critic, to the exclusion of other virtues which we should think more praiseworthy. The attitude of Macrobius is neither ignorant nor perverse; it is a reasoned estimate of Virgil's position—the natural outcome of the lines on

[1] The discussion begins in Bk. i., and is continued in iii.-iv. See generally Dill, *Roman Society in the Last Century of the Western Empire*, p. 419; Glover, *Life and Letters in the Fourth Century*, p. 174 f.

which Roman criticism had travelled, and a fair, if one-sided, reflex of Roman poetry itself.

With regard to the first charge—that they harped too much on Eloquence—we have already seen that poetic criticism was an offshoot from the study of oratorical styles, and never developed a character of its own. Indeed, it could hardly have done so, without unfaithfulness to its subject, since actual Latin poetry was so largely dominated by the rules of rhetoric.[1] Macrobius was right in seeing that Virgil had started from rhetoric; his mistake lay in failing to see how far Virgil had moved from his starting-point. Granted that the line between the orator and the poet was often fine, it was the more important to draw it firmly. Quintilian, at least, knew when the line was blurred: Lucan was to be classed with the orators rather than the poets; and Fronto was under no illusion—Lucan had flaunted the art which Virgil had concealed.[2] But, by Lucan's time, rhetoric had triumphed both among the poets and their interpreters. As Martial observed, some people might deny Lucan the name of poet, but his publisher could tell a different tale.[3] By the second century, it was possible to discuss in all solemnity "whether Virgil was an orator or a poet."[4] We are therefore prepared to find that Servius dismisses one of the most famous passages in the *Aeneid* (6, 847 *excudent alii spirantia mollius aera*) with the remark "*est rhetoricus locus*"—a criticism as true as it is painfully inadequate; or that Macrobius compares Virgil with Cicero and other orators, to their disadvantage; for, while each of the four "styles" is associated with a single orator, Virgil alone is master in all the four.[5] Greek and Latin rhetoric had adopted a large and complete system of "figures of speech," and these were transferred to poetic criticism with disastrous

[1] See above p. 16. [2] See p. 22. [3] Mart. 14, 194.
[4] Annius Florus in a lost treatise entitled *Vergilius orator an poeta*.
[5] Macrob. *Sat.* 5, 1.

results. It is needless to labour this point, since even in modern days the poets have not been entirely freed from the burden of pedantic terminology, imposed by generations of editors who have inherited the Macrobian tradition; but a single example may show how Virgil, "the orator," was treated by his ancient commentators. The power of moving to pity or anger—both affections are comprehended in the Greek term Pathos—had been exhaustively analyzed in relation to rhetoric, and Virgil—the most pathetic of ancient poets—was submitted to the same scrutiny. If the process had been confined to generalities, no great harm would have been done: it is quite proper for Servius to point out that there is *miseratio* at the conclusion of each of the first six *Aeneids*[1]—such a criticism is indeed helpful to our understanding of the poem. The real mischief began when the commentator came to details. Pathos—the most subtle and elusive appeal to the affections—became the prey of the grammarian, an emotion to be ticketed according to a number of convenient labels. How is the commentator to deal with such a passage as Virgil's description of Orpheus and Eurydice—one of the most "pathetic" scenes in the *Georgics*, or in any other poem? The passage tempts the translator, even with the certainty of failure:[2]

But on a sudden, even while she spoke,
She turned and vanished, like a wreath of smoke,
Into thin air, and saw him not again,
Clutching at shadows fruitlessly, and fain
To tell her all his heart; and Charon harsh
No more would row him over the hell-marsh.
What should he do? Twice cheated of his love,
Where should he turn? What prayers or tears might move

[1] Serv. on *Aen.* 3, 718. See some interesting remarks on pathos in Quint. 8, 3.

[2] *Georg.* 4, 498 f.

The ghosts and gods of Hades? His cold bride
Even now was nigh-across the Stygian tide.
Seven months in their procession came and went,
And still—men say—with piteous lament
He sang his tale in caverns icy-cold
Beneath a mountain crag, where Strymon rolled
Desolate waters, and the tigers grim
Fawned, and the enchanted oaks would follow him.
As a complaining nightingale hath sung
Under the poplars, for her callow young
Robbed from the nest by ploughman's cruel spite,
She, on her branch, repeats the livelong night
Her burden, and fills the country with sad songs.
So he refused all soothing that belongs
To Venus, and unmated roamed upon
Hyperborean ice and frozen Don,
A solitary wanderer amid lands
Bound in Riphæan frost's eternal bands,
Mourning Eurydice, and that trothless troth
Of Dis. At such memorial were wroth
The Cicon womenfolk, who, for the slight,
Rent him in orgies of dark Bacchanal rite,
And threw his limbs afield. Yet, at the last,
When from his marble neck the head was cast
To float down Thracian Hebrus, midstream-borne,
There came a chill voice—a mere tongue forlorn—
"Eurydice, ah, Eurydice!" and died;
And the long banks "Eurydice" replied.

On this passage the method of a Servius is helpless, because there is no obvious figure to which he can draw attention. The best he can do is to note that the nightingale (*Philomela*) is an example of *species pro genere*, "for any bird"—a note which is not even sensible, as *flet noctem* might have told him. In the Virgilian speeches, however, a Servius or Macrobius has his chance: Juno's indignant rhetoric, for example—*heu stirpem invisam*—becomes a happy hunting-ground for the discovery of ecphonesis, hyperbole, irony, and the rest.[1] It may be objected that these figures are useful, or at least innocuous: a botanist may appreciate the beauty of a flower no less because he knows its Latin name; and a reader of Virgil's beautiful lines,

> *te, dulcis coniunx, te solo in litore secum,*
> *te veniente die te decedente canebat*

need not feel their pathos the less because he is told that "repetition" is one of its causes. But the real defect of the method is that, when the grammatical terms fail, the critics perforce are dumb. Such lines as

> *sunt lacrimae rerum et mentem mortalia tangunt*

or

> *tendebantque manus ripae ulterioris amore*

refuse analysis. Matthew Arnold (who might well have included both of them among his "touchstones" of poetry) wisely refused to define the "mark and accent of high poetry in the abstract."[2] To the ancient critic the mark and accent was to be included in one of the Rules; and he could therefore choose only such touchstones as were fitted to a rule. The famous passage

> *heu, miserande puer, si qua fata aspera rumpas,*
> *tu Marcellus eris*

is worthless as material for this kind of criticism; yet we know that, when Virgil recited it in the imperial presence, Octavia fainted with emotion.[3] Augustine remembered how he had wept for Dido, and how the burning of Troy and the ghost of Creusa had strangely moved him.[4] It is from these witnesses, rather than from the rules, that we can best realize the power of the poet.

[1] Macrob. *Sat.* 4, 2 f. A list of Servius' rhetorical notes is given by E. G. Sihler in *A.J.P.* xxxi. (1910), p. 23.

[2] *Study of Poetry* (*Essays in Criticism*).

[3] Don. *vit. Verg.* 109; see Serv. on *Aen.* 6, 861.

[4] *Conf.* 1. 13, 20 f.

There remains the Learning of Virgil. Here, again, we find a difficulty in adjusting ourselves to the Roman point of view, which, as we have seen, is the natural result of the conception of a Teacher. The stock epithet *doctus* at once betrays the difference between ancient and modern notions of the poet's office. No interpretation of the epithet—and it has various shades of meaning—would be thought a compliment to a poet of to-day, at least as the final recognition of his merit. In general, the epithet connoted the idea of mastery in technique—the "learned" poet knows and keeps to the rules. But the full content of the word does not stop with the artistic meaning, as some suppose.[1] Horace might claim the laurels of "learned brows" by adapting Greek metres to the Latin genius; but, when Statius speaks of the "high fury of learned Lucretius," the *doctrina* is obviously not so much artistic as philosophic. And, most often, the learning is that curious affection for Greek mythology which came to be regarded as a hall-mark of the classic style. There were of course degrees in this taste. Catullus and Propertius were most conspicuous of all; but no Roman poet entirely neglected this form of learning. Where the whole of classical poetry is permeated by the myth, any special illustration might seem needless; but it may be worth while to quote an instance which shows not only the dominance of the myth, but our difficulty in appreciating its poetic value, as evidence of "learning". The poem on Sleep, by Statius, is deservedly famous, and may well take rank with the sonnets to Sleep by Wordsworth and Keats.[2] It has often been paraphrased, but rarely, if ever, translated into English verse, because its mythology will hardly bear translation. In a literal rendering, it would run as follows:

[1] See e.g. Plessis (*la Poésie latine*, p. 165), *savant en son métier, arrivé.*

[2] *Silv.* 5, 4. The sonnets to Sleep are collected by H. W. Garrod, *Oxford Book of Latin Poetry*, p. 496 f.

Tell me, O gentle Sleep, how I have erred,
Boy-god, who, saving me, dost all things bless!
Beasts are all silent, silent every bird,
And the tired branches droop in drowsiness;
The noise of brawling streams is lulled to rest,
And the tumultuous seas are pillowed on Earth's breast.

Seven nights the Moon has glanced on me awake,
The daystar follows evening, till the Morn
Brushes me with her whip, for pity's sake,
To cool my fever. I should be still forlorn,
Though I were cunning Argus, who could keep
A thousand eyes to watch, yet spare a tithe for sleep.[1]

Elsewhere, in dear arms prisoned, a lover lies
And bids thee, Sleep, surrender all the night:
Come thence! not overshadowing mine eyes
With pinions opened in their fullest flight
—That boon is for the happier! With thy wand
Touch me, or lightly hover by, and pass beyond!

The feeling of the original is entirely modern, or rather independent of any period; but the expression is characteristically Roman. A reference (which does not appear in the above translation) to the evening and morning star—as the lamp of Oeta and Paphos—is inoffensive, though affected; but we are then confronted with the conceit about the monster Argus, who could close some of his eyes in sleep, and still have enough for sentry-go. On these lines an excellent critic remarks that "one might almost fancy them to have been inserted later by an unhappy second thought".[2] Here modern taste has surely led the critic astray. Statius was probably prouder of this euphuism than of anything else in

[1] Compare Keats, *Lamia*:

With eyelids closed
Saving a tythe which love still open kept.

[2] J. W. Mackail, *Latin Literature*, p. 190.

his poem. His mythological learning lifted a mere human cry into the region of poetic refinement.

If we go back from this extreme case in Statius to Virgil, we find even in him some traces of recondite lore. His early work, at any rate, was not entirely free from the literary vice of Alexandria. He could write

> *cessere magistri*
> *Phillyrides Chiron Amythaoniusque Machaon.*

This has no doubt a fine ring, recalling the organ-voice of Miltonic names; but compared with the simplicity of Lucretius—if we may here venture on a "parallel passage"—

> *mussabat tacito medicina dolore*

the erudition (as modern editors have seen) strikes us as frigid and pedantic. It is even less happy than Tennyson's

> Now lies the Earth all Danae to the stars,

for the learning of that affected phrase at all events suggests a picture, whereas the parentage of Chiron and Machaon is quite insignificant—Virgil is explaining *ignotum per ignotius.*

But Virgil's claim to be *doctus* is not to be judged by his occasional lapses into Alexandrinism, nor even by his far more vital grasp on Greek culture in its finer flower. His learning is more deeply rooted in his own soil. The *Georgics* and—to an even higher degree—the *Aeneid* are perfect expressions of that form of patriotism which recognized that the present greatness of Rome was due to the past. Other poets—Apollonius in especial—had been antiquaries; but these Alexandrines had no stronger motive than curiosity. Virgil had a more serious purpose than the author of the *Argonautica:* in the reconstruction of a new Rome and a new Italy, devastated by the Civil Wars, the only hope, as he thought, was to follow the ancients—to study the *exempla maiorum*, and to recapture their way of life. The old Italian religion was to be rescued from the neglect of half a century, fallen temples were to be rebuilt, decaying priesthoods restored. In particular, the ancient ritual was to be preserved; for ceremonial was the very basis of Roman religion, and on its scrupulous performance the safety of the state depended. All this was part of the Reconstruction, the life-work of Augustus; and the chief poets of Rome found their fullest inspiration in his designs.[1]

Antiquarianism, therefore, was no mere dilettante recreation, but a serious subject pursued for a noble end. In the last years of the Republic, Varro had already set the fashion of studying antiquities, though without the practical motive of furthering the Augustan policy, which inspired the prose-writers—Livy and Dionysius—as much as the poets. Horace, as everyone knows, was the emperor's mouthpiece in urging the Restoration, and even Ovid ranged himself with the antiquaries. But the task of the *Fasti* was unsuited to his genius. The subject demanded something more than the wit and facility that rarely failed the poet of the *Amores.* It needed a sense of the moral importance of the issues, and Ovid was a poor moralist. He was lucky, as he confessed, in his own times—*haec ætas moribus apta meis.*[2] Moreover Ovid is the least enthusiastic of poets, and only an enthusiast, like Virgil, could write a poem which should not fail to be high poetry because it was also a storehouse of antiquities. In the *Georgics* Virgil had already sung of the new Italy restored by the ancient spirit, and recovering the stern simplicity of the Marsians and Sabines and Volscians no less than the virtue of the old Latin race.[3] There was reconciliation to be done as well as restoration; for, although Virgil's father was no doubt a Roman citizen, Mantua itself did not become a municipality until the young poet had left it; while Como and Garda—the great lakes eulogized in

[1] See further p. 249. On the Reconstruction generally see Heinze, *Virgils Epische Technik*, p. 465 f.; J. W. Mackail, *Lectures on Poetry*, p. 91; J. F. D'Alton, *Horace and his Age*, p. 46 f., and W. Warde Fowler, *Virgil's Gathering of the Clans*, p. 28 f.; T. R. Glover, *Virgil*, p. 76 f.

[2] *A.A.* 3, 122.

[3] See p. 115.

the *Georgics*—were also outside Italy until 49 B.C.[1] Only a few years before, Italy had fought with Rome, and the sore was still open. But history pointed the way towards healing the wound: Italian and Latin were now to be merged by Augustus in the Roman name, just as Trojans and Latins had been unified by Æneas in his new kingdom on the Palatine.

This grand moral and political idea dignifies the whole of the *Aeneid*, but especially the last six books; and it is to the credit of the later Roman critics that they fully saw the significance of the poem. Servius and Donatus knew that the *Aeneid* was more than the tale of Æneas—that it embraced the whole history of Rome, the *gesta populi Romani*, uniting the origins of Augustus and his City.[2] Macrobius has the same view, but from a slightly different angle. Living at a time when the old religion was in its last death-grapple with the rising force of Christianity, and himself a staunch upholder of the ancient traditions, he looked to Virgil as defender of the faith, the champion of an order now menaced by a new and aggressive enemy. The chief characters of the *Saturnalia*—Symmachus, Praetextatus, and Flavianus—are well known as bitter opponents of Christianity, at least in so far as it was now claiming to be the religion of the State.

For more than two centuries the *Aeneid* had been steadily rising to the rank of a Sacred Book. Hadrian—though in literary style belonging to the pre-Augustans—felt a reverence, which we may (if we please) regard as superstitious, for a poem that seemed able to prophesy the future as much as it had recorded the prophecies of the past. His use of the *sortes Vergilianæ* seems to mark the first stage of later Virgil-worship—the beatification, if not the canonization, of the poet who was destined to become the magician of

[1] See R. S. Conway, *New Studies of a Great Inheritance*, p. 30; T. Frank, *Vergil*, p. 7.

[2] Servius on *Aen.* 6, 752; Donat. *vit. Verg.* 78.

the Middle Ages.[1] By the fourth century, pagan Rome had fully acknowledged the Sacred Book, but the discovery was too late, when the better part of Rome had already transferred allegiance to other Scriptures.

It is natural that an "inspired" book should be studied for its religious or moral message rather than for its poetic charm. Half a century ago the publication of the *Literary Man's Bible* would have been regarded by many excellent people as profane. Virgil, though not formally inspired like the Sibylline Books, was of infinitely greater importance to a Roman moralist than those dull and unmoral prophecies; and there is no wonder that the poet came to be valued for his learning at the expense of his poetry. Indeed, in the early Empire the moralist looked for more edification from Virgil than he found. Seneca complained that he was not didactic enough—he sought for beauty rather than truth (we need not search for any Stoic sympathy with Keats), and that he wanted to please the reader more than to teach the farmer.[2] This uncompromising Stoicism remained to the end, the only difference being that, whereas Seneca was dissatisfied, Virgil's later eulogists found no flaw in his *doctrina*. Both Servius and Macrobius are anxious to prove that the poet is an authority in all branches of learning—*disciplinarum omnium peritissimus*. While Tennyson, reflecting modern criticism, seizes upon the essential feature of Virgil's art in a single line—

All the charm of all the Muses often flowering in a lonely word—

Macrobius curiously anticipates this eulogy with a characteristic change: "you will often find the profound *learning* of this poet in a single word."[3] He has indeed the grace to confess (again in a Tennysonian mood) that Virgil wears

[1] Spart. *vit. Hadr.* 2; see August. *Conf.* 3, 5.

[2] *Ep.* 86, 15, *non quid verissime sed quid decentissime diceretur.* See also 88.

[3] Macrob. *Sat.* 3, 2, 7.

the learning lightly—*quasi clanculo doctus*—but it is the erudition, open or disguised, that wins his praise.

If we review the results obtained from this survey of Roman criticism under the Empire, our first impression may be one of disappointment or even of contempt. Judged by modern standards, the critics were so obviously working on wrong lines, with all their insistence on principles which we have been taught to despise—the watchwords of Rivalry, of Form and Figures, of Morality and Learning. But there is another side to the picture. When not dominated by a preconceived theory, Roman criticism was as full of common-sense as the poetry itself. Instinctively, if not by rule, a Petronius or a Quintilian could appraise a poet at his true value. *Le cœur a ses raisons.* No doubt their judgments have not always been final—if there is any finality in criticism. Quintilian, for example, being under the spell of the Augustans, does scanty justice to Lucretius or Catullus. The great rhetorician was not superior to the rather exclusive ideals of classicism, and was quite impervious to romance. A sane critic of a sane poetry, he shows wide and catholic sympathy and discrimination within the range of Augustan ideals, and sums up Roman judgments on the school which most fully expresses the Roman character. Such a summary—it may be objected—is a label rather than a reasoned estimate; and no doubt Quintilian is content to dismiss each author with a brief definition. Here, however, we must remember that it was no part of his plan to enlarge on poetic criticism—his references to the poets are strictly limited to their practical value in the training of an orator. Only once, for a special reason, he expatiates; and then his criticism of Seneca proves that his shorter "labels" are not due to superficial reading, but are the concise expression of considered judgment. To say that Quintilian has the defects of his qualities is not so much to repeat a commonplace applicable to all human effort, as to remind ourselves that he keeps strictly to his business. We should not, for instance, expect that Horace would be chiefly praised for his Figures—we may prefer the label of Petronius, *curiosa felicitas*[1]—but, after all, the orator was (professionally) more concerned with figures of speech than with Chloe or Lalage.

It is usual to discuss Quintilian's poetic criticism as if it were mainly or wholly confined to the first chapter of the Tenth Book, with its famous comparisons of Greek and Latin authors. But, as we have seen from time to time, the art of the rhetorician carried with it the art of poetry, and the staple of Roman education was always a study of the poets. Just as Longinus, seeking for Elevation, makes no distinction between its appearance in prose or poetry, so Quintilian illustrates his points of a good style impartially from Cicero or Virgil or Horace. While he reminds his pupils that "the poets must not be followed by the orator in everything,"[2] he is at pains to insist that Style, in its widest sense, is common to both forms of expression. His Eighth and Ninth Books, in particular, which deal with Tropes and Figures—metaphor and the like—have really quite as close a bearing on Roman poetry as on rhetoric; and whatever may be thought of his critical methods, we must admire his deep and genuine interest in literature as a whole, even if we regret that the upas-tree of rhetoric tended to kill the poetry which had grown beneath its shade.

Of the Figures, themselves, enough perhaps may have been already said. It has been argued above, that they were harmless—as short-hand—in their place, but their proper place should be subordinate, whereas Quintilian (like all the rest) treated them as both the starting-point and the goal of criticism. The best that can be said of them is that they are signposts in the progress of literary appreciation which have now been happily passed on the way. They

[1] Quint. 10, 1, 96, *varius figuris et verbis felicissime audax*; Petron. *Sat.* 118.

[2] 10, 1, 28.

belong to a period in which the power of literature is fully recognized, but not fully understood. The later Greeks and the Romans had learnt from their own masterpieces that poetry and oratory had this abiding power to move and persuade; and they set themselves to discover and explain its causes. Language was bidden to deliver up the secret. In a sense, the discovery—and continual re-discovery—of the secret must always be the whole duty of the critic. But, whereas a Quintilian was satisfied that the key was to be found in the Word, the modern critic (having learnt all, or nearly all, that the word can teach him) looks rather to the personality behind the word. It is really the old antithesis of Art and Genius in another form; and true criticism cannot afford to neglect either the one or the other.

Quintilian—a teacher rather than a pure critic—emphasizes the place of art; but he was well aware that the Rules, without the Person, are useless. At the very outset of his task he warns his pupils that "precepts and theoretical treatises have no value without the co-operation of nature".[1] He does not seem to have read Longinus—if, as is probable, the greatest of Greek critics belongs to his era—but he would have agreed with the grand words which clinch the matter —*ὕψος μεγαλοφροσύνης ἀπήχημα*, "sublimity is the echo of a great soul." The silence of Ajax in the underworld may be more sublime than words.[2] But a text-book (on whatever subject) is not concerned with Genius. Quintilian, of course, assumed *ingenium*, and carried out the Horatian precept by supplementing genius with art. The only quarrel that the moderns can have with him lies in his deference to the Rules, where he is no better and no worse than any other ancient critic.

With Quintilian the end was close at hand, though not in sight. He lived in a period of great activity in most branches of literature; and though the Golden Age of Augustus was past, he did not despair of the present or the

[1] I *proem*, 26; cf. I, 19.

[2] Longin. 9, 2.

future. His general position is that there are living authors who can compete with the dead. His flattery of Domitian as a poet is of course to be discounted—it is on a level with the eulogy of our own Puttenham on the "learned delicate noble Muse" of Elizabeth, which "easily surmounteth all the rest that have written before her time or since."[1] Disraeli's compliment—"we authors, Ma'am"—to another royal lady (who had nothing in common with Domitian beyond a mild literary aspiration) would not be regarded as the serious and comprehensive judgment of a statesman who was also a man of letters. If Quintilian had thought or said that the Emperor's learned Muse was the only hope of literature, he might well have despaired of the poetic State; but he adds that there are others—satirists, *clari hodieque et qui olim nominabuntur* (an estimate, if not true at the time, at least shortly to be verified in Juvenal), and lyric poets, superior to all but Horace. He does not, or will not, see the signs of decay, nor will he be warned that the writing of his age is a writing on the wall. Others were not so optimistic; for good reasons or bad, his contemporaries were persuaded that literature was declining. The poets themselves knew that the resources of their art, so splendidly exploited by the Augustans, were now beginning to fail. The Models, which had once been an inspiration, had become an incubus. To the Classicist, the choice of subject is all-important, and the fountain of poetic subjects was running dry. Again and again we hear the lament that the material has been used up. No doubt the complaint was a poetic commonplace, since even Virgil had made it—and had then written the *Aeneid*;[2] but, by Flavian times, it had become unfortunately true. A later writer, reduced to the (epically) slender theme of hunting, deplores that the whole field of Greek mythology has been exhausted:

omnis et antiqui volgata est fabula saecli.[3]

[1] *Art of English Poetry*, i. ch. 31.
[2] *Georg.* 3, 3 f.
[3] Nemesianus, *Cyn.* 47. Cf. Manil. 3, 5 f.

This confession is significant. The Flavians had gleaned the scanty harvest that remained after Augustan reaping, and there was no new crop of purely Roman seed to take its place. But, though the broad fact was too obvious to be really disputed, the critics were not in a position to recognize the true causes of the decadence. In general, it was assumed that the arts, including poetry, could only flourish in an age of innocence, and that their decline was brought about by luxury. This view opened a wide field for the display of rhetoric, as we see not only from the elder Pliny but from Petronius, who should have known better.[1] But there is a more modern and scientific outlook in Velleius Paterculus, who holds that literature is subject to the universal laws of growth, perfection, and decay. With masterly insight, Velleius discovers the real root of the evil—it is impossible, he says, to surpass or equal the models of the past; the hopelessness of the attempt causes the interest to flag, *studium cum spe senescit.* He can see no remedy; we may seek for something new, but the craving for novelty is a hindrance to perfection[2]—a statement which, by the way, is at least disputable.

It is, however, in the *Dialogue* of Tacitus that the connexion between social life and literature—or at least oratory—is most fully discussed. The great and outstanding originality of the dialogue is that it makes allowance for the environment. The orator, for good or evil, is what his education, his country, and his age have made him—literature is the expression of national life. This attitude—anticipating the school of Taine—is a radical change from the older concentration on the Form, as a "thing-in-itself," independent of time or place.

[1] Pliny, *N.H.* 14, 1; Petron. 88.

[2] *Hist. Rom.* 1, 17. *sequiturque ut frequens ac mobilis transitus perfecti operis impedimentum sit.* Cicero (*Tusc.* 2, 5) had already remarked that oratory (*quod natura fert in omnibus fere rebus*) was subject to growth and decay.

In dealing with the environment, Tacitus quite rightly lays stress on the outstanding feature in Roman history—the immense political difference between Republican and Imperial Rome: Augustus had "pacified eloquence, like everything else."[1] Oratory may have declined; but, if so, it is argued that the decline is due to the excellence of the present government. The orator's opportunity comes when morals are bad. In a well-ordered state, when crimes are few, and the senate has only to register the decisions of a wise autocrat, there is no room for the barrister or legislator. This remark smacks a little too much of a courtier writing under Vespasian, and a few years later Tacitus had reason to deplore, in the *Agricola*, the fact that liberty of speech or writing was impossible during the tyranny of Domitian. For oratory and other forms of political expression, Tacitus is no doubt amply justified in pointing to a political "cause." There was no scope for a Cicero in an environment which could, at best, admit the *Panegyric* of a Pliny. But the decline of Poetry—an art so warmly championed by Maternus in the dialogue—was more difficult to explain. The cause could not be only or even mainly Caesarism. On the contrary, there should have been progress rather than decay; for the emperors, on the whole, had been good patrons. There had always been the closest relation between the poet and the court, from the time when—as Maternus reminded his audience—Virgil had been honoured by Augustus even in his retirement to the woods and groves. Juvenal was no mere flatterer when he saw that the salvation of poetry lay in Caesar's hands:

et spes et ratio studiorum in Caesare solo.

The best poetry of the Silver Age was written under one of the worst of the emperors. Plainly, therefore, the cause could not be political. But it might be moral; and Stoicism,

[1] *Dial.* 38, *eloquentiam, sicut omnia alia, pacaverat.*

which had captured the majority of thinkers, was not in doubt on the matter. As a consequence, the later Roman criticism was narrowed to a single point: the decline of art must be due to the decline of morality. The connexion of the "style and the man" was obvious enough to have already passed into a Greek proverb, and Cicero had remarked that the elder Cato's life was very like his oratory.[1] But Seneca gave a fresh start to the old proverb, which he supported, quite consistently, by Stoic arguments. To a Stoic, Nature is reason, and all faults are contrary to Nature. Good literature, therefore, must be reasonable. Virtue is clear, simple, straightforward; and a virtuous man, saying what he thinks, will express himself clearly and simply, avoiding the "obscure brevity" of Sallust, whose own morals were not commendable, or the loose speech of Maecenas, which betrayed his effeminacy.[2]

This position contains both a truism and—as generally in truisms—an error. To say, with Seneca, *talis oratio qualis vita*, or, with Buffon, *le style c'est l'homme même*, is true beyond need of argument, in the broad sense that any "style," worthy of the name, must reflect personality. We are all agreed that no poem, no work of art, can have value except in so far as it reveals the man. It need not reveal the details of his private life—many, besides Browning, have doubted, whether there is a key to unlock Shakespeare's heart—but it must express what is permanently inspiring in the artist's soul. Indeed the distinction between great and little work is simply the difference between a great and a mediocre personality. So far, we are all Senecan; and, on the "moral" side we may well concede that no thoroughly "bad" man would or could have written the *Divine Comedy* or *Paradise Lost*. To this extent, the author of *Paradise Lost* was justified in claiming that "he who would not be

[1] *de rep.* 2, 1.

[2] Seneca, *ep.* 114; cf. Persius, *sat.* 1. The subject is fully discussed by F. I. Merchant in *A.J.P.* xxvi. (1905), p. 44 f.

frustrated of his hope to write well hereafter in laudable things, ought himself to be a true poem." But the Stoic belief that a man's style—in the narrower and purely literary sense of the word—is good or bad according to his moral life, rests on the fallacy that the terms "goodness" and "badness" have the same connotation in art as in ethics—a theory killed by the ridicule of the single line

Who drives fat oxen should himself be fat.[1]

The author of this line might himself be mentioned as proof that style is not always a complete or accurate reflex of personality. If we had no Boswell, could we possibly have reconstructed Johnson's character, with all its blunt directness and absolute sincerity, from the formal and often artificial style of his own prose?[2]

As with the poet, so with his audience. The argument that the decline of poetry is in any sense due to the immorality of the age is to compare two incommensurables. Even if the Antonine age had been thoroughly immoral, this would have had no close bearing on literature. The age of Villon, and Villon himself, were immoral. But, as a matter of fact, Roman society was not more corrupt, on the whole, under Trajan than under Augustus, and the Rome of the Antonines, which saw a complete paralysis of poetry, is usually—and no doubt with truth—regarded as Rome at her happiest and best.

So far, we have criticized Tacitus and Seneca only in particulars; but there remains a wider question. How far, if at all, does the environment, whether political or moral, affect poets and poetry? In modern times there has been a strong protest against Taine's views of poetry as a mere reflection of society or the expression of its genius in any

[1] Johnson's line is quoted by R. G. Moulton, *Modern Study of Literature*, p. 253, in this connexion.

[2] I find that this point is elaborated by H. W. Mabie, *Essays in Literary Interpretation* (1892), p. 20 f.

age. We are warned, on all sides, that poetry is a "free force," which must be interpreted with reasons contained in itself.[1] Society has its own way of self-expression, by its customs and actions. We learn nothing about Keats by being told that he represents an age of romanticism. There have been good and bad poets in nearly all ages; Virgil and Bavius were contemporaries, and lived in precisely the same environment, which cannot therefore account for the difference between the poet and the poetaster.

Are we then to exclude all reference to circumstance? From the purely artistic standpoint, no doubt we should: poetry, *per se*, is timeless and placeless. Shakespeare is not the sum-total of poetical tendencies in Elizabethan England; he is just Shakespeare. None the less, Taine's opponents, in their laudable desire to distinguish art from the history of art, seem to undervalue the very real influence of environment, not indeed in creating genius—we do not know how genius is created—but in determining the subject and form of poetic expression. A poet is not a discarnate genius. He is a man; and, as such, works under the human limitations of time, race, and society. As we have seen, tradition—the experience of the past—*does* count in the determination of poetry; and environment—the experience of the present—is at least as operative. Seneca and Tacitus may have been wrong in attributing the decay of poetry to a special feature of the environment; but they may have been right in assuming that, somehow, the cause lay in that environment. Those who argue that poetic genius is a wind, blowing where it lists, forget that the wind itself is subject to law. All history shews that there have been certain periods—such as the fifth century B.C. in Greece, and the fifteenth in Italy—when genius has at least been fostered by opportunity. New ideals, new hopes and vision, new light on Nature or man have fallen on fruitful soil and have

[1] See Croce, *Ariosto*, etc. (E.T.), by Douglas Ainslie, p. 357.

blossomed a hundredfold, in what de Quincey called paroxysms of intellectual energy.[1] The freedom of Athens in the age of Pericles, the expansion of the world and the recovery of letters in the sixteenth century, the French Revolution—these are only some of the periods in which Taine may fairly demand a hearing. And if we agree that favourable circumstance is at least the forcing-house, if not the seed of talent, we must logically hold the converse—that talent may be muzzled, or diverted from poetic channels, by the unfitness of circumstance. Matthew Arnold talks sense in holding that for the creation of a masterwork the power of the moment is needed as well as the power of the man.

Now, in Rome after the days of Tacitus, there was no moment favourable to poetic genius. Even a Milton might have remained mute and inglorious in an age when poetry was threatened by so many dangers, both internal and external. Internally, a poetry, depending on fixed forms and owing a servile allegiance to masterpieces, is doomed to ultimate exhaustion. Velleius, as we saw, could not suggest a way of escape. The only hope—as Sainte-Beuve has taught us—is to substitute the relative for the absolute, to find new forms when the old have outlived their use; to honour tradition, but not to be cramped by the grip of a dead hand; to make new wine and pour it into new bottles. If there had been a new wine of ideas, the Romans might perhaps have discarded the old bottle of Form. The mischief was that, after the first century, the old ideas were petrified and there was no new stimulus to be derived from outside. The joy in a settled peace, the belief in the Julian star, the full realisation of Rome's greatness—all this had found full expression in Virgil and Horace. The later Empire had no fresh achievement to suggest new themes, while many of the earlier hopes had failed. Indeed, it was mainly disillusion which inspired such poets as shewed any

[1] See de Quincey (*ed.* Masson), x., p. 194 f.

real vitality—men like Lucan, whose whole work is a political protest, and Juvenal, whose satire, if not truly "made by indignation," was at least pessimistic. There was then the stimulus of opposition, political or moral; but a merely negative stimulus cannot vitalize poetry for long. Positively, neither Lucan nor Juvenal had any new alternative to the present political or social order. Lucan harked back to the *libertas* of the Republic; but this liberty was discredited. It meant only the return of the Senate, the freedom of a close oligarchy whose factions had brought the Roman people to civil war. Juvenal, in the moral sphere, could fulminate; but, like most satirists, he is quite barren in construction.

The Roman Empire, after its first brilliant triumph, had settled down to a peace which, for poetry, was a devastation. Neither politics nor science, neither religion nor philosophy, could supply new material for poetic imagination. In politics, the poet could do no more than flatter the autocrat of the day. Science was not merely stagnant but retrograde; and from the second century onward it was crushed beneath the weight of a superstition which had survived the attacks of Lucretius to be again rampant in the age of Lucian. As for religion, the official cult of the state had become more and more identified with the worship of the emperors. Such a religion gave scope to the panegyrist, but this motive was soon worked out—Virgil and Horace had already said as much as need be said (and perhaps more) in the praise of Augustus. Panegyric remained to the last, since the poets were nearly always dependent on an Imperial or noble patron; but Domitian and—at the very end—Honorius were poor successors of Augustus, and there was not often a Stilicho to inspire a Claudian. Of other religious creeds, which struggled in a welter of confusion from the second to the fourth century, none, perhaps, seem so suggestive of poetic interpretation as the cult of Isis, with all her wealth of symbolism, her impressive ceremonial, and her promise of immortality. That Isis had a moving power in literature is clear from Apuleius, who at least lifted the fringe of her veil. If he had lived under Augustus, his natural and inevitable expression would have been in verse; living in the third century, he adapted himself to an "age of prose". The romance of Cupid and Psyche is as capable of poetic treatment as any tale of Ovid, and has, indeed, found a fine expression in modern English verse; but though Apuleius can rise to his theme in spirit, his form is that of his time—prosaic. There is surely no clearer instance of a poet repressed, if not crushed, by his Age.

Lastly, there was the youngest religion, destined to supersede the rest. By the beginning of the fourth century it might have been expected that Christianity should have quickened the dying energies of the Classical spirit. Some of the Christians themselves did not despair of consecrating the old forms to serve a new ministry. It is true that there was strong opposition from fiery zealots like Arnobius and Lactantius, who would have no parley with the accursed literature of paganism. Augustine condemned poetry altogether, remembering, with a wistful regret, his pagan culture.[1] There were indeed others less uncompromising—Paulinus of Nola, Sedulius, and, chief of them all, Prudentius. But that poet, though both learned and zealous, shews the impossibility of reconciliation. The pagan form had too long been bound together with the Myth to suffer divorce. An ancient Roman general might summon the gods of a conquered people to quit their doomed city and join the conquerors; but Apollo and the Muses refused to enter the Christian camp. By the sixth century, the place of poetry, at best, was as a mere appendix to the seven arts of Martianus Capella.

Nothing, in fact, so clearly proves the bankruptcy of poetic imagination as the last chapter in the history of Latin literature. At no time was verse more conscientiously

[1] *Conf.* 1, 16. For the Christian attitude see Haarhoff, *Schools of Gaul* (1920), p. 169 f.

practised than in the fourth and fifth centuries, from Ausonius to Sidonius. In the earlier part of that period, literature was a stepping stone to the highest honours in the state, and Ausonius himself verified the prophecy of Juvenal—*fies de rhetore consul.* In the next century, the great nobles were indeed debarred from all political interest, but, for that very reason, they were the more devoted to literature, and especially to poetry.[1] But the old vein had been long exhausted, and no fresh quarry had been discovered. With Sidonius we reach the final stoppage of an exhausted mine. In the preface to his poems—the piece contains nearly 350 lines—he devotes over 300 to a review of the ancient subjects of poetry which he is *not* going to sing; but the bishop's own Muse, as he only too truly admits, is *valde sterilis*—hendecasyllables after Statius, panegyrics and epithalamia after Claudian, a few epigrams and occasional poems, a long way after Martial, and—in this odd company—a letter in hexameters to a colleague, dealing with subjects from the Old and New Testaments in a spirit as sincere as wholly unpoetic. Sidonius is perhaps the last melancholy illustration in Latin literature of the two worlds, one dying, if not dead, the other powerless to be born. Another bishop—Fortunatus—still tried to carry on the classical tradition, but his classics were, even more than for Sidonius, merely academic, like the Byzantine writers of epigram. His real sympathies were definitely Christian—the author of *vexilla regis prodeunt* had really broken with the past.

In this general decay the last resource was rhetoric, which had always been a danger, and sometimes a disaster, to Roman men of letters. But rhetoric, which could make a consul, could only mar a poet, if he had no greater inspiration than Ausonius. The only vital impulse that remained

[1] See Dill, *Last Century of the Western Empire*, ii., ch. 2, and iv., ch. 3. Symmach. I, 20 *iter ad capiendos honores saepe literis promovetur.* Claudian had eulogized the literary consul in Mallius.

was an honest and enthusiastic reverence for Rome—the symbol of a civilization which was already crumbling into ruins. But even this reverence was bounded by a narrow outlook, which could not merge the City of the Seven Hills into a wider vision of the Empire. Ausonius, as we have seen, very nearly broke away, moving the poetic centre of gravity from the Tiber to the Moselle. But, though he "loved Bordeaux" and only "worshipped Rome," Ausonius was not great enough to found a school which should develop a national or local poetry, independent of the Capital. Martial's fear of sending a native poem from Spain to Rome deterred the provincial, as long as Rome remained—even in theory—the head of the Empire. Tacitus, if he lived too soon to realize the whole truth, was, at least in part, a true prophet, when he saw that Roman literature was the expression of Roman life.

This is not to assert that literature is always or altogether the expression of a racial or political unit—a view which lands us in absurd results. Strictly, indeed, a poem is simply the expression of the poet himself, and the number of poems which we class together as English Poetry is nothing but a number of collected individual intuitions. This collective poetry may have very close contact with the poetry of other nations, especially if (as between England and America or Ireland) there is community of language. In modern poetry, at least, the influence of a dominant nationality, though by no means negligible, must be severely limited. For Rome, however, the influence was overwhelming. She had "imposed" not only peace but poetry upon the whole of civilized Europe, and the decay and death of classical poetry followed the fate of the City which had always been the true scource of Roman inspiration.

CHAPTER IV

NATURE IN LATIN POETS

I

WE are often told that to contemplate a landscape or to observe any natural phenomenon—a flower, a bird, or a sunset—is strictly an intuition, an exercise of the aesthetic activity, without the participation of the logical faculty. It is admitted, of course, that such pure intuitions are rare; they are almost inevitably blended with an intellectual process, and the fusion of these two elements forms a new and more complex intuition. Further, it is argued that a poet can multiply these intuitions to an indefinite number, so that in his capacity as artist, his whole view of Nature may be intuitional—his logic is of value only so far as it assists or directs his feelings. While the philosopher's duty is to unify, impersonally, the facts which underlie the phenomena of Nature, the poet's business is to express the impressions which Nature makes to him personally, through the medium of the senses. Hence Nature—whether in her totality or in her meanest flower that blows—is merely an object for science or philosophy, unless she suggests or reflects human emotions. A poet may express the beauty of a rose in terms of feeling alone; or, if the short life of this beauty suggests the brevity of human life, this "thought" is itself emotional. Poetry, however, would be a simple matter if it were confined to the expression of

> Gather ye rosebuds while ye may;

and great poets have penetrated more deeply into Nature than Herrick, or than the late Latin author who here anticipated him. And, the deeper the penetration, the greater is the part played by the intellect, however much the logical faculty may be directed and controlled by the emotions. A poet, in fact, like any other artist, must not simply transcribe Nature. He must interpret her; and as she is too vast to be interpreted under all her aspects, he must select. Whether this selection is conscious or unconscious, it must be prompted not merely by his physical environment but also by his intellectual attitude towards external Nature.

Now, in the course of human history, man's views of the external world, in relation to his own life, have been very diverse. Nature has been regarded as animate or inanimate; as friendly or hostile; as a thing apart from man, or intimately connected with his life and fortunes. We may hold—if we wish—that there is no such thing as an aesthetic progress of man; but we are bound to admit that the objects of aesthetic appreciation must change with changing views on the meaning of the world. In the words of a prominent writer on aesthetic, "So long as art is alive, its range of appreciation and expression extends itself by a natural process, in which the 'apperception' of later artists is prepared by the recorded perceptions of their forerunners".[1] Modern historical knowledge has taught us to be more catholic in our tastes; if we claim to be more appreciative than the eighteenth century, the reason is that we have a wider experience, a larger field from which to choose our objects for expression.

If the twentieth century has here an advantage over the eighteenth, it follows, *a fortiori*, that our field of observation is far broader than that of the Greeks and

[1] B. Bosanquet, *Hist. of Aesthetic*, p. 91.

Romans. This fact is patent enough, though many writers, anxious for the honour of the "Classics," have tried to overlook or discount it. When the wave of Romanticism was hardly spent, the chief concern of some critics was to show how the ancients—Homer or Lucretius or Virgil—had anticipated Romantic ideas. Romance was the only wear; and it was therefore a point of honour to read into the Classics as much Romanticism as possible. It is of course an excellent thing to recognize that Homer or Virgil had a real feeling for Nature; but nothing is gained by an attempt to confuse the record. One of the chief reasons for studying ancient poetry is that we thereby widen our knowledge of man's views on the universe; and this knowledge is simply obscured by well-meaning efforts to accentuate the likeness, and so to neglect the differences, between the ancients and ourselves.

Apart from this occasional tendency to modernize the Classics, the general difference between ancient and present views of Nature has of course never been disputed. It has become a commonplace to say that the Greeks and Romans very largely took their scenery for granted. They belonged to a purely humanistic stage, in which man is so far occupied with himself that he regards his environment as a mere background to his own activities. Landscape is not studied objectively until man has exhausted—at least for a time—his own proper study of mankind. The Græco-Roman world passed through the first stages of this transition. Between Homer and Aristotle the Greeks had explored the depths of human life and personality, and it was left for the Alexandrines to lay more stress on external nature. In much the same way the Romans (as we shall see) became less purely humanistic in Ausonius than in Virgil. But the Romans themselves stood on the shoulders of the Greeks, and were in a position to profit by their "recorded perceptions".

To the Greek poets, with a religion based on the worship

of elemental forces, Nature was not only animate, but beneficent. The Earth was a kind mother, and the gods, no less than men, were sprung from her womb, and thus were linked together by participation in a common parenthood. The elements might be capricious or even hostile; but, for the most part, they were friendly, or could be placated. Greek poetry assumed—long before Socrates—that Nature was purposed for the service of Man; and later, when the Epicureans denied purpose, pointing out the faults of a lifeless Nature, the Earth was still regarded as a kindly parent rather than a cruel stepmother. Part of the world, no doubt, was useless to Man—there were tracts of ice and torrid sands, barren rocks and untrodden mountains, but—as Lucretius remarked—such places could be avoided.

With this outlook, the wildness of Nature seemed to call for apology rather than admiration. The Greek, in fact, was so thorough a humanist that, during the best period of his literature, he disregarded external Nature, except in so far as she could be translated into terms of humanity. An oak tree must be observed as a Dryad, before it became a subject for the painter or sculptor. Even the poet, though his medium of language gave him a wider scope, moved most freely in the region of humanized Nature. It may be argued that this anthropomorphic view does not prevent the poet from appreciating natural beauty: on the contrary, he may show more imagination by turning the tree into a Dryad than by observing it directly as a plant. But the attitude is fatal to a clear *description* of Nature. If the landscape is peopled with Dryads, there is no room for the scenery itself. Nor could philosophy stimulate the poet, at a time when Socrates was a stranger to the country and declared that trees did not want to teach him anything. There were, indeed, many Athenians who did not follow Socrates in his thirst for knowledge—men who preferred the plane-trees of the Ilyssus and the "well-side violet-patch" of the farm to the market place of Athens. But, though these found a spokesman in Euripides or Aristophanes, the dominant note of poetry in the age of the City-state was humanistic and urban—the mirror of a social life which found its analogy in the eighteenth century, when Johnson preferred Fleet Street to Greenwich Park, and Lamb confessed to Wordsworth that he found London good enough, "without your mountains".[1]

The nemesis of civilization is over-civilization, and later Greeks, like Rousseau, sought for escape in a Return to Nature. The phrase—as the prince in *Rasselas* discovered —is ambiguous, and may stand for various experiments in simplification. It has been interpreted as a return to more "natural" conditions, without the relinquishment of city life; or as a refuge from the city altogether, either to the country or to the wilderness. The Greeks stopped short of the wilderness, but they tried the other ways of escape; and of these, one at least made its mark on their poetry. The growth of large cities such as Alexandria, without the compensation of a free political life, obliged the townsman to look beyond his walls, and Theocritus turned to the orchards of Cos and the pasture-lands of Italy and Sicily. But Theocritus was no Thoreau. For him the lure of the city was still powerful; the country, at most a means of relaxation; and the old Greek ideal of the Polis still lingered as the highest and most natural sphere of human energies. And even when Theocritus wholly leaves the town, his interest is still with human nature rather than its environment. A love of the country, for itself, and apart from its human associations, is hardly a prominent feature of the Idylls, in spite of the delightful scene in which he places his characters. Even so, the gain to literature was immense: between Theocritus and Words-

[1] Boswell, *Life*, i., p. 283; Lamb to Wordsworth, Jan. 30, 1801.

worth there is a long distance to travel; but Theocritus alone had made the journey possible, and it was left for Virgil to move a stage further on the way.

II

The *Eclogues* of Virgil must have come as a revelation to the Roman public. Even those who had read Theocritus could not have failed to realize that a new province had been conquered, a new note struck in Latin Poetry. On the formal side alone, the *Bucolics* were full of rhythms and cadences unknown to Catullus, giving promise of the "stately measure" which was soon to be perfected in the *Georgics*. The learned might complain—later, at least, Gellius complained—that the young poet had missed, in places, the native sweetness of the Greek, which defied translation into the rougher Latin.[1] But the Roman reader would also have felt—as we feel now—that there was compensation for this loss in the strength and dignity of the Virgilian hexameter. In spirit, the new poems were even more remarkable. They were Alexandrine, it is true, in so far as their original was of Alexandria; but Theocritus was greater than his age, and the *Bucolics* turned Roman poetry from the cold polish and affected pedantry of the Callimachean School, into which even Catullus had fallen, to the fresh air of the fields. Their outstanding merit was to dethrone the trivial prettiness of the *Coma Berenices* and its kind. They displaced the Egyptian court for the countryside of Italy.

Virgil did not discover Italy, as the *Sirmio* of Catullus amply proves: but he saw the district, to which Sirmio itself belonged, with a vision entirely new. Northern Italy was no longer to be the preserve of an artistic noble, spending more time, and living a fuller life, at Rome than in his country villa. Mantua and the Mincius had dwellers,

[1] *N.A.* 9, 9, 4 f.

more humble, but more permanent—the farmer (Virgil's own stock), the shepherd, and the goatherd, whose lives were bound to the soil, and who could only imagine Rome as like their country town. It was transpadane Gaul, not the Sicily of Theocritus, which Virgil knew and set out to describe. But here comes the inevitable criticism. The charge is often made that, even in his own country, Virgil still took a foreigner as his guide. A close scrutiny can detect at most one or two passages suggesting a definite Italian locality, as in the lines:

qua se subducere colles
incipiunt mollique iugum demittere clivo
usque ad aquam,

which may be identified with the poet's home at Andes.[1]

Elsewhere, Virgil has clouded his own observation—keen as the *Georgics* prove this to have been—in the midst of his Greek original, so that glimpses of Mantua (or is it Naples?) are scarcely seen in a golden haze of Sicily and Arcadia. The fault is not entirely due to the reverence for Theocritus. It was contrary to the classical spirit to particularize. Local colour was out of place in a landscape as ideal as its inhabitants, who are themselves Theocritean. In the main, however, the charge is true that, if Virgil kept his eye on the object, that object was more often Theocritus than Nature. The *Bucolics*, in fact, show that the young poet had reached, as yet, only the "conventional" stage, which Arnold called the first or lowest mode of handling Nature. Yet, even here, there are flashes of the poet who was to become the "landscape lover" as well as the "lord of language." There are times when he rises to Arnold's

[1] *Ecl.* 9, 7 f.; see R. S. Conway, *New Studies*, p. 97 n. 2. Tenney Frank (*Vergil*, ch. 10) thinks it doubtful whether Virgil ever again saw Mantua after his boyhood; the pastoral scenery (except in *Ecl.* 9) rarely pretends to be Mantuan: it is Neapolitan. But, even if we grant this, we must allow that the poet "generalizes."

higher modes, in which the eye is not only on Nature but "lightness and brightness are added." In lines like:

et iam summa procul villarum culmina surgunt,
maioresque cadunt altis de montibus umbrae

we can surely recognize something better than the mere "faithful way"; and there is the final charm of the highest mode, which Arnold unfairly denied even to the Greek, and appropriated to the Celt, in the magical rhythm and diction of at least one passage:

sic tibi cum fluctus subterlabere Sicanos,
Doris amara suam non intermisceat undam.[1]

It is therefore quite unjust to see in the Virgil of the *Bucolics* a sedulous ape of the Greek pastoral. The young poet, dazed by the glamour of a brilliant masterpiece, was satisfied to re-echo, in part, the Syracusan Muse; he had yet to pass from the No-man's land of his pupilage to the real Italy of the *Georgics* and the Seventh *Aeneid*, from the model to Nature herself. The *Bucolics* were a prelude and a training for the great work in which Virgil—as he describes his own development in the proem of the *Aeneid*—left the woods and made the neighbouring fields obey the husbandman. Even here, the Roman would willingly give credit to a Greek, but the patronage of Hesiod is little more than nominal. The *Georgics* differ from the *Works and Days*, not merely in bulk and scope and general treatment, but (which is more important) in their spiritual content. Hesiod's advice to a lazy brother is to work, for only work can keep the wolf from the door. Virgil—as Conington long ago remarked—raises work to a higher power; it is the dignity of labour, rather than its necessity, on which he insists. The way of the farmer is not easy, for Jupiter has

[1] Since Arnold, the term "magic" has perhaps been overworked to express the highest poetical appeal. But it has an honourable tradition, rooted in the κήλησις of Greek criticism.

8

so willed it, but the farmer must do for agriculture what the ancestors of Romans did for Rome:

tantae molis erat Romanam condere gentem.

There was a rich reward, as the second *Georgic* testifies in a conclusion of matchless beauty. The farmer may be fortunate in any land if he only knew his own good—but he will be by far most fortunate in Italy. For, although the Latin poet might believe that he sang a "song of Ascra," he could speak of his native land with a love and admiration unknown to Hesiod, whose Ascra was a stony hill-side "evil in winter, grievous in summer, never good." The rest of Greece—from a farmer's point of view—was little better; and if Xenophon tried to praise the fertility of Attica, Thucydides and Plato had no such illusions about a land "not good enough to tempt an invader."[1] An Italian—and especially a North Italian—was far luckier not only in his soil, but in its associations. While the Greek states were largely maritime, with a hold on agriculture at best precarious, the history of Rome, from the Kings to the Punic Wars, was bound up with the land.[2] There is no Greek counterpart of Cincinnatus. The whole fabric of religious and social institutions was based on agriculture; and, if Latin poetry strikes its highest note in the world-empire of Rome, its accents are more tender when its theme is nearer home, in the pastures of Mantua or the farm of Tibullus. To the Roman, indeed, the empire was a direct outcome of the land. A belief in the unity of Land and People was the first principle of classic anthropology: racial characters were fixed by the climate and the soil; and even Strabo, who accepted this Hippocratean theory with some mistrust, was firmly convinced that the natural advantages of Italy were the chief cause of Roman greatness. The famous antithesis, "Divine Nature gave the country; human

[1] See the author's *Anthropology of the Greeks*, p. 80 f.
[2] I need only refer to Heitland's *Agricola*.

art built the City," is a text of Varro's fine tribute to Italy, in the preface of his book on Agriculture; and this eulogy was repeated, in a still more noble form, by the poet of the *Georgics*, who saw in his native land not only the bearer of the Massic vine and the flocks of Clitumnus, but the mother of the Scipios and the Caesars:[1]

Yet neither Median woods, of wealth untold,
Nor lovely Ganges, nor that river of gold,
Hermus, nor Bactria, nor the Indus-land
And all Panchaea's perfume-laden sand
Can match the glories of our Italy. Here
No dragon-teeth were sown, nor ever came
The yoke of bulls that, breathing deadly flame,
Prepared the harvest of the helm and spear.
But bursting corn abounds, and Massic vine,
And olives, and the delight of herded kine.
Here are the plains that know the warrior-pride
Of galloping charger; hence thy white flocks come,
Clitumnus! hence the bull that, sanctified
As chiefest victim by thy holy tide,
Brings Roman conquerors to the gods of Rome.
Here Spring remains, and the long summer-span
Counts alien months for measure; twice the fold
Is white with lambs, and twice the orchards hold
The fulness of their ministry to man.
But the fierce tiger and lion's cruel breed
Are strange to the land; nor is there any need
To trust the aconite unwarily,[2]
And learn, too late, its poison, nor to see
The long snake coiling with a monstrous trail,
Or gathered into a spire of glittering mail.
Here, too, are miracles of human hand—
Fair cities numberless, towns that upstand
High on the mountain-precipices, and all
The rivers lapping many an ancient wall.

[1] *Georg.* 2, 136 f.

[2] Compare Shelley, *Queen Mab*:

The nightshade's tempting bane
Poisons no more the pleasure it bestows.

Or shall I leave unpraised the Italian seas,
That bathe the higher and the nether strand?
Or the great meres, and—lordliest of these—
Lake Como? Shall I pass thee by, unsung,
Garda, whose far-resounding surge is flung
As high as Ocean's? Or shall I forget
The harbours and the giant barriers set
To guard the Lucrine, where in sullen mood
Vainly the sea chafes at the piles that save
The Julian channel, and Etruria's flood
Streams intermingled with the Avernian wave?
A land of copper veins and silver ore
And golden-flowing founts—she also bore
The flower of men: heroes of Marsian stock,
Sabellians, Ligures, stubborn as their rock,
And pike-bearers, whom Volsci brings to war.
She has given Rome that chivalry of fame,
Decii and Marii, and the noble name
Borne by the brave Camillus: she has sent
Those sons of mighty Scipio, aye, and thee,
Great Caesar, of them all most excellent,
Who now art driving India's broken horde
Far across Asia in astonishment,
A rabble urged before the Roman sword.
  Hail, Mother of Corn! mother of glorious sons!
To thee, Saturnian Land, I dare to raise
A song of ancient art and ancient praise,
Striking the rock, whence sacred water runs,
And sing, through towns of Rome, Ascraean lays.

We need not set bounds to Virgil's genius, but we must at least note the limits of his aesthetic horizon. His Italy is a land of corn and wine and oil rather than the dream of a Turner. And here—it may be added—Virgil comes into line with Lucretius. He confessed that he could not follow his predecessor in the contemplation of the Universe, nor could he feel a "divine pleasure and shudder" in the most awful and majestic spectacle of Nature; but, when Lucretius left the worlds of clashing atoms and descended to the solid earth, the scenery which he loved to depict was not the forest or mountain but that of a Nature conquered by man, who by long experiment and ceaseless toil had "compelled the woods to move up the hills and to yield place below for cultivation."[1] In this Lucretian country, where a grey strip of olives runs over hills and valleys and plains, marking orchard from orchard with varied charm, Virgil finds his own conception of natural beauty realized to the full.

The "love of the country"—so often discussed in connexion with Latin poets—is a genuine thing; but it is almost entirely limited to those phases and aspects of Nature which are nearest and most serviceable to Man. In Horace there is hardly a trace of "Romanticism"; and though the critics of the nineteenth century did their best to claim him as a "lover of scenery," even Keble was compelled to admit the lack of evidence. More modern critics have from time to time attempted to revive the claim,[2] and it has sometimes been suggested that Horace at least grew to love the country in later life. The evidence, however, hardly shows that his view was changed from the early period of the *Epodes*, when he put the praise of the country into the mouth of a money-lender.

So curious an association has caused some trouble. Tyrrell compared the ironical end with the method of a Calverley, working up a poem, ostensibly serious, to an unexpected conclusion. Such a method, however, is rather humorous than witty, and Horace—though he has plenty of humour—is above all things a wit. He is far nearer Marvell than Calverley, and there is close analogy in one of Marvell's most characteristic poems. The theme of his famous "Garden" is "delicious solitude," and we are therefore prepared for the praise of a place where the mind may

[1] *Lucr.* 5, 1361 f.

[2] See e.g. Wight Duff, *Literary History of Rome*, p. 539; J. F. D'Alton, *Horace and his Age*, p. 137 f.

withdraw into its own happiness. But we are not prepared for the final conceit—that Eve spoilt the happiness by her mere presence:

> Two paradises are in one
> To live in paradise alone.

Marvell intentionally strikes an unromantic note. He admires the Garden, but though his motto is not the Horatian *nil admirari*, it might well be the kindred warning *ne quid nimis*. Neither he nor Horace can contemplate a natural scene as purely objective; and when the intrinsic beauty of the scene carries them unwillingly beyond the human sphere, they return—as if with an apology for enthusiasm—to the same ground of wit.[1]

But where, after all, does this enthusiasm lie? Horace —to judge from his later work—demanded no more from the country than his moneylender. The life of a wit, a pleasure-seeker, and a court-poet could only be lived at Rome. There were times when, like other townsmen, Horace fled from "the smoke and wealth and noise" of the capital, to seek refuge in his Sabine farm, where a remote valley tempered the heat of Sirius. But his exclamation *o rus quando te aspiciam?* is not prompted by any yearning for the beauties of the countryside; Horace looks only for leisure and quiet, for freedom from social duties, for books and philosophic talk instead of politics. It would be absurd to suppose him insensible to the pure impressions of Nature; but his choice of natural beauty seems almost entirely to depend on its utility. He can draw, with a few masterstrokes, the picture of a tall pine and white poplar blending their hospitable shade, and a stream hurrying underneath in a twisted channel. But the shade and the stream—he hastens to point out—are useful for a picnic, as Lucretius had already discovered. If, in a less Epicurean vein, he may sometimes describe Nature by

[1] See p. 13.

way of pointing a moral, he nowhere seems to regard her beauty as an end in itself. He has the seeing eye, but surely not the soul of a Nature-lover.

Here, as so often, Horace is a true mirror of normal Roman feeling. He falls into line with Pliny the younger, who valued his villas at Laurentum or Como for their opportunities of study rather than for the charm of their surroundings; or—at the very end of Roman life—with Symmachus, who looked to the country to give him rest, good air, and time for literature, with hardly a word of appreciation for the scenery.[1] Partly, no doubt, the attitude of a Pliny or Symmachus is a pose—a serious Roman senator had more important things to think about than the merely picturesque. But the pose is none the less significant: Nature could make no sensuous appeal strong enough to counteract the ethical views of Roman philosophy, or the practical views of Roman life.

If Nature appealed to the Romans only, or mainly, in her cultivated trim, we are not likely to go astray in turning to the literature of the Garden as the surest index of their aesthetic standards. A garden, whatever its style, must always be artificial; but the art may either be concealed or paraded; and, in the long history of gardening, the changing views of Nature and Art have been accurately reflected in the changing fashions of horticulture. Broadly speaking, we may group these styles under the head of two principles: in Schopenhauer's words, the object of a garden may be to express either the will of Nature or the will of Man.[2] As extreme illustrations of the two principles we may take the "English" garden of the eighteenth century, and the "French" garden of the same period, a direct descendant of the Italian and ultimately of the Roman style. In practice, there has generally been some give-and-take between the

[1] See Dill, *Roman Society from Nero to M. Aurelius*, p. 174 f.; Boissier, *Fin de Paganisme*, ii. p. 215.

[2] See A. F. Sieveking, *The Praise of Gardens* (1899), p. 254.

two principles, and infinite gradations are possible within the extremes; but the Romans, at least, were almost wholly consistent. Despite some lip-service to the doctrine of "following" Nature, their gardeners were determined—in Cowley's phrase—to over-rule her. To a nation both practical and highly disciplined, the beauty of a garden lay either in its order or its usefulness. Of these qualities, the idea of order was plainly uppermost in the pleasure grounds of the Roman nobles, who could scarcely boast that their *horti* were useful. Pliny's gardens, with their long box-bordered walks, their colonnades and statuary and fountains, must have had all the charm which we can still feel at Versailles; but it is the charm of a Nature not only conquered but almost crushed.[1] There was little sympathy even with *l'arte che tutto far nulla si scopre*, since there was no attempt at concealment. In Pliny's garden, like Tasso's, the cultivated may sometimes be mixed with the wild—*si misto il culto col negletto*—but these negligent beauties are merely a foil for the refinement of the *topiarius*, who laid no more stress on Nature unadorned than Bacon on his "heath or desert in the going forth." As for the city garden, perhaps with more excuse, the triumph over Nature was even more complete. A Roman was said to "build" his garden; and the word implied not merely that he carried out the plan and style of the house—a modern gardener should do no less—but that he made the grounds as architectural as the house.[2]

There is no reason why the most formal garden should not inspire the poet. We may remember that Marvell's *Thoughts in a Garden*—the finest poem, of its class, in English or any other language—was suggested by stiff Italian pleasure-grounds, in which the skilful gardener had drawn a sun-dial of flowers and herbs. But the Roman *horti* were as barren a theme to the ancients as the French garden was uncongenial to Pope, who (for all his classicism)

[1] See Plin. *Ep.* 2, 17; 3, 5; 5, 6, and the elder Pliny, *N.H.* 19, 4.
[2] Cf. the town-garden of Vettius at Pompeii.

became one of the chief critics of box-tree animals, and one of the first to champion a return to Nature in the landscape style.[1]

If the Roman poets could get little pleasure from the *horti*, they found compensation in the *hortus*. The word, in the singular, stood for the orchard and kitchen-garden, and both of these fulfilled the canon of beauty in usefulness. They were a part of the land; and, as we have seen, the Italian land was fruitful and beautiful enough to satisfy the needs of poetic fancy. Instead of Homer's magic fruit, Virgil was content with the reality of the allotment where his Corycian farmer spent his declining years. For even that poet, who yields to none—except, perhaps, to Catullus—in a love for flowers, is careful to restrain his imagination within the bounds of fact. Nothing in the *hortus* is merely pleasant or picturesque, where roses and hyacinths can only claim a mention by virtue of their service to the bees.[2] Here, perhaps, the suburban (and even the country) gardens of England —in which the line between Beauty and Service is often too rigidly drawn—may hinder our appreciation of Virgil's *hortus*. The true tradition has been handed down in the gardens of Italy and Provence, where one may see the *potager*, brilliant in April with the graded reds and pinks of peach and cherry and almond blossom, overhanging the lettuce and artichoke —all enclosed by a rose-hedge, whose beauty is not lessened because even the rose has a purpose as well as a delight.

But Virgil's description of a garden is no more than incidental. He left the subject "to be sung by others after him." The elder Pliny noticed the omission, and thought that Virgil was deterred by the humbleness of the theme; but it is difficult to believe that the poet of the plough would have thought a garden humble, and we need not question the sincerity of Virgil's own excuse that he had no room—

[1] See *Moral Essays*, *ep.* 4, and the *Guardian*, 173; Addison, *Spectator*, 412.
[2] *Georg.* 116 f.

spatiis exclusus iniquis; since he doubtless held, with Callimachus, that a great book—at least on husbandry—was a great evil. His invitation was accepted by Columella, whose work is a curiosity of literature; for this very practical writer added a poem in praise of gardening, with due acknowledgment to Virgil, at the end of his prose treatise on farming. It must be confessed that Columella's poetry is more akin to his own prose than to the *Georgics*. Yet he shows some imagination, and a discriminating critic has called him at least as good a laureate of the garden as Thomson of the Seasons.[1] He could describe the Spring in graceful verse at a time when such descriptions were still unhackneyed.[2] He has a real love of flowers, even though—as the same critic has remarked—he enumerates them in the manner of a seedman's catalogue. He feels the beauty of these *terrestria sidera*—a flash of fancy less bright, perhaps, than Shelley's

> Daisies, those pearled Arcturi of the earth.
> The constellated flower that never sets,

but deserving the credit of priority which was given to a German poet by Longfellow, and by others to Cowley or Rousseau.[3] Nor is the list merely conventional, like Ovid's, who satisfied Proserpine with the stock-in-trade of poetic flowers, adding as a make-weight, *et sunt sine nomine flores* —a half-line which is less a reflection on ancient botany than on Ovid's own want of interest. Besides the roses and hyacinths and lilies, Columella notes other flowers, less familiar to Latin verse—snowdrops (*leucoia*), marigolds (*calthae*), the snap-dragon (*leo*), and the pansy, with its petals of purple and gold,

> *quae frondens purpurat auro.*

Even when the flower is "common", Columella can de-

[1] H. E. Butler, *Post-Augustan Poetry*, p. 146 f. [2] 255 f.

[3] Longfellow, *Voices of the Night* (*Flowers*); Cowley, *The Garden*, 9; Rousseau, *Conf.* 7.

scribe it with a characteristic touch, as when the violets "open their winking eyes"

et conniventes oculos violaria solvunt

—a passage which recalls the "winking Mary-buds" of *Cymbeline*, though Columella's violets can hardly rival those of Perdita. His poetry suffers in a very marked degree from the defects of Roman qualities. As we should expect—even after Virgil—his list of garden flowers passes, without the least breathing-space, into medical herbs and vegetables, as if to show that no line can be drawn between the useful and the beautiful. Unfortunately his sense of use too often overpowers the beauty. A follower of Virgil, he could understand his master's realism, but not the unfailing charm which Virgil knew how to pour over common things. The greater poet drew the picture of a country scene—the farmer driving to market with a load of oil and cheap apples, and returning with a millstone or a lump of black pitch.[1] This is a poetic realism that might well find a place in Crabbe or Wordsworth, but Columella must needs go further. His market gardener (*holitor*) sends narcissus and violets to neighbouring towns and returns with pockets full of cash. So far Virgil would not have disowned the scene; but his pupil spoils the picture by adding that the carrier returns *titubante gradu multo madefactus iaccho*—very drunk.[2]

If Columella stood alone, we might discount his evidence on the ground that a didactic poet is concerned with utility. But even in the last period of Roman literature, when new ideas of beauty, and new conceptions of Nature were beginning to transform the classic spirit, we find the same practical treatment in the garden-poem of a certain Asmenius, who lived about the end of the fourth century.[3]

[1] *Georg.* 1, 273 f. [2] 309.

[3] Baehrens, *P.L.M.* 4, 151; H. W. Garrod, *Oxford Book of Latin Verse*, 354.

To my Garden, let us raise
Daughters of Jove, a song of praise!
Orchard of unfailing fruit,
Grape and apple, herb and root,
Of all the wealth that gardens give
Whereby man may eat and live.
Here, in fellowship, agree
Pleasure and utility:
Silver freshet-streams are drawn
Round about the channelled lawn,
Where the beds are rainbow-hued
By a flower-multitude.
Hark, and you'll hear the bee awing
On dew-brushed petals fastening;
Look, and you'll see the married vine
With amorous arms, that intertwine
Over the loving elms, and press
The trellis with their fruitfulness.
Tall trees there are, whose warp and woof
Keep the August sun aloof,
And tuneful birds the trees among,
Making a paradise of song.
In that quiet haven Care
Hath no abiding-place; but there
The gardener, for his easy pains
Repaid a hundredfold, in gains
Of lighter limb and clearer sight,
Reaps a pure harvest of delight.

Asmenius was no great poet. His iambics are a little bald and stiff, and contain no thought which, even in the fourth century, could be called original. But his love for the garden, if limited, is sincere, so that (except for the traditional appeal to the Muses) he can afford to dispense with conventions, such as a reference—decent or otherwise—to Priapus, who adorns or disfigures nearly all Latin poetry of this class. Severely practical, he would have agreed with Dr. Johnson that the best garden is one "which produces the most roots and fruits."[1] His subject does not inspire him, like Marvell, to "create other worlds"

> Annihilating all that's made
> To a green thought in a green shade.

For Asmenius, the visible world is enough, and the gospel of his *hortulus* might be summed up in a single line:

> *multisque mixta commodis iocunditas.*

The Roman garden, in fact, has no room for spiritual suggestion. At best, it is the garden of Epicurus—a place of quiet and refreshment, well situated for high thoughts on philosophy; and perhaps—though no Roman seems quite to have anticipated Bacon or T. E. Brown—it was the purest of Roman pleasures, and the veriest school of peace. But the philosophy and the poetry were rather *in* the garden than *of* it. We must look beyond the range of Latin thought for the poetic belief that God Almighty had first planted a Garden, and might still be found walking there in the cool of the day.

III

From the foregoing account, it will, I hope, be evident that the *general* outlook on Nature was bounded by certain well-marked lines, beyond which the eye of the Roman poet rarely travelled. Consciously or instinctively, he chose those aspects of Nature that best harmonized with his philosophy of life.

These limitations bound not only "minor" poets but one at least of the four whom we regard as belonging to a different class. As we have seen, Horace has little claim to be considered a poet of Nature, if we interpret Nature in a wide sense, as existing by itself, independent of human interest. It remained for the other three, each in a different

[1] Mrs. Piozzi, *Anecdotes*; see Johnson's *Life of Shenstone*, 10.

characteristic way, to enlarge the scope of this narrow Roman vision, by glimpses of a Nature whose beauty was not conditioned by utility. Of these three, Lucretius stands in a place by himself. Concerned with the Universe rather than with the Earth, and dealing with infinities rather than with the petty bounds of human life, he finds his complete aesthetic satisfaction in the great forces of Nature—the "celestial quarters of the world, and the ether set above with glittering stars, the moon, the day and night, and the severe stars of night."[1]

With Catullus, we exchange the majesty of the Universe for the more intimate beauties of the earth. A traveller over many lands and seas, he found no country to be more beautiful than Italy, and no part of Italy a match for his northern lakeland, with Sirmio, the eye of peninsulas and islands, where the waves rejoice with all the laughter of their home—*quidquid est domi cachinnorum.* We may think of the Aeschylean *ἀνήριθμον γέλασμα*, but we feel that Catullus has seen the smile and heard the laughter with his own eyes and ears—there is no question of borrowing. Indeed, a yachtsman among a race of landsmen, Catullus is easily chief among Romans for his love of water, both in his own lakes and in the Mediterranean or Adriatic seas. No poet has ever described more finely and truthfully a calm sea, first ruffled by the morning breeze that wakes the little waves to laughter, and then rising with the rising wind, until the billows can be seen far off in the purple light.[2]

Apart from its charm, the passage has an interest in the history of aesthetics, since it accurately marks the limit of classical appreciation. Nature, in order to be admired, need not always be cultivated or subject to human discipline, but she must at least be in harmony with human life; not wild, or rugged, or awful, but *amoena*—pleasant and gentle. It

[1] 5, 1188 f. [2] 64, 270 f.

was this *amoenitas* that led the Roman nobles to build their villas on moles that gave an uninterrupted view of the Mediterranean. The angry sea roused no emotions of pleasure; and though the "poetic storm" became a commonplace in rhetoric, it served only as an example of the horrible in Nature.[1]

It needs, perhaps, a seafaring people to admire a rough sea, even in safety on the shore. The *Aeneid* is no sea-poem like the *Odyssey*, though it opens with a storm; and, throughout Latin poetry, we look in vain for the splendid observation of the Greeks, who may not have loved the sea, but at least knew it in every phase of calm or fury. The Romans have not unfairly been called a nation of land-lubbers, for whom a fleet was an unpleasant necessity of empire. In pursuit of this empire, a Roman fleet would sail, stolidly and conscientiously, over the undiscovered seas of Scotland. But there was no joy in the discovery, and no stimulus to the imagination. To push beyond the pillars of Hercules was—in Pedo's phrase—to violate the sacred waters and disturb the peace of the gods; in plain prose, to be foolhardy.[2]

Catullus may claim to be called a poet of Nature, because he was an artist, responsive to the beauty of a flower or a sunlit sea, who delighted to turn aside, from time to time, to the pleasant things of Nature from the world of men. But his real business was with man. Apart from the mastering passion of his life—for all other joys or griefs were nothing when Lesbia smiled or was false—Catullus was almost wholly wrapped up in the life of a Roman aristocrat, in the feverish years immediately preceding the Civil War.

There remains Virgil, who, alone of the four greater Roman poets, was qualified, both by temperament and environment, to be a real lover of country life. Unlike

[1] Juv. 12, 22.

[2] *Oxford Book of Latin Verse*, p. 232.

Lucretius and Catullus, he was spared the distractions of politics or philosophy. Unlike Horace, he was hardly touched by the lure of the city and the court; and there was no Lesbia to draw away his affection for Nature.

As we have seen, Virgil starts on the common basis of all Roman poets in their view of Nature. Primarily, he chooses those aspects of her beauty which illustrate her usefulness, whether direct as in agriculture, or indirect as in the cool and pleasant woods that minister to man's material or spiritual comfort and refreshment. On the formal side of aesthetics, we may say that he holds the definition (so far unchallenged), which regards beauty as inherent in order and symmetry—the proper relation of the part to the whole. Plotinus had not yet risen to reject this classical theory, and to pronounce that beauty is a spiritual light that plays over the symmetry of things rather than that symmetry itself.[1] But the poets have often anticipated the philosophers, and Virgil, in particular, may be called a Plotinian before Plotinus. For more than any other poet of his day, he feels the light on the symmetry of things. Choosing objects and forms of Nature which have no "use", he shows the beauty that is independent of material purpose. He knows the pure aesthetic pleasure of colour and sound—of colour, when "saffron Morning shines in her rosy car"; of sound—when he listens to the wind on the heath, or hears the voice of the falling water:

> *nam neque me tantum venientis sibilus Austri,*
> *nec percussa iuvant fluctu tam litora, nec quae*
> *saxosas inter decurrunt flumina valles.*[2]

For water, indeed, Virgil has a love which links him, on the one hand, with Catullus, and on the other hand—as we shall see—with Ausonius. This love is not merely utili-

[1] Bosanquet, p. 116. For the aesthetics of Plotinus cf. *Enn.* 1, 6; see W. R. Inge, *Philosophy of Plotinus*, ii. pp. 210-215. For the idea of symmetry as beauty cf. Plat. *Gorg.* 525; Cic. *Tusc.* 4, 13; Augustine, *C.D.* 22, 19.

[2] *Ecl.* 6, 82.

tarian, though no Roman poet scorned the pleasure of taking refuge from the heat by a shady stream—*propter aquae rivum;* it is as an artist that he admires the great Italian lakes, and his own Mincius, fringed with green reeds, and the Tuscan Tiber, where Æneas heard the birds singing on its tree-clad banks, while the waters and unaccustomed woods wondered at the bright shields and painted vessels. He was the first poet, apparently, to play on the conceit that there is a reality in the "inverted scene"—as Wordsworth calls it—of the reflecting water. The ships of Æneas "cleave the woods in the calm waters"; and though some have thought that Virgil only meant to describe the Tiber as dividing the trees on either bank, Servius is surely right in explaining the woods as mirrored in the stream.[1] We know that observers like Pliny and Statius took pleasure in noting the reflection of a clear stream;[2] but the strongest evidence for Servius is to be found in the fact that Ausonius, the constant imitator of Virgil, develops the conceit, in describing the Moselle:[3]

> What beauty, when the star of evening shines,
> And the late shadows lengthen, as the river
> Lies interfused with the green mountainside,
> And all the swimming hilltops dance and quiver,
> And all the tendrils of the absent vines
> Tremble, the vintage of a crystal tide!

The same idea has appealed to many poets—to Pope, who follows Ausonius in his *Windsor Forest*, and scarcely improves on his original in such lines as

[1] *Aen.* 8, 96. This meaning has been recently disputed by Warde Fowler, *Aeneas at the Site of Rome* (1917), p. 47; but see J. W. Mackail in *Class. Rev.* Aug. 1918, who says that "what was not too modern for Servius was certainly not too modern for Virgil." Mr. Mackail might have added the evidence of Ausonius.

[2] Pliny, *Ep.* 8; Stat. *Silv.* 1, 3, 17; 2, 2, 48. Virgil's own patron Maecenas wrote of gardens reflected *verso vado;* see W. C. Summers in *Class. Quart.* ii. (1908), p. 1702.

[3] Aus. 10, 61 f. and 195 f.

> The headlong mountains and the downward skies,
> The wat'ry landscape of the pendant woods,
> And absent trees that tremble in the floods:

—to Wordsworth:

> That uncertain heaven received
> Into the bosom of the steady lake;

and to Shelley, who more than once describes the wrinkled image of a city:

> as there it lay
> Immovably unquiet, and for ever
> It trembles, but it cannot pass away.[1]

—the last line borrowed, by conscious or unconscious reminiscence, from Wordsworth. Virgil himself has but just hinted at the conceit which a long line of poets developed, but that is Virgil's manner. He never allows the "scenery" —in either sense of the word—to divert his attention from his actors. The environment of his epic is never thrust to the front. In his "Gathering of the Clans"—to adopt Mr. Warde Fowler's expressive title for the Seventh *Aeneid*—Virgil had a unique opportunity, if he had cared to use it, of describing the natural features of Italy. A Romantic poet would have seized the occasion; but Virgil is content with a passing reference (often a single striking epithet) to mark the Place, and concentrates on the People—on their arms, their way of life, or their fortunes in the war. Place and People, it is true, are closely linked together—the grove of Anguitia and Fucinus, with its glassy water, weep for their loved Umbro; but it is the man, and not his circumstance, that matters.[2] The pathetic fallacy, of which this passage is a good example, never serves as an excuse for landscape-painting.

It is here that the latest Roman poetry assumes an im-

[1] Wordsworth, *Peele Castle;* Shelley, *Ode to Liberty;* so *Evening* (Pisa) and *Witch of Atlas.*

[2] *Aen.* 7, 750 f.

portance to which, on its general merits, it is hardly entitled. For, after all, Claudian and Ausonius, as thinkers, add nothing to the poetry of Humanism, while, as artists, they are immeasurably inferior to Virgil. But, if they shew no advance in their conception of Man, considered by himself, they at least struck a new note in relation to his environment. Poetry, in fact, had reached a stage when the purely human interest had been throughly explored—as far as the classical range of ideas permitted—and attention was turned from Man in Nature to Nature herself. Even so, the break was not complete: the Virgilian tradition was too powerful to be overthrown, and the Farmer (or the Philosopher), rather than the Artist, remained in almost undisputed possession of the land. It is the place where the simple life can best be lived—the phrase itself (*simplice cultu*), which sounds with so modern a ring, is at least as old as Claudian,[1] who develops the idea in the most celebrated of his poems:[2]

Happy the man who all his life has kept
His father's homestead, from the world aloof,
And hobbling now, where as a child he crept,
Tells the long history of a single roof.

Not his, to follow Fortune's varied lure,
—To drink, a hurried traveller, streams afar;
—To brave the storm, for traffic; to endure
The battle, or the clamouring of the Bar.

Unskilled to mingle in the affairs of men,
Strange to the neighbouring town that meets his eye,
He finds a joy, denied a citizen,
In the free vision of an ampler sky.

[1] *In Rufin.* 1, 196 f.

[2] *Epigr.* 2 (*de sene Veronensi*). Other translations (including Cowley's) are given in the *Oxford Book of Latin Verse.*

Seasons, not consuls, set his annual mark
—The fruit, for autumn; for the spring, the flowers;
And in one field, from daybreak to the dark,
His labour registers the passing hours.

He views the tall oak, where he sowed the seed,
And ages with his own coeval trees,
Still hale and vigorous, with a sturdy breed
Of children's children gathered at his knees.

To him lake Garda seems the Arabian sand,
Verona, distant as the darkest Moor:
—Travel, then, if you will, from land to land;
He knows that Life is knocking at his door.

Here (except for the rather narrow-minded application of the last stanza), the range of thought is pure Virgilian—the *Senex Veronensis* might well be the Corycian of the *Georgics*. Claudian is carrying on the true Roman tradition to the end. But, by Claudian's time, the land had ceased to be the monopoly of the Farmer, philosophic or otherwise, and had acquired a dignity and a beauty of its own. The new movement towards Nature seems to have started early in the fourth century, and is well illustrated by a fragment from Tiberianus, a poet slightly older than Ausonius, and apparently a high official in the court of Constantine. The context is unknown, but the fragment is complete for our purpose. There is nothing very remarkable in the language or metre—the trochaics were perhaps as trite in Latin as they have become in English—but the lines have a peculiar interest in the evolution of poetry. They link Tiberianus with Tennyson, and, though the following translation cannot claim a Tennysonian felicity of language, it may at least shew a kinship of spirit between the fourth and nineteenth centuries:[1]

[1] Tiberianus in *P.L.M.* 3, p. 264.

Down the cool depth of the valley, through the fields, the river sped
Flower-fringed, with smiles of water rippling on a jewelled bed.
In the green bay-thickets, in the myrtle-copses, high above,
Little breezes stirred and told the leaves a whispered tale of love.
Underfoot, the grasses flowered; the lily and the crocus-gold
Lined the green with light, and violets broke in fragrance from the mould.
Spring had scattered all her colours, all her scents; and, Queen of those,
Bright as Phosphor, flamed the glory of Aphrodite's golden rose.
Everywhere the wood was moist with singing rivulets, every cave
Wreathed with moss and myrtle leaf, bright with the spray of wandering wave.
Over all the shady places echoed joyful carolling
—Myriad birds, in unimagined hymns of beauty, greet the spring.
Here the river softly murmured; answering tree to river spoke,
As the west-wind touched the branches, and the minstrel leaves awoke.
So his path was filled with odours, voices, visions of the glade,
Loveliness of bird and river, wind and woodland, flower and shade.

It will be seen that, since Virgil, the relation between Man and Nature had been exactly reversed. Nature has advanced from the background to fill the whole canvas; humanity has shrunk to a single word in the last couplet—*euntem.*[1]

Side by side with Tiberianus we may set an extract from a marriage hymn by Claudian. Here the context determines

[1] On Nature in fourth-century poetry see F. T. Palgrave, *Landscape in Poetry*, pp. 8, 87; J. A. Symonds, *Essays*, p. 100.

the attitude towards the scenery—the poet is describing a "Garden of Venus" to show the source of the passion that was to inspire Honorius and his bride. The epithalamion itself, for pure poetry, is unworthy of a place beside that gem of marriage-songs, the *epithalamion* of Catullus—with which, indeed, it does not attempt to compete, being not strictly a song but an epic idyll in hexameters. But it has an interest in this place, for more than one reason: it shows the growing love of description, and—a still more striking change—it introduces a note of sentimentality, which, however foreign to the Augustan age, we have already seen to be creeping into the poetry of the decadence. The passage, though part of a much longer description of the Venusberg, may stand by itself.[1]

A Mountain, unprofaned of human feet,
Hangs over Cyprus, on the Ionian main,
Looking toward the Egyptian island-bed
Of Proteus, and Nile's sevenfold-hornèd head,
Where never rages wind nor ruinous rain
Nor snow to clothe the peak in icy sheet.

To Idleness and Venus dedicate,
This Mountain harbours such eternal spring
As shall exile all fiercer heat or cold,
And on its spreading top a hedge of gold
Fences the upland with a flashing ring,
And keeps the level lawns inviolate.

With this for wedding-gift did Vulcan win,
Uxorious, the kisses of his bride,
Offering—so runs the tale—this golden wall
To guard a land of flowers perpetual,
That needs no gardener, Zephyrus beside,
A land of many birds, singing therein;

[1] *de nupt. Honor. et Mariae*, 49 f.

But birds have entry to that pleasant lea
Only if Venus, their sole arbitress,
Adjuge the singing worthy of the place:
So must each comer supplicate her grace
And gain admittance by his songfulness,
Or, failing, lose the forest sanctity.

There, every leaf lives but for Venus' sake,
And every fruitful trees loves, and is loved:
The palm is bent, its fellow palm to reach,
The sighing poplars murmur, each to each,
The platane to its mate is softly moved,
Alder to alder whispering vows doth make.

All magic gardens are perhaps in lineal descent from the domain of the Phæacians; but Claudian owes little to Homer and less to Virgil, here. The garden of Venus looks forward, rather than backward—to Tasso and Spenser; we think of Armida more than of Alcinous.

There remains the notable poem in which the new movement is most clearly manifested. The *Mosella* of Ausonius has a peculiar importance, because it holds fast to the old tradition, and yet speaks with an accent unknown to Virgil. Ausonius is a Virgilian, for no fourth-century poet could escape—even if he wished—from the domination of the great Augustan. In the true classical spirit, he re-echoes, with full intent, the phrases and cadences which Virgil had consecrated. He salutes his beloved Moselle in a line:

Salve, magne parens frugumque virumque, Mosella,

which recalls the invocation of Italy:

Salve, magna parens frugum, Saturnia tellus,
Magna virum.

The "foreign" Moselle is thus introduced into the comity of Latin rivers, dignified by the suggestion of the noble apostrophe in which the Italian poet had honoured the motherland.

Again and again, the echo is heard, as when the beautiful line of the Georgics

fluminaque antiquos subterlabentia muros

becomes

moeniaque antiquis te prospectantia muris.[1]

But the "imitation" is not merely in rhythm or verbal similarity; the whole conception of the *Mosella* has been drawn from the "Praise of Italy" in the second *Georgic.* Yet the difference is far more striking than the resemblance. Virgil's eulogy is a mere episode; Ausonius has chosen the river as his whole subject. Virgil has been too much occupied with the richness and fertility of his land to find space for its scenic beauty; Ausonius knows that it is just the beauty of his river that makes his subject worthy of a poem. It is true that the Moselle has other merits in his eyes—there are the fish (and Ausonius enumerates their species with all the thoroughness of the Roman catalogue); there are the rich vines on its banks—a concession to utility; and, lastly, there is (as indeed there should be) the human element, in the boat-races and water-parties, in the fishing, and in the magnificent country-houses which overlook the stream. Ausonius would not have been a Roman if he had passed by these aspects, but he is more than the Roman in subordinating them to Nature herself. *Naturae mirabor opus,* he announces, and keeps his word. He is not a Romantic, for he seems to take less pleasure in the half-lights of the forest than in the bright atmosphere of a land, which he has reached after travelling through woody wastes unknown to human cultivation. But he is at least a Caroline—one who could anticipate Marvell's "*green* shade" when others thought only of its blackness[2]—one, moreover, who cut adrift from the panegyrics of men (often, like Claudian's Honorius, quite unworthy of praise), setting a new fashion, which the poet of

[1] *Georg.* 2, 156; *Mos.* 454.
[2] *Mos.* 15, *quaeritur exclusum viridi caligine caelum.*

Cooper's Hill was the first to follow. For Denham's *Thames*, after twelve centuries, takes its place as the next and direct successor of the Mosella, in whose bed Ausonius had marked the bright pebbles appear and disappear in the shifting light and shadow, and the green river-weed set off by the yellow gravel

> *—lucetque latetque*
> *calculus, et viridem distinguit glarea muscum—*

while, on the banks, he had noted the *naturale theatrum* of the vine-clad hills, and his eye had rested on the mirror of the landscape in the evening light.

IV

This evidence of Virgil and his Roman successors appears to prove that Latin poetry may be rightly regarded as a connecting link between the strict classicism of the Greek and modern romanticism. No doubt the Roman outlook on Nature was nearer to the Greeks than to the moderns—in many respects the Latin view is hardly in advance of the fifth century—but, on the whole, the change is real, and a proof of "originality" in Latin thought. Virgil may be more akin to Sophocles than to Wordsworth; but whereas we instinctively contrast the Greek and the English poet, when we think of Virgil we begin to compare as well as contrast. In the words of one who wrote wisely on both Virgil and Wordsworth, there are passages in the *Georgics* so Wordsworthian in tone, that it is hard to realize what centuries separated them from the *Sonnet to Lady Beaumont* or from *Ruth.*[1] None the less we must not make the mistake of discounting the wide difference between the ancient and modern conceptions of natural beauty, which, after all, are deeper and more striking than their resemblances.

By Classical canons, the objects of Romantic admiration were strictly excluded. The impenetrable forest and the

[1] F. W. H. Myers, *Wordsworth*.

bleak mountain were not only remote from man, but, actively or passively, were hostile. It is true that Stoics, in their attempts to prove a purpose in all things, held that old woods and mountain caves were evidences of the divine,[1] thus giving a high meaning to the popular belief in the wild deities of the woods and mountains, which Lucretius had rejected. But this religious awe left no room for aesthetic satisfaction. A sacred grove, in Lucan's words, is a place where men "make way for the gods."[2]

With regard to mountains, the insensibility of the ancients is so well known that some apology is needed for even touching on the subject. Since Humboldt and Ruskin it may well seem to have been worn threadbare. But Ruskin was mainly concerned with the broad difference between ancient and modern appreciation, and failed to trace a subtle change within the limits of the classical period—a change so delicate that it may easily be overlooked, although it marks, I think, a real development in this particular feeling for Nature.[3]

We shall again find that the Romans added to the aesthetic experience of the past—that Virgil is in advance of the Greeks, who appear to have been wholly unmoved by the beauty of their own mountains. After ransacking all Greek literature, scholars have only found a single passage, in Plato, which (at first sight) seems to recognize the charm of mountain-scenery. In the *Critias*,[4] mountains are called *καλά*, a word which we are accustomed to translate by "beautiful," reading into it, instinctively, the modern sense of "picturesque." Such a sense—in this connexion—is an

[1] Seneca, *Ep.* 41, 3, *fidem tibi numinis facio.*

[2] Lucan, 3, 423. The Romanticism of the Forest is really the creation of the Middle Ages; see Vernon Lee, *Euphorion*.

[3] In general see Humboldt, *Kosmos*, Bk 2; Ruskin, *Modern Painters*, Bk. 3, ch. 13. More recently, Palgrave, *Landscape in Poetry*; Shairp, *Poetic Interpretation of Nature*; Geikie, *Love of Nature among the Romans* (1912); Hardie, *Lectures on Classical Subjects*; Friedländer, *Roman Life*, Vol. I, p. 380 f.; W. W. Hyde in *Amer. Class. Journ.* 11 (1915-16), p. 70.

[4] 118, B.

anachronism. The adjective has, of course, many shades of meaning, according to the various definitions of τὸ καλόν, abstract Beauty; but it is important to remember that, before Plotinus, the Greeks never identified this abstract Beauty with aesthetic value, as the artistically beautiful.[1] Socrates, with his strong sense of utility, had defined τὸ καλόν as "answering the end," and Plato himself hesitated between the definitions of truth, goodness, measure, or divinity. In the *Critias*, the context shows that Plato is returning to his master's favourite conception—the mountains are beautiful precisely because they are useful, well fitted with their rich woods and fertile valleys to serve the needs of man.[2]

Here, as so often, we must resist the temptation of reading Greek literature with modern eyes. That literature could not dispense with the mountains, for the simple reason that mountains are almost the whole of Greece. From Homer onwards, Greek poetry abounds in pictures of snow-clad Olympus; of Ida, with the flowery marriage-bed of Zeus and Hera; of Pan roaming over the hills; of Bacchants following Dionysus on Cithaeron. But the motive of the picture is always the human interest. Theocritus followed the shepherd to the Sicilian mountains; but, as a poet and artist, he stopped, with the sheep themselves, on the lower slopes. Religious instincts, again, when thwarted by the official cults, might find an outlet in orgiastic worship on the mountains; yet, even so, it was the human-god, Dionysus, that attracted the Maenads, and Cithaeron meant only freedom from discipline and restraint.

The Roman lived in a broader, less precipitous land, whose mountain ranges, however conspicuous, were a small part of the whole country. As a background, there was less need for them in Latin literature, and their imaginative

[1] H. W. Carr, *Philosophy of B. Croce*, p. 255 f.

[2] W. R. Hardie (*op. cit.* p. 18), in his otherwise admirable study of the feeling for Nature, misunderstands this passage.

value was no stronger for the Italian than for the Greek. Indeed, the Roman had even more cause for prejudice; in religion, at all events, he steadily set his face against "those who worshipped on the mountain," and he had a short way with dissenting Bacchanals. There was no stimulus to counteract the classical view of mountains as both formless and useless, and therefore outside the ordered scheme of Roman ideas.

Livy saw nothing but *foeditas*—sheer ugliness—in the Alps, and Silius was only struck by their inclemency; *nullum ver usquam nullique aestatis honores.*[1] This is the farmer's point of view; and Cobbett, who called Hindhead the most villainous spot that God ever made, would have cordially agreed. Mountains might have some sentimental value, as symbols of patriotism or landmarks of home; aesthetically, however, the best that could be said of them was Cicero's admission that, by force of habit, we may find pleasure in mountains and forests, if we live long enough among them.[2] Pliny's Tuscan villa was surrounded by hills; but his "view" is not of the Apennines; on the contrary, "you will be delighted" he says, "if you look at the prospect from the hills."[3] Pliny, in fact, approves of Quintilian's test of charm in scenery—*speciem maritimis, planis, amoenis*;[4] and it is probable that he would have seen no humour in the story of a Welshman who, asked for his impression of English scenery, replied that England was a beautiful country—as flat as a penny. To the average Roman, a mountain needed human interest to be tolerable, and Roman art is eloquent of this limitation. In a Pompeian wall-painting Prometheus, bound to a rock, is being rescued by Hercules; and here, at least, we should expect that the artist would have left the frosty Caucasus alone, especially as there was the "human interest" of Prometheus himself.

[1] Livy 19, 32; Sil. 3, 477; so Petr. 122, 144 f.; Claud, *de bell. Get.*, 340 f. and often.

[2] Cic. *de amic.* 19.

[3] Plin. *Ep.* 5, 6, 7.

[4] Quint. 3, 7, 27.

But taste is too powerful for propriety—the painter must needs add a temple and a statue in the foreground.[1] Mountains—according to the Autocrat of the Breakfast Table—can be domesticated; and this was the Pompeian method of bringing them within the sphere of the home-circle.

Apart from the presence of humanism, it has often been suggested that the root of the matter lies in the insensibility of the ancients to delicate shades of colour. The shifting shadows which pass over the mountain-side, the pink heather on a hilly slope, the violet evening-glow, the dark mass of some projecting peak—all this beauty was unmarked by a race who took pleasure in bright and often violent colours, as we see from the reds and yellows of Pompeian decoration. In a great measure I think this suggestion is the truth. There is no doubt that Roman poets—like Roman artists—delighted in the warmer, intenser colours, and their vocabulary is full of words connoting brightness—*splendens*, *purpureus*, and the like.[2] On the other hand, there is no question of colour-blindness. It is probable, indeed, that Gladstone's well-known theory does not deserve the contempt once heaped upon it—if Homer himself was not colour-blind, his language may well be a survival of an earlier defect in colour-sense, such as can still be observed among savages.[3] But the Classical Greeks and Romans were certainly not deficient in sensitiveness to colour. The Romans were interested in the question whether the Greeks were more appreciative of colour than themselves, and Gellius remarked that Latin has a very wide range of colour-words, to express "shades"—*rubidus*

[1] Figured in W. Zahn, *Pompeii*, i.-v., ii., 30. The landscapes from Boscoreale (B.M.) are similar.

[2] On Virgil's use of colour-words see T. R. Price in *A.J.P.* iv. p. 1 f., for Ovid, N. G. McCrea in *Class. St. for H. Drixler* (1894), p. 180 f.

[3] See W. H. R. Rivers, *Primitive Colour Vision* (*Popular Science Monthly*, lix. May, 1901, p. 44).

(dark red), *spadix* (chestnut), and others.[1] But it is significant that the poets almost entirely neglected these words—the gradations of colour were of no aesthetic value. Roman painting shows at once a physical sensitiveness to colour and a lack of poetic interest. At Pompeii the mountains on the horizon are quite correctly indicated by a slate-blue tone,[2] but the absence of any reference to this colour seems to be good evidence that it gave no satisfaction to the poet. In the same way, the artists of the Renascence, from Jan van Eyck to Claude and Ruisdael far outran the poets of their age, proving the beauty of the mountain long before literature was ready to accept the proof.[3] Athens was violet-crowned; but a people who themselves wore chaplets of flowers did not need to look towards Hymettus, suffused with a violet lustre in the evening sun.[4] The power of seeing the fact must not be confused with the power of seeing beauty in the fact. Campbell's lines on the azure mountain, to which distance lends enchantment, have now become the tritest of quotations: but we are apt to forget that, although the enchantment was not new when the *Pleasures of Hope* was written in 1799—even Pope had admired the "bluish hills"[5]—an Elizabethan or Jacobean poet would scarcely have understood it. The Roman, at least as much as the Elizabethan, was stimulated only by a nearer prospect which he could accurately appraise

[1] *N.A.* 2, 26.

[2] See the coloured illustration in Zahn, *Ornamente*, 9, 89. So in a Roman mosaic (B.M.).

[3] A. Biese, *Feeling for Nature in the Middle Ages* (E.T.), ch. 7. Giorgione (1477-1511) is said to have transferred "figures with landscape" into "landscape with figures"; but the credit of painting scenery without any human interest seems due to the Flemish school. A river-scene, with distant blue hills (Nat. Gallery. No. 1298) is attributed to Patinir (1485-1524). It is interesting to remember that Ruisdael, the last of a long line of landscape painters, died in 1682, a century before the Romantic poets.

[4] For this romantic explanation see *A.J.P.* (1911), p. 366.

[5] *Windsor Castle* (1704).

—one that left nothing to be guessed, but presented a clear-cut and definite picture to the eye. Mountains must have looked as blue to Lucan as to Campbell, but the Roman poet takes no pleasure in the aerial perspective, in terms of colour. He rather turns the aesthetic fact into an intellectual concept—distant mountains, viewed from the sea, are *dubii*, merged in the skyline, so that the mind cannot discriminate between sea and sky and land.[1]

Nevertheless, it would be unfair to class the poets with Livy. If Virgil nowhere seems to recognize the positive beauty of the mountains, he would surely have denied their ugliness. His famous apostrophe to the country includes not only the rivers and woods and plains but the ranges of Taygetus :

> *virginibus bacchata Lacænis*
> *Taygeta.*[2]

Here, it may be objected, Taygetus is not mentioned for its own sake, as a grand outline in the sky ; it is merely the place of Bacchic revelry, and Virgil can at most be said to have recaptured the Greek point of view. No doubt the passage need prove no more than this, but, even so, it would be much that the poet should have conquered the old Roman repugnance. And I think that Virgil goes further. His description of Maenalus, with its whispering woods, and its pines that hear the shepherd's love-song, show at least the germ of Romanticism. Maenalus, already beautiful for its human associations, is on the way to become beautiful in itself. Before the mountains can reach that stage, they must lose the terror, which makes them, even more than the forests, a place for gods—or devils. It was late in the Middle Ages that a bold explorer of the thirteenth century climbed Canigou in the Roussillon, and roused a monstrous dragon from a lake near the summit. Such folk tales could be multiplied,

[1] *Phars.* 3, 7. [2] *Georg.* 2, 487.

as any reader of Stephen's *Playground of Europe* knows. When superstitious fear was passed, there still remained other terrors—the physical danger of climbing and the risk of brigandage. Beyond all this, there is a vague, indefinable feeling of unfriendliness, which some minds may still feel in the presence of mountains; and it was left to the eighteenth century to mitigate this melancholy with a growing sense of pleasure, "a sort of agreeable shuddering," in Addison's words, "at this most mis-shapen scenery". In this vein, Collins was moved to feel "awful gloom" by the Highlands, and Gray was frightened by the peaks of Borrowdale—"let us not speak of them, but look and pass on"—while his attitude to the Alps may be summed up in the characteristic words *severi religio loci*, which he inscribed in the album of the Grande Chartreuse.[1]

The taste for mountain scenery comes from various sources, all more or less outside the borders of Classical thought. In the oldest phase, it was perhaps mainly religious or ethical. Under this aspect, Petrarch is the acknowledged pioneer—we know, from his own account, how his ascent of Ventoux figured the arduous pilgrimage of a saintly life. In a moral rather than a religious spirit, Rousseau admired the mountains as a symbol of simplicity, a protest against luxury and convention. In the first half of the eighteenth century the praise of Alpine scenery, as Stephen remarks, is curiously connected with praise of the unsophisticated peasant. Closely connected with this social Arcadia, the Alps became the home of political freedom—an idea developed by Rousseau's disciples, though, long before Rousseau, Freedom had sat on the heights and Milton had sung of the Mountain-nymph, sweet Liberty. Side by side with this philosophic

[1] Collins, *Ode on the Popular Superstitions of the Highlands*, 1788. Gray's grand tour was in 1741. In Germany, Von Haller's poem, *Die Alpen*, had already appeared (1734).

view, there rose a literary revolt from the neo-classic school. The very "horridness" of the mountain was a welcome change from the symmetry of Boileau and Pope. With the Romantic movement, the Alps were appropriated by Byron as a refuge for the individual soul from the "hum of human cities". Finally, as a "playground", they have won—as we all know—a popularity of which Leslie Stephen himself could hardly have dreamed. Nor must it be forgotten that science—both geological and botanical—has shown the poet as well as the artist a new vision of the hills.

But even this is not all that separates the modern poets from Virgil. The mountains are only a part of the world which has been re-interpreted and re-valued. In the words of a great Romantic leader, "Glades, flowers, and streams satisfied the poets of paganism; the solitude of the forest, the boundless ocean, the starry heavens, can scarcely express the eternity and infinity with which the Christian spirit is filled".[1]

Is Mdme de Staël right in attributing the change to the spirit of Christianity? If we confine the phrase to the actual dogmas of Christians, there is little warrant for the theory. It is often argued that a taste for natural beauty has been derived from the Christian view of the world as a thing of divine significance, permeated by the presence of God.[2] But Roman Stoicism held this belief, and was yet unable to widen the ancient aesthetic values. The early Christians themselves were too much occupied in regarding the world *sub specie aeternitatis* to admire the passing show of visible things.[3] As late as the fifth and sixth centuries cultivated and broad-minded Christians like Sidonius or

[1] Mdme de Staël, *de l'Allemagne*.

[2] See e.g. W. P. Begg, *The Development of Taste* (1887), p. 96 f.

[3] P. T. Forsyth (*Christ on Parnassus*, p. 255) admits that "to love Christ is not to love Nature . . . St. Paul had no sense of natural beauty whatever."

Fortunatus retained a purely classical outlook on nature; while, to the more ascetic holders of the faith, all phenomenal beauty was repugnant. Nor, as is often supposed, could the change have arisen from the fusion of Hebraic thought with Greek and Latin Christianity. The book of Job is full of the wonders of creation, and the Psalmist delights in the hills that stand about Jerusalem. But the wonders and the delights are purely religious, untinged by aesthetic appreciation. A race which almost wholly rejected the arts of painting and sculpture could hardly have recognized nature as beautiful in and for herself.

Still, if early Christianity added little or nothing to the stock of aesthetic perceptions, it paved the way to a radical change in the function of art. The medieval spirit produced, as its immediate result, only a contempt for the body in contrast with the soul; but this very change implied a recognition of the soul as an element without which art is purely formal. The mortification of the flesh turned the artist to the objects of spiritual vision—to the infinite, the eternal. Sophocles and Virgil in poetry, like Pheidias and Praxiteles in sculpture, had striven for an ideal which could be completely apprehended and expressed. Their art aimed at a mark before their eyes. It is of course mere ignorance to call this mark "unspiritual." All these great artists were concerned with the things of the spirit, whether it might be Pheidias "adding to the received religion" in his great conception of Zeus, or Virgil, showing that the Roman empire was fore-ordained of God. But it is true that, for the Classic artist, the spiritual rarely eludes the material, rarely soars into regions of infinity and eternity where the body may not follow. The medieval sculptor could no longer rest content with the symmetrical beauty of a Polyclitus. Dissatisfied with formal perfection, he grasped at something beyond the senses, and therefore incapable of full expression. Art became symbolic, significant of the reality that underlies the objects of sense-perception.

Are they perfect of lineament, perfect of stature?
In both of such lower type are we
Precisely because of our wider nature;
For time, theirs—ours for eternity.[1]

In this sense, the Christian spirit has undoubtedly been a prime cause of the new outlook; but there have been other influences at work. Since the days of Virgil, civilization—if it has not shifted its centre from the Mediterranean—has at least enlarged its circumference; and both painters and poets have been in contact with types of scenery unknown to Virgil. Northern mists, green Atlantic breakers, Alpine snow-peaks, saffron sunsets over the canals of Holland, have added to the beautiful but rather narrow store of impressions which an Italian poet could receive. And, with a widened field of vision, there has come a new interpretation, to which Christianity has contributed, but only in part. Science has not merely taught us more of the world than Virgil knew, but has also revealed to us our ignorance. To the classic mind the universe was finite and intelligible. Lucretius yields to no poet, ancient or modern, in admiration for its grandeur—*maiestas cognita rerum;* but the word *cognita* is eloquent. He knows too much, and the sense of mystery is almost wholly absent. His philosophic horizon lacks aerial perspective—it is sharp and clear-cut to the very end, leaving no region of the unknown beyond the human eye. We have learnt that Nature has a secret, which Art can but imperfectly express; and just as Painting has tended to replace the strong outlines and bright colours of a Mediterranean scene by the half tones of Northern cloud and sky, so Poetry has found its fullest expression in the vaguer, more mysterious aspects of the Universe. With Goethe—if not before—poetry and science met together in the study of Nature; and the chief gift of Science has been to show that

[1] R. Browning, *Old Pictures in Florence;* the contrast is familiar in *Andrea del Sarto* and others of his poems. See generally Bosanquet, *op. cit.* pp. 4 f., 130.

Nature is not simply subservient to Man. In consequence, we no longer regard her utility as an integral part of her charm. Her beauty, and the poetry which seeks to express it, is not to be confined within the limits of a few special types, formal, expected, and symmetrical; but it may strike upon us suddenly with a fresh and unexperienced pleasure, whether the vision is revealed in the peaceful lake or the stormy ocean, in the fruitful plain or the barren precipice.

To credit Virgil or Ausonius with the larger outlook, which has come from centuries of slow development, would be a gross anachronism. These poets have nothing in common with what may be called the Byronic side of Romanticism. But this is not to say that Virgil has been superseded. The spell of the Romantic has been broken, so that we have no longer much sympathy with Nature in her Titanic moods, and the cult of the wild—simply because it is wild—has lost its interest. Aesthetically, the Alps have ceased to be a fashion, although it is not many years since Mr. Hardy wrote that the time would soon come "when the chastened sublimity of a moor, a sea, or a mountain will be all of nature that it is absolutely in keeping with the moods of the more thinking among mankind."[1] But poetic taste of the present day has not fulfilled this rather pessimistic prophecy. Our younger poets have rediscovered the quiet beauties of England—the England of Sussex and Kent and Gloucestershire rather than of Westmorland. The great poet of Westmorland had himself "two voices." One was of the mountains, and this Byron in his own way re-echoed; the other, of "the meadows, grove, and stream"—a voice which Byron despised, but which is still heard in modern poetry, as it was heard two thousand years ago. Even when we seem to have travelled so far, we are nearer, perhaps, than we think to Virgil. It is even possible that we may be nearer to Virgil than

[1] Hardy, *Return of the Native.*

to Wordsworth. For, although Virgil has so much in common with the great English poet, there is a profound difference between their views of Nature. Virgil would have shared in the purely sensuous admiration of Wordsworth's youth—in

> A feeling and a love
> That had no need of a remoter charm
> By thought supplied, or any interest
> Unborrowed from the eye.

But, as we all know, Wordsworth moved from this simple, unphilosophic delight in a visible beauty to a

> sense sublime
> Of something far more deeply interfused.

Nature became a guide and teacher, the soul of his moral being; and here he parted company with Virgil, and indeed from all his predecessors. Both had started from the same point, for Virgil was at least prepared to admit divine immanence in the natural world:

> *—deum namque ire per omnes*
> *terrasque tractusque maris caelumque profundum—*

but Wordsworth alone pushed the theory to its logical conclusion, that, if God pervades Nature, He must reveal himself to Man through the teaching of Nature. Her beauty and harmony can pass into the mind, and even the body, of one who contemplates her aright, so that her favoured child should be moulded by the motions of the storm, or the murmur of the rivulet.

If the Wordsworthian view is admitted at the present day, we cannot call ourselves Virgilians. But do we really "believe" in Wordsworth in any literal sense? Is his natural philosophy tenable? At first sight, his case seems hopeless; for, whatever may be the ultimate meaning of Nature, it is certain that the phenomena of the external world are in flat contradiction to his teaching. Here his own friend Coleridge deserted him, in the famous Ode:

> O Lady! we receive but what we give,
> And in our life alone does Nature live.

Modern science—to Wordsworth a sealed book—refuses to allow that Nature can be a pattern for human life or morals.[1] If man is the child of Nature, he must be a rebellious child. The Victorian poets were dismayed by the damning evidence of tooth and claw, and Matthew Arnold warned his generation that " Nature and Man can never be fast friends." In France—not to multiply the instances—Alfred de Vigny had prayed not to be left alone with Nature, who is called a mother and is only a tomb.[2] So deeply do some of our poets feel the difficulty that they are tempted to turn altogether from Nature to Man. Mr. Hardy comes back to the Socratic conclusion:

> Since, then, no grace I find
>   Taught me of trees,
> Turn I back to my kind,
>   Worthy as these.
> There at least smiles abound,
> There discourse trills around,
> There, now and then, are found
>   Life-loyalties.

The true Wordsworthian, however, is not disconcerted. He appeals from biology to the higher court of philosophy. There is a real and intimate connexion—he will argue—between Nature and Man. In Emerson's words—illustrated by his own poetry—every natural fact is a symbol of some

[1] Sir W. Raleigh (*Wordsworth*, p. 142 f.) remarks that the poet was not insensitive to the cruelty of Nature, and that no doctrine of the struggle for existence would have changed his faith in the law of happiness. Perhaps not; but the doctrine certainly affected his successors, although poets like Meredith have come to terms with Nature.

[2] *La Maison du Berger*.

spiritual fact.[1] Nature, like man, is imperfect; but we are part of her, and our lives, at their highest, are in unison with her. The pathetic fallacy is not altogether fallacious. Poetically, therefore, and philosophically, we have still the right to follow Wordsworth, whatever men of science may say. Yet, in spite of his continued and even growing popularity, it may be doubted whether his admirers can accept his teaching in a literal sense. The disharmonies of Nature, which Wordsworth was able to ignore, are now too patent and insistent.

From this difficulty there are two ways of escape, and either path leads directly back to one of the two greatest poets of Rome. We may return to Lucretius, and acquiesce in a natural environment, inanimate and careless of human fate. Or, if that creed appals us, we may find refuge in a halfway house. There we shall contemplate a world, providentially adapted to human life, but with an external rather than an internal relation to mankind; a world where Design is general but not particular; where Nature and Man cannot be fast friends simply because Man is intended to conquer Nature, and the conquest is hard. If we follow this path, we shall, like Dante, take Virgil as our guide.

It is dangerous, as we have just seen, to prophesy the future of poetry, whether in relation to Nature or Man. At any time and in any place a great poet may arise, who shall point out an unsuspected bond of unity between man and his surroundings. But, for the present, it seems probable that Nature must resign the predominant place which she claimed from the poets of the early nineteenth century. Whatever may be our attitude towards Nature, the first concern of Poetry is with Man. Quite apart from any philosophic or religious theory, it was good that Nature should be as fully expressed in language as the character of that medium allows. But pure description has its limits

[1] See A. A. Jack, *Poetry and Prose* (1911), p. 116 f., where this view is upheld.

—no "word-painting" can represent a landscape with the same satisfaction to the mind that the landscape-painter can give to the eye. Poetry is not likely to go back to the artificial school before Thomson and Gray, for we have learnt too much from Wordsworth to tolerate convention. But she may well return—indeed she seems already to have returned—to a phase in which Nature, however lovingly and accurately described, will not compete with Man as the prime source of inspiration. As long as there are woods and rivers, the modern poet, no less than Virgil, is certain to love them; and there are some to-day who rest contented in that love; but the prevailing tone of modern poetry is surely that of Virgil in his maturer years—the Virgil who sang of an Italy beautiful for herself, but more beautiful as the mother of men. There may be no longer room for a didactic or even an epic poem, and modern psychology and self-analysis offer themes and methods of which Virgil was ignorant; but this is no great matter. The real lesson of Classical poetry is that human nature—whether viewed in action or thought—must always stand out, in clear and sharp relief, from any background of its environment, however beautiful the scene may be. Odysseus and Nausicaa, Æneas and Dido, will always be more than even the snow-capped mountains of Greece and the sunny olive-gardens of Italy.

CHAPTER V

POETRY AND PHILOSOPHY

I

SINCE Plato remarked on the ancient quarrel between Poetry and Philosophy, the question has often been asked, whether this estrangement is inevitable, or based on some misunderstanding. Have they the same, or a different End in view? Shall we agree with Keats, that

> all charms fly
> At the mere touch of cold philosophy,

or with the contradiction, that "No man was ever a great poet without being at the same time a profound philosopher".

Rightly interpreted, both statements are true. Keats claimed—and magnificently proved—that poetry is outside the range of logical judgment. The truth of Beauty is reached by a process quite different from that by which we seek the truth of philosophy. For, while philosophy attempts to comprehend the whole universe by reason, poetry is content to apprehend some part of the universe in relation to man.[1] To the philosopher, the transient experiences of sense are of value only so far as they corroborate the convictions of the mind; to the poet, reality can only be seen (if seen at all) by some individual experience. Poetry is not concerned with the abstract, but with a concrete embodiment; not with logic, but feeling. Keats thought, it would appear,

[1] See Sir A. Quiller-Couch, *Poetry*, p. 19 f.

that not only is the truth of Beauty all we *need* know, but all we *can* know, since the values of a given philosophy are bound to shift, whereas the sphere of feeling is constant and unchanging. The parting of Hector and Andromache, in Homer, the lament for his brother, in Catullus, the Ode to Autumn, in Keats himself, belong to the highest sphere of pure poetry, self-sufficient and perfect. But poetry has rarely such moments; nor does it evade its proper province, if it passes beyond its own sphere of intuitive feeling to annex other spheres, provided that the material which it gains thereby is transformed through the poet's imagination. And if there is no sphere which, rightly annexed, cannot provide a stimulus for the poet, the highest region—the Nature of Things—must surely provide the finest stimulus.

On this ground, not only Lucretius, but Virgil and Dante, Milton and Wordsworth, are all profound philosophers. Their systems may have become antiquated; but the link that binds Lucretius with Wordsworth is not a particular mode of philosophy—their conclusions were as antagonistic as is possible—but a common attitude of mind. Both were inspired by the same reverence for Nature, and—as we have already seen—neither had any doubt that his mission was to teach her secrets.[1] To the classical poet, at least, the propriety of this teaching was never in question. If Agriculture or Astronomy was a fit subject for poetry, the Nature of Things—which embraced the whole of human activities—must be the fittest of all. But modern criticism is not so easily satisfied, since it regards poetry as emotional rather than intellectual. The ascertained facts of science, or the speculations of metaphysics, are not to be excluded from the poet's material; but the facts and speculations must be treated poetically: as De Quincey was fond of insisting, it is not *by* teaching that didactic poetry moves, but *in spite of* teaching.[2] Even if we do not agree with Croce that poetry,

[1] See above, p. 147 f.

[2] De Quincey's *Works*, *ed.* Masson, xi. pp. 96 f., 215 f.

as a process, comes before the intellect, we must admit that, if the poet makes use of scientific ideas, he does so only to change logic into imagination. "We allow him to sing to us, while other men are only allowed to talk, not because he argues more logically than they, but because he feels more deeply and perhaps more truly."[1]

But where in all this (it may be asked) is there a ground for quarrelling? Why cannot Poetry and Philosophy agree, if only to go their separate ways? Plato, at least, thought agreement impossible; and as no other philosopher has ever felt the call of poetry so deeply, or rejected it so sternly, his point of view—even if mistaken—deserves a sympathetic hearing. In banishing the poets from his ideal City, he certainly did not misunderstand the meaning of poetry. He knew it as a *μανία*, a divine inspiration: "whilst a man retains any portion of the thing called reason, he is utterly incompetent to produce poetry".[2] So, in another dialogue, "whoever comes to knock at the doors of poetry, thinking to become a poet by force of art, departs with ruined hopes, and his poetry of reason fades before the poetry of madness."[3] To him, therefore, the two were really incompatible, and neither would brook a divided allegiance. One of the two must go, and Plato would cleave to Reason. Yet his own practice—if not his theory—allowed for the truths of poetry, when reason failed. He called in the Myth to supplement Dialectic, acknowledging thereby that there is a reality which the philosopher may conceive, but which only the poet can figure, since even the philosopher cannot fully grasp abstract ideas without symbols drawn from the world of sense. But this is no quarrel; it is rather an alliance for mutual help. Why, then, does Plato, as philosopher, reject his co-partner, the poet? He was not a Darwin, to confess (and deplore) that long scientific study had killed all taste for poetry; he

[1] T. Watts-Dunton, *Poetry and the Renascence of Wonder*, p. 11.
[2] *Ion* 534 (Shelley's transl.).
[3] *Phaedr.* 245; cf. *Laws*, 682 *a*, 701 *a*; *Gorg.* 502 f.

was far more akin to a Jerome, putting aside, although not without sorrow, the culture that seemed to stand in the way of truth.[1] For—apart from any mistrust of "imitation"—Plato's dislike of poetry is deeply rooted: intuition *may* illuminate the truth concealed from reason; but it may rather be a will-of-the-wisp. As early as Hesiod, the Muses had confessed, "we can speak many lies like the truth, and when it pleases us we can speak truthfully".[2] To Plato, the poet was the ignorant mouthpiece of the Muses, and they might deceive him, as Dionysus deceived the Bacchanals, "who when possessed by the god draw honey and milk from the rivers, in which, when they come to their senses, they find nothing but plain water".[3]

Plato would surely have avoided the philosophic myth, if he had not believed that there are times when the intuition of the poet may help the philosopher; but he must also have felt that intuition and reason might be in antagonism. He would have agreed with the modern philosopher-poet:

> But when I sit down to reason, think to take my stand, nor swerve,
> While I triumph o'er a secret wrung from Nature's close reserve,
> In you come with your cold music, till I creep in every nerve.[4]

None the less, it was the philosopher's business to avoid the immediate intuition and to seek for truth by logical argument. In the end, no doubt, truth may be suddenly revealed to the philosopher; but this flash of insight is not immediate—it is the culmination of a long and laborious process of reasoning; and Plato was not one to think that the kingdom of truth could be taken by poetic violence. In any case he could not ally himself with those who were ignorant whether the thing called madness came from Apollo or from Dionysus.

Some such mistrust of art, as commonly defined and

[1] Jerome, *Ep.* 22, 30, *Ciceronianus es, non Christianus.*

[2] Hes. *Theog.* 27.

[3] *Ion* 534; see generally *Apol.* 22c; *Laws* 719c.

[4] R. Browning, *A Toccata of Galuppi.*

practised, seems to have prejudiced the mind of Plato, before he found, or at least developed, a philosophic theory of the universe which had also a bearing on poetry.[1] In the tenth book of the *Republic*, he states his famous doctrine that *all* poetry is to be condemned as "imitative"—the poets copy sensible things, which are themselves only copies of reality.[2] It is unnecessary to point out that Plato misconceived the nature and function of representative art, (which is certainly not a "copy" of sensible things); but, whatever the value of his premisses, he shows unerringly that the real quarrel is between sense and thought.

This, however, was not his original position. In the early part of the *Republic*, he had condemned only such poetry as imitates what is bad.[3] He had no case against the imitation of what is good; on the contrary, it is the mission of all arts to educate by such imitation.[4] Plato, in fact, says no more than Aristophanes had said, protesting against the "immorality" of Euripides. In this sense, the quarrel was ancient enough—it was started at least a century before—but it had nothing to do with aesthetics. From Homer to Empedocles (that is, till the middle of the fifth century), the distinction between the literature of power and the literature of knowledge would have been meaningless. In Homer and Hesiod, verse had been the only medium, and both Parmenides and Empedocles carried on the tradition, without suspecting that any line of demarcation could, or should, be drawn between the poet and the philosopher—provided that the poet told the truth. It was here that the trouble arose. By the end of the sixth century, the frank anthropomorphism of the old epic no

[1] Plato must not be understood as wishing to abolish art (including poetry), but to idealize it. See R. L. Nettleship, *Lectures and Remains*, II, p. 112 f.

[2] *Rep.* 505*a*. [3] *Rep.* 376 f.

[4] The difference between Plato's earlier and later criticism of poetry is pointed out by W. C. Greene, *Harvard Studies in Class. Phil.* xxix. (1918), pp. 1-75, the most complete article on the subject.

longer satisfied the religious thinkers of Greece. The Myth had become a scandal. How could it be believed that Cronos had swallowed his own children? How—asked Xenophanes indignantly—can the gods be thieves and adulterers? But Xenophanes himself wrote in the epic metre, and both ancients and moderns have doubted whether to call him a poet or a philosopher. His protest, in fact, was not concerned with the difference between sensation and thought; it was a question of truth or lies.

Such was the simple issue when Plato took over the controversy; and, as we have just seen, he was at first prepared to rely wholly on the moral argument. He was quite ready to admit hymns and edifying poems; and if Homer and Hesiod had told no lies about the gods, he might well have allowed the poet a better place in the hierarchy of souls than one below the professor of gymnastics, if above the sophist or demagogue, and (of course) above the absolute monarch. Anyhow, his unfortunate, if only apparent, antagonism to *all* poetry was without influence on later thought, for Aristotle soon put the doctrine of Imitation in a clearer light. The theory that all imitation is necessarily bad was quietly dropped—it would have stultified the whole of Greek poetry; and no Greek, except Plato, in certain moods, would have tolerated that.

Yet Plato's contribution to poetic criticism was of supreme importance. Directly, he gave the immense prestige of his authority in favour of the moral significance of art. Indirectly, he did even more: during the next three centuries—until the advent of Lucretius—he prescribed the line of demarcation between poetry and philosophy. Indeed, he may be said to have started, in a new form, the quarrel which he thought so old. Up to his time, it was still possible to confuse the spheres of sense and reason. The tradition of Xenophanes and Empedocles might well have continued, and verse have remained as at least a possible mode for the philosopher. Plato made it impossible. His master, Socrates, had invented a new method in dialectic, and Plato's own splendid prose seemed to have settled the question once for all. Henceforward, there was an open breach between the verse-writers, who clung to the Homeric myth, and the philosophers, who either discarded it altogether, or turned it—like Prodicus and Plato himself—into a mere allegory to serve the purpose of ethics or metaphysics.

In the generation after Plato, the case against philosophic verse was even stronger. Philosophy had become systematic and encyclopædic; the vast range of Aristotelian theory would have been as ridiculous in verse as Bacon's *Novum Organum* or Spencer's *Principles.* Moreover, Aristotle had laid the foundation of literary criticism in the *Poetic*, showing that, if the provinces of science and art might approximate, their methods and ends were different: to the philosopher, the particular serves only as a help for comprehending the universal, whereas the aim of poetry is to give a concrete embodiment of a universal truth.[1]

But the gulf was still further to be widened. Although Aristotle is rightly regarded as the founder of the inductive method, its full application was left to his successor Theophrastus. With an accumulation of observed facts such as we see in the *History of Plants*, the writing of a philosophic poem became more and more difficult. The growth of descriptive science, as an offshoot of metaphysics, overpowered the poets, who could no longer draw simply on their imagination with the easy freedom of an Empedocles. It is true that Aratus and Nicander, the contemporaries of Theophrastus, attempted to turn science into poetry, in departments ranging from astronomy to bee-keeping and the bites of poisonous snakes. But the exposition of a philosophic system, as a whole, was beyond their powers.

[1] S. H. Butcher, *Aristotle's Poetics*, ch. 3, p. 191 f.

There were Stoic poets, but no poet of Stoicism. Cleanthes composed a noble hymn to Zeus, holding that metre could alone express the majesty of God; but, though Stoicism, as a religious creed, was an inspiration to Aratus, the systematic exposition of its tenets was strictly confined to prose.

The rival creed of Epicurus was unable to produce any poetry at all. There was to be no Greek Lucretius, even at the time when philosophy had become all-important in the general life of Greece. How are we to explain this fact? Some may answer that no explanation is required, or even possible: poetry, they may argue, does not proceed on logical grounds, so that a poet should always be ready to hand, whenever a subject is waiting for his appearance. Positively, no doubt, the genesis of a great poet cannot be predicted with the assurance of a weather-prophet; but negatively we may "predict"—at least after the event—the causes which seem to hinder his appearance at any given time in the history of literature. It has been argued above that, in later Rome, there were certain definite hindrances to the production of a poet;[1] and it seems that the case against poetry is no less strong for Hellenistic Greece. Philosophy was then a dominant notion, a subject of supreme interest, and all history proves that such notions are bound, sooner or later, to affect poetry. The question is, therefore, why this inspiration was delayed until the advent of Lucretius. The obvious answer, of course, is that Hellenistic Greece was decadent; that Greek poetry was exhausted before the rise of post-Aristotelian philosophy, and too feeble to be receptive of great ideas. But, after all, the Alexandrine age gave birth to Theocritus and Apollonius, no mean poets. Why should philosophy have failed, when the new stimulus of the pastoral and the revived interest of the epic succeeded?

[1] See p. 101.

If we look a little closer, it will appear that philosophy itself, rather than poetry, was responsible for keeping up the quarrel which remained for Lucretius to settle. New systems, such as those of Zeno and Epicurus, were long in reaching the point at which they could be material for the poet. The founders of the two creeds were fervent missionaries, but their gospels were essentially practical. The brilliant cosmical speculations of Empedocles had been replaced by controversies on the value of Virtue or Pleasure in human conduct. Physical theories mattered only in so far as they affected the happiness of the individual. As Epicurus himself remarked, "if it were not for human fears, we could do without physics." Hellenistic Greeks, in fact, were tired of guesses about the framework of the world. They were not anxious to construct a model of the universe; all they wanted was a sanction for human morality, a way of life. Here the struggle was bitter, and more suited to the partizan than to the poet. Fundamental differences must be fought out in the arena of prosaic debate before they can give scope to the imagination. Poetry needs a perspective of its own: we have only to remember that Christianity was attacked and defended for three hundred years before Prudentius; that Dante represents the culmination of medieval theology; that *Paradise Lost* is no early protest of Puritanism, but its triumph. In fields other than theological, the wars of Napoleon waited a full century for a poet; and the present generation, which has taken part in an even vaster struggle, can hardly expect, in its own lifetime, a full interpretation of that Titanic upheaval.

If, therefore, Alexandria could create no philosopher-poet, it may fairly be claimed that, apart from the general decadence, the special conditions of philosophy were unfavourable. On the other hand, the phenomenon of a Roman Lucretius—strange as it may appear that Rome succeeded where Greece failed—is not difficult to explain, as far as genius can be explained by time or environment.

By the middle of the first century B.C., the feud of Stoics and Epicureans had long ceased to be novel, not only for the Greeks, but for the Romans, who had been familiar with the rival sects for more than a hundred years. A stage had now been reached in which the controversy could be lifted to a higher plane. Controversial, indeed, the two schools always remained; but the issues were now clear, and there was room for combatants other than the lecturer and the pamphleteer. In particular, there was room for an enthusiast who should value philosophy, not—in the narrow view of Epicurus—as a mere ethical guide, but as a complete revelation of the Universe. It is of course a fact that, for the Romans, the conduct of life was at least as important and engrossing as it had been to the Athenians of the third century. But they were also keenly interested in the external world, and approached physical problems with a zest and freshness which the contemporaries of Epicurus had lost. Speculation gained a new lease of life. There was good reason for Lucretius to pay a glowing tribute of praise to Sicily as the land which had produced no marvel more wonderful than Empedocles. Lucretius was himself the incarnation of the great physicist of Agrigentum.

More than three centuries had passed since Empedocles had expressed his vision of the Universe, and the intervening period had witnessed Greek philosophy, as well as Greek literature, flourish and decay. After Plato and Aristotle, it might have seemed impossible for a later poet, in an alien language, to recapture the spirit of the old philosopher. Hazlitt once complained that "there can never be another Jacob's dream. Since that time, the heavens have gone farther off, and grown astronomical."[1] Lucretius anticipated Hazlitt, almost to the letter, for he denied the Stoic myth that a golden rope was let down from heaven to earth. No

[1] *Lectures on the English Poets.*

less than Keats, he knew that the rainbow was no divine Iris, as the age of Empedocles still believed. To Lucretius the heavens had grown astronomical, however crude his astronomy may have been. He would certainly have claimed to have unwoven the rainbow, and would have classed it in the catalogue of common things. But, unlike Keats, Lucretius never thought that the catalogue was "dull." From these common things, rightly understood, he could carry on the great task of Empedocles, in the fuller light which his master Epicurus had thrown on the Nature of Things. The key of Atomism alone could unlock the door in the flaming walls of the Universe, so that heaven and earth should be seen, undistorted by the false glamour of mythical religion.

From his nominal teacher, Lucretius, as a poet, had little to learn. Epicurus, with all the "apathy" of which he was so proud, had failed to discover the least poetic spark in the great system of Democritus. His crabbed style and dry, unimpassioned tone are unredeemed by any flash of imagination. He can find no value in atomism—the most brilliant and far-reaching speculation of the ancients—except as a basis on which to build a gospel of quiescence. But Epicurus had a personality, a power of inspiring affection and admiration; and it was a point of honour for his followers to present their master's teaching with absolute fidelity. It was just here that, for Lucretius, the danger lay. He has been accused—and not without reason—of following Epicurus too closely, and so of sinking the poet in the philosopher. Instead of assuming the truth of his system, and omitting details which no language could turn into poetry, Lucretius takes nothing for granted. He lectures on his subject, in all its *minutiae*, like a professor, and spares his pupil no argument, although he claims to have other proof in reserve, if Memmius is still unconvinced. Science, in fact, as nearly crushed the poetry of Lucretius as Superstition—in his belief—had crushed mankind. In consequence, his poem now appeals only, or mainly, by virtue of his "purple patches"—his wonderful digressions on the majesty of the Universe, his deep knowledge of human nature, his eloquent protests against luxury and ambition, his keen sense of the pathos and littleness of life, his scorn of an effete religion. With the scientific part of the poem we are unsympathetic, not because the science is often bad, but because, even when good, it seems out of place. We cannot help judging Lucretius by modern standards, and a modern poem on entirely Lucretian lines would be impossible. Didactic poetry, on a scientific subject, came to an inglorious end with Erasmus Darwin; and, since his time, the methods of science have become so special, and its material so vast, that, although a poet may still bring his imagination to bear on the results of experiment, he cannot, like Lucretius, attempt to trench on the ground of the physicist or biologist. Even for Lucretius the attempt was dangerous. As he confessed, it was difficult to explain the obscure discoveries of the Greeks in Latin verse. But Lucretius was saved by the very defects of ancient philosophy. We may condemn Greek science as guess-work, because it was almost entirely unsupported by experiment. On the other hand, the physical conclusions of the Greek Atomists nearly always rested on observation (however inadequate); and, in the sphere of Science, observation is all that poetry can well assimilate. Atomism, in fact, could give material to a poet, precisely because the dry bones of argument were clothed with the flesh of natural analogy. A few instances, from a highly technical part of the *de Rerum Natura*, will illustrate this power of poeticizing the most stubborn material. Atoms are in perpetual motion: direct proof is indeed lacking, since they are far beneath our senses; but reason requires them to move, and proof is found in the analogy of the motes that dance in the sunbeam. So, even a solid body, which appears to be at rest, is composed of moving particles, just as a flock of sheep on the hillside seems at a distance to be a white spot resting on the green slope; or just as, when we stand on a mountain, an army manœuvring on the distant plain appears to be motionless. Again, atoms must be of infinite variety, since each living thing differs from any other; and, as an analogy, Lucretius "digresses" into the pathetic description of a cow which knows the footprints of her calf, torn from her side to be slaughtered at the altar: "gazing on every place in search of her lost offspring, she stops to fill the shady groves with her lamentation, or often returns to the byre, smitten with yearning for her calf." These observations—all comprised in an argument of less than three hundred consecutive lines—are sufficient proof that Lucretius saw, in the atomic theory, not the bare and passionless system of his master, but the answer to the riddle of a world pulsating with life and colour, a world where the artist and poet can take pleasure in watching the lambs that play on the dewy grass, and in marking the shells that "paint the bosom of Earth, where the level sea with gentle lapping touches the thirsty sand upon its winding shore." [1]

After this, it is scarcely necessary to discuss the question whether Lucretius welcomed Science "for its own sake," or whether, like Epicurus, he viewed it as a mere means of escape from the terrors of death and damnation. Virgil, in a plain reference to his predecessor, favours the latter alternative—he who knows the causes of things can crush underfoot the fear of Fate and Hell. Lucretius himself would not have denied its truth; for he often insists that the reason of Epicurus has dispelled the terror of divine punishment. But, for the poet, this is not the whole truth. In one sense, no doubt, every poet must interpret Nature in human terms. Even to a Wordsworth, the external world has only a value in relation to man. A poet who tried to regard Nature as entirely dissociate from man would be—as Aristotle might have said—either a monster or an (Epicurean) god. And

[1] 2, 114-376.

Lucretius, with his intensely human sympathies, was least of all poets inclined to study the Universe with a coldly scientific detachment. None the less, he has the same sense of wonder, and the feeling for beauty, which distinguish the artist from the moralist. The "majesty of things" moves him to a divine pleasure, quite apart from their consequences. For proof of this, we need not merely consider the form of the poem, though three-quarters of its bulk are devoted to physical theory; what really counts is the poet's obvious enthusiasm for pure science. It is of little consequence that his methods are primitive and his conclusions often puerile—that is only a defect of the age, and is nothing in comparison with a scientific imagination which so far transcends the limits of the actual system. Indeed, it is remarkable that, only when Lucretius passes from pure science to its human application, is his enthusiasm tempered by pessimism. As a physicist, he can whole-heartedly admire the law and order of the natural world. The Universe is as much a marvel—*adlaudabile opus*—to him as to the writer of *Job*. But Nature holds out no satisfaction to the race or to the individual, beyond the short span of human life. His acquiescence in the inevitable is serene and splendid, but it strikes, at best, the note of resignation. That he is more than resigned, that he has fire and energy, that he is a poet as well as a philosopher, is surely due not to the tameness of his moral code, but to the sublimity of his physical imagination.

Nevertheless, Lucretius would have been no true Epicurean if he had regarded Science as an end in itself. The nominal End at which Epicurus aimed was Pleasure; but this was merely a means to *ἀταραξία*—a quiet life. The arch-enemy was superstition, and science was the redeemer. Only by a knowledge of Natural law could man escape from the fear of angry and capricious gods. It has often been suggested that Lucretius (like his kindred spirit, Condorcet) overrates the baneful influence of superstition—that he protests too much. Yet the protest seems to ring true. No doubt the official state-religion of Rome was little concerned with the after-world, and it was easy to keep on good terms with a Pantheon which only needed its proper dues of spelt and salt. But underneath this Olympian brightness there was in Italy, even more than in Greece, a nether stratum of furies and hobgoblins, of witches and ghosts. Cicero and Juvenal might laugh at these old-wives' fables; but the mass of Italians learned their first lessons in religion from old-wives, and the fear remained. Even in the poem of Lucan—a cultivated Stoic—the marks of a real belief in witchcraft are plainly visible; and there was a recrudescence of superstition in the age of the Antonines. Against demons, the gods of light were powerless or indifferent; and so there is no mere rhetoric, but profound conviction, in the burning words with which Lucretius condemns the whole of an outworn creed:

Here thou mayest shrink, and fear to be the Fool
Who saith: "There is no God"—in Reason's school
Treading the path of sin. Nay! many a time
Not Reason, but Religion, counsels crime.
That impious word the Danaan lords obey'd,
Dooming to death Iphigenia fair
Upon the altar of the Huntress Maid.
The fillet, bound about her virginal hair,
Dropt, covering either cheek in equal bands,
And she beheld her father, where he stands
Mute on the altar-steps in dull despair;
And mark'd the sacrificers at his side,
Holding the deadly knife they fain would hide,
With all the townsfolk in a mournful ring
To see her die. And then she fell to earth
Voiceless: it could not help her that the King
First won the name of Father by her birth.
Roughly was she upraised, and quivering
Brought to the altar, not with escort meet,
Or ceremony, or song of marriage-bliss,

But haled, a girl immaculate, ripe to wed,
Victim of her own father, that the fleet
Might leave the harbour, fortunately sped.
Men hearken to Religion—and do this![1]

The tale of Iphigenia—though familiar enough in literature and art—may seem a little remote from Roman life, and Lucretius might easily have found examples of superstition nearer home. But his choice of the subject is significant. He makes straight for the fountain-head: the "Greek bible" had sanctioned cruelty in the name of the gods. Religion was not even a "useful lie," and it must go. This, for Lucretius, is the ultimate aim of philosophy—a science worthy, in itself, as the true interpretation of the Universe, but still worthier as the sole refuge from the haunting fears of ignorant humanity.

But there is even more than this. In the story of Iphigenia, Lucretius is steadily setting his face against *all* Myth. Elsewhere, he inveighs against religious Myths—Cybele, Pan, the Nymphs and Fauns are figments of the brain; here, and here alone, he quotes an heroic myth (though in a religious connexion), as if to shew that philosophic poetry is alien to all mythology, however blameless and beautiful. He cuts adrift from the characteristic material of Greek and Latin poetry. A poet may be a philosopher; but the price is heavy—he must renounce all the charm of all the Muses. He must give up the splendid inheritance of Homer and Aeschylus and Sophocles, and turn from the pleasant path which the Romans had already begun to explore. There must be no dallying in the romantic groves where Ovid was to lay the scene of the *Metamorphoses*, or in the nymph-haunted waters, where Propertius was to revive the story of Hylas. A mythic Hercules must make way for the historic Epicurus.

Lucretius had good reason for holding that if philosophy

[1] I, 80-101.

was to unite with poetry, the Myth must be dropped. It was too intimately bound up with popular religion to be tolerated by the seeker of truth. Virgil, during his early phase of Epicureanism, seems to have felt the same difficulty. In a youthful poem he had proposed to give up not only rhetoric but poetry itself, though he hoped that his philosophy might accept the Muses as rare visitors.[1] Later—to the lasting benefit of poetry—Virgil was to reverse the order, choosing the Muses, with the rare visit (in his Sixth *Aeneid*) of philosophy. Lucretius, however, remained constant to his creed, knowing that if Myth was allowed an entrance to Poetry, Religion would creep in by the same door.

Yet the Myth might be admitted, on terms, and as a rare visitor. More than once Lucretius does not disdain to make poetic use of a myth which his reason condemns : you may call the earth Cybele, he says, or the sea Neptune, provided that you do not stain your mind with foul superstition. And—as if to emphasize the exception which was to prove the rule—Lucretius began his poem by what seems a flat negative of his principles, in the famous apostrophe to Venus. Of course, in a sense, this is no real exception—any average Epicurean would have said that Venus and Mars were not personal gods, but meant the two principles of Love and Hate, or Peace and War—that mysterious pair, by whose equal and antithetic power (*aequo certamine*) the order of the world was balanced : Lucretius was not staining his mind with superstition, but simply using a poet's undoubted right to personify. This would be the exoteric, common-sense reply to any criticisms ; but I do not think that Lucretius himself would have been content with it. He was not merely destructive in his attack on orthodox religion. Epicurus, once absurdly thought to be an atheist, aimed at reconstruction. His gods, it is true, were not

[1] See p. 23.

touched by human affairs, but none the less—on their own side—they could influence humanity. Their images continually poured into the minds of men, and it was in the act of prayer or worship (which Epicurus specially enjoined) that the mind became receptive to their influence. The gods themselves lived in eternal peace, and this intermundane calm, which the Epicureans so ardently desired, could be communicated to the human mind. There were other motives, no doubt, for the Epicurean belief in the gods—the supposed consensus of opinion seemed to them conclusive—but the highest, and the most religious, as well as the most poetic reason is surely that the gods were needed as an ideal which could be realized by man. Viewed in this light, Venus is no wanton, nor even a fair goddess of beauty; she is the giver of Life, and also the giver of Peace, without which life has little of pleasure to bestow on mankind.

The *de Rerum Natura* both marked and made an epoch. Politically, it expressed the culmination of a philosophic school, which was to last until nearly the end of paganism, but which was never so popular as in the middle of the first century B.C., when religion and morality had been rudely shaken by the struggles leading to the Civil War. As literature, the poem was the greatest Roman achievement since the *Annals* of Ennius. But, in politics and literature alike, it was the close, rather than the opening of an epoch that Lucretius represents. Published only a few years before the War, its message, no less than its style, was antiquated by the Peace. It may be objected that, in the Augustan age, Lucretius received the practical flattery of constant imitation. But, except for two references by Ovid[1]—a practical Epicurean, if "unattached"—the poets of this period never mention Lucretius by name. This silence, in itself, would not conclusively prove neglect, for

[1] *Amor.* i. 15, 23; *Trist.* 2, 4, 25.

the omission of the name was a point of style in certain classes of poetry; but the prose-writers are no less silent. After Cicero, his contemporary,[1] there is no mention of Lucretius in Augustan prose, except passing allusions in Nepos and Vitruvius.[2]

The fact is that the whole spirit of the Epicurean poet was out of harmony with the New Age. Quietism may have brought consolation to spectators in the Civil War, and the combatants themselves may well have disbelieved in the Roman gods who could not, or would not, interfere. But, after the war, the new hopes and strenuous aims of Augustus had no use for Epicurean apathy—calm might be "well," but it was no longer "life's crown." The revival of religion was one of the most prominent features in the imperial policy, and it was the business of the court-poets to support the emperor. Virgil and Horace had been attracted by Epicureanism in their youth, but both abjured it. From all we know of Virgil, we may feel sure that his renunciation was genuine—the author of the Sixth Book of the *Aeneid* could not long be satisfied with a negative creed, even if his own vision of Truth might issue darkly through the Ivory gate.[3] Horace, too, was no doubt sincere in calling the philosophy of his youth "a mad wisdom," for he certainly learnt to appreciate the finer qualities of Stoicism; and, if the cause for his conversion (he had heard thunder in a clear sky) seems to us inadequate, he may have had other and stronger reasons.[4] It is unfortunate that a conversion—as Johnson said of Dryden—"will always be suspected that apparently coincides with interest"; but as Johnson added—"truth and interest are not by any fatal necessity at variance." Among the other poets, Ovid alone imperfectly disguised

[1] *ad. Q.F.* 2, 9, 3. See p. 57.

[2] Nepos, *Att.* 12, 4; Vitr. 9, 17.

[3] See p. 182.

[4] *Od.* 1, 34. It must be remembered that the Epicureans laid stress on the presence of clouds (Lucr. 6, 400). Horace may really have thought that the rationalistic theory had broken down. For Horace's religion see D'Alton, *Horace and his Age*, ch. 3.

his irreligion, a Voltaire among the orthodox, with his cynical frankness

expedit esse deos et, ut expedit, esse putemus;

but Ovid was never an official poet, and paid for the character of his verse by its exclusion from the library of the Palatine Apollo.[1]

There was thus no room for Lucretius in the Reconstruction; the poets were occupied with the glory of Rome and the splendour of the new dynasty. Nevertheless, the sect of Epicurus was still a power, if perhaps only in opposition; and Lucretius had challenged an answer: "if I speak the truth"—he had exclaimed—"surrender; if I lie, gird yourself to fight." After half a century, when the theme of Rome's grandeur had been exhausted, the turn of philosophy came again, and the challenge received a rather belated answer from the Stoic camp. We need not search for a political reason to explain a counterblast which, on purely philosophical grounds, was due or overdue; but it is worth while to note that Stoicism was now rapidly becoming a political as well as an intellectual force, and was soon to develop into open hostility toward the principate. Even under Augustus, when Stoics were still welcome at the Court, the creed must have been a satisfaction to those who saw that the empire was a despotism in disguise, and who were debarred from any real activity in political life. The attack on Lucretius took the form of an astronomical poem, written by Manilius in the second decade of our era.[2]

II

Astronomy, as a science, had started in Greece with the speculations of the Ionian philosophers; but in the great age of humanism, its interest declined until, with Democritus,

[1] *Trist.* 3, 1, 59.

[2] Apparently between 9 and 15 A.D. See H. W. Garrod, *Manilius*, II, p. lxiv.

it had almost vanished. The Democritean system, resting on the truth of sense-perception, and resolving the Universe into atoms, could find no importance in heavenly bodies which were no bigger (and no better) than they looked. But all Greeks were not atomists; and, just at this point, the waning stream of astronomy was fed by a new influx of Oriental star-worship, and henceforward astronomy was almost merged in astrology. Greek rationalism—the inheritance of Anaxagoras—was still a force against superstition; and, not long after Democritus, the astronomer Eudoxus rejected the horoscope. But the pseudo-Platonic *Epinomis* shews that astrology was gaining ground, and—though Panaetius stood out[1]—it found a strong champion in Stoicism. That school was an easy prey, with its basic conception of the world as a living thing (ζῷον), whose parts are in sympathy with each other. Man is the highest product of the Universe, and his life is mapped out by Destiny. The stars are undeviating in their courses, and their movements can be foretold with certainty. If, therefore, these heavenly bodies predict their own movements, and if they are in sympathy with man (whose soul is a particle of heavenly fire), it follows that they must also predict the future of man.

The importance of astrology did not end with a belief in mere sympathy. Man's soul was akin to the stars, and some favoured souls, at least, would return to their celestial home, although the common sort would be absorbed in the fire of the Universe. There was to be a place not only for the Caesars, but for Lucan's Pompey, in Stoic apotheosis. We cannot here blame the Stoics, when even Raleigh could hold that "the stars are instruments of far greater use than to give an obscure light, and for men to gaze on after sunset"; indeed, once the geocentric view of the universe is

[1] Cic. *de Div.* 2, 29; see F. Cumont, *Astrology and Religion* (1912), pp. 48 f., 82 f.

granted, the Stoic position is natural, and—unless we follow Democritus—inevitable.

The final step was taken by Posidonius,[1] the pupil of Panaetius, whose lectures Cicero had attended; and henceforth the alliance between astrology and Stoicism was finally sealed. Roman philosophy was willing to accept the arts of the East without compunction; Augustus himself—a firm believer in the "Julian star"—was not too emancipated to consult an astrologer,[2] and Virgil—to name no other poet—described the presage of a comet or an eclipse with evident credulity.[3]

The alliance was philosophically a drawback, by opening the floodgates to a superstition which it was the business of philosophy to restrain. On the other hand, the science of the stars was a strong poetic motive. The subject was hallowed by antiquity, for a lost poem on Astronomy, attributed to Hesiod, was known to the founder of Stoicism, as well as to the Alexandrine scholars,[4] one of whom had earned a fame which we find very difficult to appreciate. Ovid's eulogy of Aratus—

cum sole et luna semper Aratus erit—

seems hyperbolic to modern readers who (as a rule) know little of astronomy and care less for astrology; and an age which has lost all interest in the original is not likely to be moved by the translations of Cicero and Germanicus. But Ovid correctly voiced the ancient view at a time when—as Quintilian said—one who was ignorant of the stars would not understand the poets—a statement only too true for most readers of Manilius.[5] Aratus (himself a Stoic) was the best model and ally for an opponent of Lucretius. There was a further advantage to be gained. The physical theories

[1] *Fatalium siderum assertor*, Augustine, *C.D.* 5, 2.
[2] Suet. *Oct.* 94.
[3] *Georg.* 1, 33, 336. Cf. *Aen.* 4, 519 *conscia fati sidera.*
[4] Garrod on *Manil.* 2, 12.
[5] Quint. 1, 4, 4.

of the Stoics, as a whole, were dull and uninspiring, even if Munro is perhaps too contemptuous of "their one wretched world, their monotonous fire, their rotund and rotatory god".[1] But they had a conception of the heavenly bodies at least more adequate than Lucretius could offer. Misled by Democritus, the Epicurean could only regard the stars as pin-points, making the night wonderful and beautiful—"when we gaze on the celestial quarters of the great universe, and see the ether set with glittering stars"[2]—but meaningless and unimportant for mankind. It is astonishing that, with this ignorance of relative magnitudes, Lucretius was still susceptible to "the majesty of things"; and here, no less than in the moral sphere, we may well see an illustration of Patin's *l'anti Lucrèce chez Lucrèce*—the striking and patent fact that the poet was greater than his philosophy. To the Stoic, for whom Reason was superior to the senses, Lucretius presented an easy target, at the very point—his physics—where he seemed most invulnerable.

Stoic Reason was here, no doubt, as inadequate as Epicurean sense-perception, for the Stoic failed to recognize both the vastness and the mystery of the Universe, as a secret beyond human intelligence: man's ways seemed plain, and Nature was constructed on human principles, so that the stars must be marshalled in their appropriate ranks, as senators, knights, and plebeians, after the Roman model.[3] But while the Epicurean, looking at the heavens, could only *fear* that there might be a divine Power that ruled the stars in their courses, the Stoic saw in the *insigne spectaculum noctium* a proof that a beneficent Providence was revealed in the starry heavens as well as in the moral law.[4]

A casual reader might assume that Manilius was first and foremost an astronomer, and only in a minor degree a Stoic concerned to refute Lucretius. But a closer study will shew

[1] *Lucr. Introd. vol.* 2, p. 6. [2] Lucr. 5, 1202. [3] Manil. 5, 734.
[4] Sen. *Ep.* 90, *non impendebant caelata laquearia, sed in aperto iacentes sidera superlabentia, et insigne spectaculum noctium.*

that the *Astronomica* is controversial from beginning to end. At the very outset Manilius picks up the gauntlet. He is anxious to prove that the Epicurean anthropology—which, more than any other part of the system, has stood the test of modern science—is based on error. Lucretius has described the miserable condition of primitive men, naked, defenceless, a prey to wild beasts, each one a law to himself, and careless of the common good.[1] With his eye on the Golden Age, which the Stoics accepted (though not without some higher criticism), Manilius traverses the argument step by step. Lucretius, sensibly enough, had said that the first men took the process of day and night for granted; the astronomer-poet, on the contrary, represents man as frightened by nightfall and joyful at the rebirth of day.[2] In dealing with the next stage of society, the Stoic shews to more advantage: while Lucretius is compelled to deny any altruism in social evolution, Manilius rightly sees that society cannot be formed by self-interest alone. Taking the actual words of Lucretius—*commune bonum*—he insists on the influence of society as a natural and not merely a conventional bond. The wild and selfish cave-man of Epicurean fancy is replaced by the "noble savage", who is led upwards to civilization through the providence of God.

It is this belief—that the Universe has a meaning and a divine plan—which gives the *Astronomica* its chief distinction. Again and again Manilius leaves the dull recital of what he supposes to be astronomical facts, to point out their significance.[3] The world is reasonable, and man, the microcosm—*quibus est et mundus in ipsis*—is part of the world-deity. Hence Reason is the sole and ultimate authority—

ratio omnia vincit,
nam neque decipitur ratio neque decipit umquam[4]

[1] Lucr. 5, 925 f.; Manil. 1, 66 f. See *Anthropology of the Greeks*, p. 100.
[2] Lucr. 5, 973; Manil. 1, 69.
[3] E.g. 1, 246 f., 483 f., and often. [4] 2, 131.

—a thrust at the Epicurean criterion of the senses, which Manilius disdains to refute with direct allusion. Curiously (it may seem), he is but little attracted by Ethics, which all others of his school rate so highly. He utters the usual protest against luxury and ambition;[1] but this was common form, and even a rigid Stoic could hardly have found fault with the stern denunciation of vice by Lucretius himself. However much the two sects might differ on the sanctions for morality, they were largely agreed about the actual conduct of life. It is as a theologian rather than a moralist that Manilius attacks Lucretius in the eternal antagonism between the two ultimate interpretations of the world—a rational government or the blind forces of unconscious Nature. The Stoic theology, from which all the accretions of popular religion had been refined away, was not, perhaps, so far removed from the Epicurean creed as the ancients thought. The "rotund and rotatory" god, devoid of all personality, is no great improvement, for human needs, on the *Natura gubernans* of Lucretius, even though the former was sentient and the latter inanimate. But the great power of Stoicism lay in the recognition that this World-god stood for a moral order and a high place for man in the scheme of things. Stoics could claim this supreme advantage without renouncing the rationalism of the Epicureans. Except for their weak spot—astrology—the Stoic armour was strong enough to avert the superstition, of which Epicurus believed himself to be the sole opponent. Not less than Lucretius, the Stoic poet is proud of his victory over popular ignorance and fear. Manilius, at least, would not have been converted to Stoicism by thunder in a clear sky. Reason has nothing to do with such superstition—it has once for all wrested the thunderbolt from the Jupiter of false imagination:

eripuitque Iovi fulmen viresque Tonanti,
et sonitum ventis concessit, nubibus ignem.[2]

[1] 4, 1 f.

[2] 1, 104.

From the above account, it will be seen that, while nominally confining himself to a single and—for a Stoic—unessential branch of his creed, Manilius really attacks Lucretius on a wide front. The anthropology and ethical system of the Epicureans are condemned as strongly as their theological and cosmical views; and, in particular, the doctrine of Chance is opposed by that strict belief in Fate which has been called the corner stone of Stoicism, but which might equally well be called a millstone about the philosopher's neck. The best that could be done was to follow one's fate bravely and willingly, since—as Cleanthes said, and as every Stoic repeated—cowardice and unwillingness were of no avail. Here, at least, Manilius does not fall behind his Stoic masters: *sors est sua cuique ferenda.* He can even extract comfort from a doctrine which really sapped the springs of energy as much as the quietism of Epicurus. Why should we spend life in seeking for wealth, he asks, when our destiny is mapped out for us at birth—*nascentes morimur, finisque ab origine pendet?*[1] But the comfort is, at best, acquiescent; it has not the strength of a more virile Stoic, who strives, not so much to follow willingly, as to be the master of his Fate, the captain of his Soul. This triumphant note is often sounded in ancient Stoicism, from Cleanthes to Seneca—*non pareo deo sed adsentior*[2]—but it is not characteristic of Manilius, who rarely rises above the commonplaces of his school.

One may regret that, in this tremendous duel, Lucretius found no worthier antagonist. Philosophically, indeed, Manilius was fighting in a noble cause; but his choice of weapons was unfortunate; for his poetic imagination was no match for Lucretius. So far, Stoicism was not to blame. But it may be fair to urge that even a better champion might well have been beaten. No creed which denies the value of the senses can be a fit subject for poetry. The

[1] 4, 16.

[2] Sen. *Ep.* 96.

Stoics relied on pure Reason, neglecting the emotions as unphilosophical; and—as a recent critic has remarked—it is impossible to imagine the *Critique of Pure Reason* in a poetic form.[1] On the other hand, Epicureanism, with its strong, if often misguided reliance on the senses, was a mould ready to receive external impressions. Apart from this advantage, Epicurus had laid great stress on the value of Friendship; and if—in his strict logic—the acquisition of friends was ascribed to a selfish motive, the Epicureans soon recognized that this selfishness could lead to altruism, so that the friend was loved "for himself." We think of Horace, to whom Virgil was "half his soul," and wonder if a Stoic would have felt, or at least uttered, the sentiment. For friendship cannot exist without sympathy, and the chief fault of Stoicism was the self-sufficiency which too often masqueraded as independence. In theory, no doubt, the Stoic widened his society to include a world-brotherhood, and it would be unjust to deny the great value of the school in this expansion; but, in practice, the philosopher was too apt to be narrowly individual. Socrates had spied vainglory peeping through the holes of the Cynic's threadbare mantle, and the same charge might have been brought against some of those Stoics who were fond of wrapping themselves in their virtue; but, even if their moral cloak was sound, poetry needs other singing-robes.

It is useless to "compare" a respectable, second-rate writer with a poet who can rank with Dante or Milton, but it may be worth while to shew, by a single illustration, where the difference lies. Both Lucretius and Manilius dealt with a pathetic subject—the sacrifice of a fair girl as a victim for the sake of others. What Lucretius made of the subject may be seen, even if dimly, in the passage translated above.[2] Not a word, in the original, mars the scene of infinite pity, leading to the indignant outburst at the folly of superstition.

[1] J. A. K. Thomson, *The Greek Tradition*, p. 176.

[2] p. 167

The whole apostrophe is unaffected, uncontaminated by any rhetoric. Manilius, on the other hand, cannot forget to be clever. His heroine, Andromeda, "hangs on a virgin's cross," and even so, remembers her modesty. Perseus envies the very rocks and chains that hold her fast. What a little prey is she for so vast a sea! And so on. Manilius can do better than this; but he sinks just where the subject should have given him wings.

It is not surprising that there was no later Epicurean poet. Lucretius had left nothing for a follower to say. His diction could be imitated, but he had made the subject his own, and there could no more be a second *de Rerum Natura* than a second *Aeneid* or *Paradise Lost.* Manilius had gained no such prescriptive right. His treatment of Stoicism was only partial and incidental, so that there would have been room for a more thorough presentment of the subject if a poet had been forthcoming. But such a poet would have needed to be a peer of Lucretius, and the Silver age produced no such genius. Physical poetry, of a sort, survived, at least till the generation after Manilius, for the *Aetna* is probably Neronian.[1] The author, whoever he may have been, was apparently a Stoic—not, as has been held, an Epicurean—since he admitted Providence, and apostrophized religion and virtue:

> *o maxima rerum*
> *et merito pietas homini tutissima virtus.*[2]

But he was content with this passing testimony to his creed; his real interests are elsewhere—not in heaven, but earth; for "what greater madness is there than to explore the realms of Jupiter, and to neglect so vast a task before one's feet?" This—whether intentional or not—is a criticism of

[1] It has been attributed to Lucilius, the friend to whom Seneca dedicated his *Natural Questions;* but see W. C. Summers, *Select Letters of Seneca*, p. 270. E. K. Rand in *Harvard Studies in Class Phil.* xxx. (1919) returns to the tradition of Virgil as author. T. Frank (*Vergil*, p. 58 f.) dates it about 46 B.C., and thinks it may possibly be Virgilian.

[2] 194, 631.

Manilius no less than of Lucretius. Philosophy was to make way for pure science, and that science itself was to be something less remote than the stars—the natural causes of volcanic eruption. The writer had one quality which makes for scientific research: he rejected mythology, and all his care—he claimed—was for the truth. Unfortunately, the truth turns out to be nothing but wild hypothesis, as absurd as the despised mythology, and unredeemed by the poetic imagination which gives the myth a value of its own. Theories, such as we find in the *Aetna*, were best left to the medium of Seneca's *Natural Questions*.

Stoicism, in fact, as a direct motive, soon relaxed its brief and rather feeble grasp on poetry, and was now confined to prose. After Seneca, even Latin prose was largely excluded; and not only foreigners, like the Phrygian Epictetus, but Romans, like Marcus Aurelius, preferred the original language of philosophy. Didactic verse eked out a sort of existence almost to the end, but it had lost its highest theme. From the first century onwards, although Stoicism continued to impress its strong character on the best Roman poetry, this influence was indirect. The Stoic poet ceases to be a teacher, while he still retains the moral fervour of his creed. Sometimes—so strong is the didactic impulse of Roman poetry—he is still apt to teach or preach; but the instruction is informal, and by the way; he no longer attempts to invade the province of a Lucretius, expounding his creed as the proper subject of poetry.

III

To discuss the indirect influence of philosophy on Roman poets with any fulness, it would scarcely be possible to omit a single poet; since Roman education—as far as it was not merely rhetorical—was derived from philosophy; and a poetry so devoted to Reason could not be far removed from the particular lines on which Latin reasoning was taught to move. In this sense, even Ovid could testify to a philosophic training; for, though he may have despised philosophy no less than religion, Ovid shows the influence of the Schools simply because he was an educated man. But between Lucretius and Ovid, as the two extremes, there is a class of poets—including the greatest of them all—who, though not professional apologists, were seriously concerned with philosophic problems, either as followers of a particular sect, like Lucan, or as more or less independent students, like Horace and Virgil. Neither of these claimed to be a schoolman; but both felt the need of some credible explanation of the Universe, and went through something of the same experience in their search for the truth. Both, as we have seen, became discontented with the Epicureanism which only offered the depressing theory of a fortuitous world; both were attracted by the stern virtues of a Stoicism which at all events gave a dignity and a value to human life and endeavour, while, on the other hand, they were repelled by the self-sufficiency and priggishness of the Stoic sage. But Horace, in the main, was satisfied with a negative position, criticizing Stoic and Epicurean impartially, but feeling no imperative need, it would seem, for a really constructive creed. Virgil, anxious, in spite of his modest disclaimer, to know the causes of things, could not rest on a mere negation. He had tried the *docta dicta Sironis*, and found Siro's lore inadequate. The *Eclogues* show traces of the thought as well as the diction of Lucretius, but it is impossible to believe that the poet of the *Aeneid* (or even of the *Georgics*) was in any sense an Epicurean.

To judge from certain notes of Servius, the Epicureans claimed him as their own during the whole of his life; but Servius himself rightly protested that only philosophers, like Lucretius, were bound to a single sect—a poet might borrow from any source [1]—though it must be confessed that the

[1] Serv. on *Georg.* 4, 219, *quidam accusant, quod sit Epicureus, alienam sectam usurpare.* See his note on *Aen.* 10, 467.

commentator was too often ready to find Epicureanism in Virgil at the slightest provocation.[1]

The question would hardly deserve to be mentioned, if it had not recently been reopened by a distinguished scholar, who holds that, although the eschatology of the Sixth Book was adopted as a *mythos*, for purposes of the plot, Virgil really continued in his earlier faith.[2] His arguments are by no means conclusive. The fact that there are about two hundred reminiscences of Lucretius in the *Aeneid* only shows —which is obvious—that Virgil admired and "imitated" the poetry of Lucretius. If it proved more than this for Virgil, it would prove that Manilius—also an imitator—was equally an Epicurean—a conclusion which might provoke Euclid to an even stronger comment than is his wont. The further argument, that Virgil's conception of Fate is not purely Stoic, does not make him an Epicurean. At most, it points to eclecticism, and this philosophic position may well explain the fact that all the schools quarrelled over his creed, just as various churches have claimed Shakespeare for their own communion. It might also explain a statement of Suetonius that, after the completion of the *Aeneid*, the poet meant to devote himself to philosophy.[3] He had not yet "attained," but was still a seeker after truth. But we need only examine the actual "sources" of Virgil's eschatology, which are those of no one school, nor (in part) of any school at all. The material is composite: from Homer, who (in the eleventh book of the *Odyssey*) suggested the general motion of a Descent into the Underworld; from the Orphics, Pythagoreans, and Plato, who all taught the doctrines of rebirth and of rewards and punishments beyond this life; and from eclectic philosophers in their attempts to harmonize the contradictions of their predecessors.[4] Chief of these was

[1] E.g. on *Aen.* 6. 264, 376, 596, 885.

[2] Tenney Frank in *A.J.P.* 41 (1920), p. 115 f. Prof. Frank restates his arguments in his *Vergil*, p. 182 f.

[3] Suet. *vit. Verg.* 35.

[4] See H. E. Butler, *Sixth Book of the Aeneid*, *Introd.* p. 19 f.

Posidonius, whose influence, though perhaps recently exaggerated, is almost certainly to be traced in the Sixth Book.[1]

That book clearly shows the influence of the Porch. Virgil has borrowed the doctrine of the *anima mundi*—the fiery soul that pervades the universe and is the source of all life. But, in the very same passage, the poet changes this Stoicism for the Orphic-Pythagorean doctrine of *Metempsychosis*, and describes a purgatory on the lines of Platonic myth.[2] If we were only concerned with the Sixth Book and its eschatology, we could only infer that Virgil was an impartial contemplator of all creeds. But the rest of the *Aeneid* tells a rather different tale, indicating that in spite of eclecticism, Virgil's theology is more deeply interfused with the ideas of the Stoics than with those of any other school. His Jupiter—it is true—is very far removed from the Stoic deity, being modelled after the Homeric Zeus; but Virgil has contrived to throw a philosophic mantle over the old Greek sky-god. The King of Heaven is no longer a jealous god, at once tyrannical and hen-pecked, good-tempered in the main, but liable to throw things—and gods—about if annoyed. While Zeus is only *primus inter pares*, Jupiter has become omnipotent. Of course this omnipotence is not entirely a Stoic notion, for all the schools (except the "atheists") were searching for monotheism, and even the Fatherhood of Jupiter—so prominent in Virgil—is not exclusively Stoic. But the outstanding problem for the ancient mind was not so much the character of the supreme god as his relation to Fate; and here Virgil is most indebted to Stoicism. The difficulty was how to make a personal deity consistent with an impersonal Law, binding not only men but—in some way—even gods.

[1] See E. Norden on *Aen.* VI.; Heinze, *Virgils Epische Technik*, p. 286 f.; E. Bevan, *Stoics and Sceptics* (1913), *lect.* 3; J. F. Dobson in *Class. Quart.* xii. p. 179 f., and in general E. V. Arnold, *Roman Stoicism*, p. 389 f.

[2] See Butler on *Aen.* 6, 724 f.

To the Stoic, Jupiter cannot be above the Fates, but neither can he stand below them; he must rather be the personal representative of the universal Law. This is precisely the conception of Jupiter in the *Aeneid*, if we allow for the fact that the poet is not always careful about absolute consistency.[1]

But, after all, the character of Jupiter, or his relation to Fate, does not greatly affect the *art* of Virgil; and, since we are mainly concerned with the aesthetic qualities of the *Aeneid*, it is much more important to discover whether there are any Stoic ideas which really touched the poem as a work of art. Here we are at once confronted with the hero of the poem. Possibly the *Aeneid*, without Aeneas, would not be so vacant as the play of Hamlet without the Prince of Denmark; but still the Prince of Troy *is* the protagonist —the only actor who holds the stage throughout. At the present day, we might perhaps condemn Aeneas and yet admire the *Aeneid* as a whole; but to a Roman such a compromise was impossible, for two reasons: in the first place, he regarded poetry from an ethical point of view, so that, if he condemned Aeneas, he would have been forced to reject the whole poem as immoral; and in the second place, we may feel sure that, in Aeneas, Virgil intended to sum up the distinctive features of the ideal Roman. Was this Roman hero Augustus himself? The question is not so absurd as it seemed a few years ago, when there was a strong reaction against the eighteenth-century belief in the *Aeneid* as an "allegory," with Augustus under the disguise of Aeneas.[2] On this view we may remark that there is no *a priori* poetical reason why the *Aeneid* should not be as much allegorical as the *Faerie Queene*. The pertinent objection is that Virgil certainly treated the foundation of

[1] See esp. I,257 f.

[2] See e.g. John Hughes, *On Allegorical Poetry* (1715). The theory was carried to an extreme by Dunlop, who was properly criticized by Sainte-Beuve (*Étude sur Virgile*).

Rome as history: Aeneas was a real person, not—as we should regard him—a mythical hero. Nevertheless, Virgil may have believed, or half-believed, in the cyclic theory of which he makes poetic use in the Fourth Eclogue—that history repeats itself, and that, in all essentials, Aeneas was to be reincarnated in Augustus, the second founder of Rome. In any case, it was only reasonable to hold up Aeneas as an *exemplum* to the Emperor, and to think—or at least hope—that the spirit of the great hero had passed, metaphorically if not literally, into the body of his successor. As Professor Conway remarks, "Virgil has given us an ideal ruler confronted with the same kind of troubles as beset Augustus."[1]

Clearly, therefore, a character, which was to be a forerunner or prototype of the Emperor, must have been drawn with care and full consciousness of its importance. Whether we moderns sympathize with Aeneas or not, the Romans were expected to admire him. In some respects, indeed, we have no difficulty in sharing the admiration. Aeneas is a "fine figure of a man," strong in body and mind, magnanimous, moderate in success, and, above all, religious. Ethically his character is best summed up in the title *pius* —an adjective which has caused critics to blaspheme, because they have read it as "sanctimonious," whereas its full content, for a Roman, would imply the three-fold virtue of respect to family, country, and religion.[2] *Pietas* implied a duty to be performed, and no human weakness must interfere with its performance.[3]

Such—in the briefest outline—is the character of Aeneas; and, so far, it is "sympathetic" enough. He may not appeal to a modern reader as possessing the charm of

[1] *New Studies*, p. 141. On the relation of Aeneas and Augustus see generally Glover, *Virgil*, p. 163 f. I cannot agree with Frank (*Vergil*, p. 172 f.), who denies all identification between the two.

[2] See Warde Fowler, *Death of Turnus*, pp. 75, 147.

[3] See especially *Aen.* 11, 126; 12, 311 and 435; contrast the *vis consili expers* of Turnus, Heinze, p. 206 f.

Achilles or the versatility of Odysseus, but he is at least a Roman and a man. If this were all, we should not need to go further than the *exempla maiorum*—a Fabius or Camillus or Scipio—to understand him. These heroes owe nothing to philosophy; they are simply types of Roman *virtus*, such as Horace found in his Regulus, whose character he might have described in the same terms even if the Stoic creed had never been invented.

But Aeneas is something more than Regulus. His virtues and (as they seem to us) his failings are not entirely those of the typical Roman; and it is just here that we may look for a philosophic influence in the moulding of his character. To disentangle the philosophy from the purely "Roman" elements is no easy matter; for the Roman spirit was *anima naturaliter Stoica*, so that the virtues of the race were merged, almost imperceptibly, in the virtues inculcated by the Stoa. The ethical system of that school was built (or re-built) upon the sure foundation of the old Roman ideal; and the Stoic was in essentials so Roman that we are apt to forget how far the Roman may be stoicized. But Virgil has invested his hero with certain qualities which are outside the common stock shared by the Roman who was merely a "natural" Stoic; Aeneas has been given a philosophic cast, altogether distinct from the more heroic type, whether Greek or Latin.

In the first place, Virgil could not fail to be impressed by the search for the Wise man, which, since Plato's time, had engaged philosophy. All the schools were in quest of a Pattern of humanity—Epicureans as well as Stoics. But the former were hard pressed to find a flawless example in Epicurus; and though Lucretius loyally calls him a god, the divinity appeared more clearly in the "revelation" of his teaching than in his personal qualities, which, if amiable, were in no way superhuman. The Stoics were more fortunate. They could claim Socrates as a pattern; yet, as even that great philosopher was not perfect, but only a traveller towards perfection, it was safer, on the whole, to find their model among the Epic heroes, in Hercules and Ulysses, both of whom were praised for their unconquerable soul.[1] Hercules, in especial, became a Stoic saint, and in consequence was duly criticized by Lucretius, who was not greatly impressed by Herculean labours.

With this precedent, it was unlikely that Virgil would have allowed his own hero to lack all graces of philosophy. Aeneas—a Roman, by anticipation, as well as a Trojan—must needs be a pattern at least the equal of Hercules or Ulysses. As a fact, he is far more "virtuous" than either. He may deceive Dido, but he cannot lie with the pleasing facility of the Greek Odysseus. He can fight as well as Hercules, but he does not relax, like that warrior, in his cups, nor become a slave of the Tyrian, as Hercules of the Amazonian queen. Here again, it may be objected, there is no proof of Stoic influence—the change may be merely due to the natural growth of civilization between the Epic (or Tragic) period and the age of Augustus. If, however, we look a little deeper, we shall see that the change has been largely, though not entirely, brought about by Stoicism. Aeneas is not a mere Fabricius or Regulus; he has learnt his lesson at the feet of Zeno, or at least Posidonius. The keynote of his character is complete submission to fate, as represented by Jupiter; but he does not submit blindly. As Servius noted, he has a Stoic foreknowledge of his fate.[2] He could have resisted—so much of freewill the Stoics allowed within the sphere of compulsion—and, "forgetting his fate," he might have stayed in Sicily, and so have defrauded his son of the kingdom promised by the fates.[3] But Stoicism demanded a willing acquiescence, and Aeneas

[1] Cic. *de fin.* 4, 20, 56; Seneca, *Const.* 2, 1. For Hercules in particular see Mayor on *Juv.* 10, 361.

[2] See Norden on *Aen.* 6, 103. Cf. Seneca, *Ep.* 76, 33, and Virg. *Aen.* 8, 131 f., 334; 10, 467 with Servius on the last two passages.

[3] *Aen.* 4, 355; 5, 703. On fate in the *Aeneid* see MacInnes in *Class. Rev.* (1910), p. 169; L. E. Matthaei in *Class. Quart.* xi. (1917), p. 11.

obeys against his wish—*Italiam non sponte sequor*—but with the full assent of his will. As Seneca noted, the hero's words *dis aliter visum* are a Stoic motto.[1] To bear one's fortune—*superanda omnis fortuna ferendo est*, in words addressed to Aeneas—is the supreme duty of Stoicism.[2]

Up to this point, perhaps, we have no just ground of complaint against the intrusion of philosophy. In the ordinary conduct of life, Aeneas is a dignified character, worthy to be the founder of Rome. One may admit that the Stoic trend of thought which has transformed the Greek hero is, in itself, no drawback for poetry, however much we may prefer the "romanticism" of Homer's Odysseus. Unfortunately, this is not all. The crucial test of his character lies in the episode of Dido, where modern judgment seems to be dead against Aeneas; and some part at least of the blame must be laid on Stoicism. For, judged by the Stoic creed, Aeneas was entirely innocent in his desertion. Cato could resign his wife Marcia to his friend Hortensius, after she had borne him three children, and Lucan counts it for righteousness. How much more rightly should Aeneas give up his mistress, when Jupiter himself commanded? Stoicism, therefore, would have approved his conduct without a twinge of scruple.

Once more, I may be told that here, too, Virgil had no occasion to philosophize: Aeneas is simply following the old Roman code of morals, in refusing the lawlessness of Dido's passion and returning, after an interval of temptation, to the ordered and stable life of the Family. He had been seduced for a time, just as Julius Caesar had succumbed to the wiles of Cleopatra, who had almost corrupted even Augustus—a point, as Warde Fowler observes—of enormous importance in the history of Rome.[3] Roman morality of course tolerated an *amour de voyage;* the sin would have lain in constancy to that love.

[1] Seneca, *Ep.* 98, 3. [2] *Aen.* 5, 710.
[3] *Roman Essays and Interpretations*, p. 185 f.

I think there is cogency in the argument—Aeneas would have passed muster, without the advocacy of a Stoic, who could have done little more than approve a general verdict of acquittal. If, therefore, we resent his behaviour, we must at all events acknowledge that the fault lies with Roman rather than Stoic opinion. But did Virgil, as a poet, really approve of what, as a Roman, he recognized as the right conduct? Did his sympathies wholly follow his reasoning? We know that his voice faltered, when he recited Dido's pathetic appeal:

hoc solum nomen quoniam de coniuge restat;

and her sorrow moved men so dissimilar as Ovid and Augustine.[1]

To some minds, the question will seem unprofitable, perhaps even absurd. The answer looks so obvious—that the Fourth Book is a tragedy, and the essence of tragedy is a conflict, not only of wills but of rights. Both Aeneas and Dido have their points of view, which demand our sympathy, though of course we are not required to sympathize equally. Virgil—it will be added—may have intended Aeneas to have the greater right; and if, in spite of that, our sympathy is more with the deserted queen, this only proves a change of moral and social opinion between Romans and ourselves.

But is this the last word? Did the poet really mean his hero to be blameless (since he only follows his destiny) and Dido to be blamed, as a rebel against Fate, a mad woman who had broken her vow to her husband Sychaeus?[2] Probably Virgil set out with some such idea. He seems to have planned the tale of Dido as a mere episode, which was to increase rather than diminish the fair fame of Aeneas. Like Odysseus—or Caesar—he was to leave his Calypso-Cleopatra—without a stain on his character, tempted to dalliance,

[1] Suet. *Verg.* 47; Ov. *Heroid.* 7; cf. *Trist.* 2, 535; Aug. *Conf.* 1, 13, 21. See p. 85. On Dido see especially Glover, *Virgil*, ch. 8.

[2] *Aen.* 4, 27.

but in the end obedient to Destiny. But Virgil himself was destined to fall in love with a Dido, who grew in his imagination from a mere enchantress like Circe or Medea, to be a loving woman—*amans et femina.*

This view of Virgil's development in the conception of the whole episode is by no means novel. Conington fully realized it, observing that Virgil struck the chord of modern passion and it responded more powerfully, perhaps, than the poet himself expected.[1] Prof. Norwood, taking up this hint, quotes the analogy of Shylock, whom Shakespeare developed in the course of the play, until the grasping moneylender of the first scenes becomes a character whose final punishment fills us with a sense of injustice. It is well known that characters may take the bit between their teeth, even when—or because—they are guided by Genius; but if a second analogy is required, we might point to a still more striking evolution of character in the *Pickwick Papers*, on which I cannot better Mr. Chesterton's words: "The strange and stirring discovery which Dickens made was this—that having chosen a fat old man of the middle classes as a good thing of which to make a butt, he found that a fat old man of the middle classes is the very best thing to make a romantic adventurer."[2]

The result of this unforeseen development might have surprised Virgil himself. Later critics were pained and puzzled by the sympathy which the poet extorted from their hearts if not their heads. They allowed that Dido's punishment was a necessary consequence of her infidelity and rebellion, but they felt that something was wrong somewhere. And so they took refuge in the rather crude assertion that Virgil was mistaken in his facts—that he had

[1] See his edition on *Aen.* 4, p. 13; and generally H. W. Garrod, *Vergil* in *English Literature and the Classics* (1912). R. S. Conway, *New Studies*, p. 140 f.; H. H. Yeames in *Class. Journal* (Chicago), viii. p. 139 f.; G. Norwood in *Class. Quart.* xii. (1918), p. 146 f.

[2] G. K. Chesterton, *Charles Dickens.*

invented the whole story. In a late Greek epigram (of which there is a Latin version) the statue of Dido asks: "Why, muses of Pieria, did you arm holy Maro against me? Such were the falsehoods he told against my chastity." [1]

How does Aeneas stand now, when the world has outgrown at least the rigidities of Stoicism? Charles James Fox condemned him vigorously; and this is perhaps a serious matter, since Mr. Fox ought to have been a lenient judge—his own standard of conduct was not severe, and quite untainted with Stoic morality. His disapproval, of course, was based on the fact that Aeneas, in deserting Dido, did not behave like an English gentleman, and that the excuses for his behaviour only made matters worse. Is it enough to point out—as I have tried to do—that Aeneas must be judged by the standards of his own times, and that both Stoic and Roman codes absolved him? Such an apology may not satisfy our feelings, even if it is sufficient for our logic; but we may at least remember that Aeneas is no common deserter or vulgar libertine. Compared with his fellows in the same circumstances—with Theseus, or with his own "model," the Jason of Euripides and Apollonius, he may be honourably acquitted. Of these, Aeneas alone can shelter behind "the President of the Immortals," and can claim to have obeyed the call of duty before pleasure. For within the tragedy of Aeneas and Dido there is an inner tragedy in the mind of Aeneas himself. If he fails to win our sympathy, the failure is due—paradoxical as it may seem—to an excess rather than a defect in virtue.

Aeneas is not the only poetic hero to suffer for his "piety". He has been compared with Tennyson's King Arthur, whom it is now fashionable to condemn. Indeed, the pair have much in common, since both were the ideals of their respective times, while they were delineated—to some extent—from a real model; for, if it is probable that

[1] *Anth. Pal.* 16, 151; *Pseud.-Aus.* Riese, *A.L.* 263; Macr. *Sat.* 5, 17, 5 f.; Priscian, *Perieg.* 185 f.

we can see traces of Augustus behind Aeneas, we can certainly discover glimpses of Prince Albert behind Arthur.[1] Both Virgil and Tennyson intended their heroes to be "the highest and most human too", and unfortunately—though in different ways—they confused the provinces of ethics and poetry. Of the two heroes, Arthur is poetically the less convincing. His standard of duty is at least as high as that of Aeneas, but Tennyson forgot that the sphere of poetry is not the pulpit. There is no ground for condoning Guinevere's lapse, but there is no excuse for a poet to sermonize over her. Meredith justly complained that the injured King preaches to his queen "like a curate", and a distinguished churchman, making a slight change in the hierarchy, exclaims: "As he stands over his wife and talks like an Archdeacon, I am reduced to something like frenzy".[2]

Poetry, as we have seen, is concerned with morality, but it must treat ethics in its own manner, which requires the poet to be, above all things, sympathetic; and here, at all events, I think that Virgil's sympathy is far deeper than Tennyson's. The Roman failed less signally than the English poet, precisely because Aeneas was less of a copybook moralist than Arthur; he might not have failed at all, if Aeneas had been a little less excellent. If Dido had been a mere Circe, the Trojan might have left the shores of Carthage with flying colours, instead of stealing away silently by night. As it is, the overwhelming pathos of the Fourth Book has spoilt our view of Aeneas as he appears in the other eleven books, a very gallant gentleman —unless we hold the opinion that a Roman gentleman did not exist—with the saving grace of human weakness. It is surely this human weakness that makes him so much less tiresome than the true Stoic hero or—it must be confessed—than Arthur himself. Virgil was too great a poet

[1] See L. Strachey, *Queen Victoria*, p. 232.

[2] [Bishop] W. Temple, *Mens Creatrix*.

to force his creation into a single mould. The Stoicism of Aeneas is moderated by that broad humanity, which one might say is borrowed from the Greek Epic, if it did not plainly spring from Virgil's own knowledge of human nature. In the storm, Aeneas groans, and his limbs are loosened with fear. We think of the Homeric heroes, whose terror of the sea is open and unashamed; but if Virgil borrows *λύτο γούνατα,* he borrows, through Homer, from Nature herself.[1] A true Stoic (of fiction) would have been utterly unmoved, or indeed might have usurped the function of Addison's angel, riding in the whirlwind and triumphantly directing the storm. Aeneas, after all, is but a moderate philosopher. It remained for Lucan to step in where Virgil had no desire to tread, by depicting the authentic Wise man of Stoicism.

IV

The *Pharsalia*, like *Paradise Lost*, has been said to want a hero; and, in the popular sense of the word, the criticism is quite true. Caesar is no more, if perhaps no less, the hero than is Milton's Satan, being rather the villain of the piece, although Lucan is forced to admit his greatness. Pompey is at least on the side of the angels, standing for law and order, for the established constitution, and for the unenlightened oligarchs whom Lucan thought to be champions of "freedom". But, in the Civil War, Pompey had become "the shadow of a mighty name", and, with the best will, Lucan could not make him a worthy match for Caesar. His death inspires some fine rhetoric on his former glory, but no rhetoric could disguise the weakness which marked the last phase of his life; and the poet could do no more than make excuses for his failure.

But there was one man whose part in the war, from

[1] Sainte-Beuve rightly condemned Saint-Evremont's criticism of this "weakness" (*Etude sur Virgile*, p. 217).

Lucan's point of view, was perfect. Cato had a double claim to his admiration. In the first place, he was—after Pompey's death—the leader of the Senatorial party, for which Lucan hardly cares to conceal his sympathies. In the second place, Cato was a thorough Stoic, and—though Lucan was not perhaps an orthodox philosopher—the general tone of the *Pharsalia* is patently Stoic.[1] From the moment of his death at Utica, Cato had been cast for the rôle of hero in any epic on the Civil war. His suicide had raised him to the rank of a martyr for the Republic, and a whole literature of pamphlets took him as subject for praise or blame. Caesar himself answered Cicero's eulogy with an *Anticato*, and, later, Augustus joined in the fray. It is to the credit of that emperor that Cato could be safely praised, if not for his politics, at least for his *nobile letum.*[2] Horace was as free as Marvell, whose ode to Cromwell, fitly called "Horatian", is no less generous—did Marvell think of Cato when he wrote of Charles? After the death of Augustus, Cato's fame grew with the growing Stoic opposition to the empire. Men like Thrasea took him as their model; Seneca preferred him even to the official Stoic patron, Hercules; his dying speech suggested a stock theme for recitation; and his life, no less than his death, had become an *exemplum virtutis*[3]—the type of the Wise man pitted against adversity, whom Seneca thought a "peer of God".[4]

The real Cato may, or may not, have deserved this canonization; but at all events, he was something more than the Don Quixote of the aristocracy, "one of the most

[1] See Heitland's *Introd.* to Haskins' ed. p. xlviii f.

[2] Some of the praise in Augustan poetry (Virg. *Aen.* 8, 670; Hor. *Ep.* i. 19, 13), *may* refer to the elder Cato; but in Hor. *Od.* 1, 12, 35; 2, 1, 23 Cato Uticensis must certainly be meant. So Manil. 1, 797.

[3] Sen. *de const.* 2, 1 and often; Pers. 3, 45. On the *exempla virtutis* see H. W. Litchfield in *Harvard Studies Class. Phil.* xxv. p. 1.

[4] *de prov.* 2, 9, *ecce par Deo dignum—vir fortis cum mala fortun compositus.*

melancholy phenomena in an age so abounding in political caricatures."[1] Mommsen's biassed judgment is itself a caricature of the truth. The Romans were good judges of a man, and Cato's own contemporaries would not have trusted and followed a mere eccentric. As a politician he was no doubt unpractical and uncompromising—a visionary who spoke as if he lived in the *Republic* of Plato instead of the dirt of Romulus.[2] In his private life he was obsessed with the idea of the stern Roman, and either inherited or copied the rough manners of the elder Cato, although Cicero once reminded him that there was a gentler side of the great Censor's character.[3] But his real honesty and dogged purpose were assets to a party whose chief characteristics were self-seeking and vacillation. He was at least a sincere Stoic, as his death was to prove; and, a certain eccentricity being the hall-mark of a Stoic, Lucan may well have accentuated, though he did not invent, the strict and rather ostentatious virtue of the Wise man.

During the first period of the war, Cato was of course obscured by Pompey; but, even so, the poet manages to bring him, if not into the limelight, at least on to the stage. The second book gives Lucan an opportunity of describing his hero's character:

> Stern and undeviating, Cato showed
> The constant practice of a rigid code:
> Steadfast to make the Mean his only guide
> —Never from Nature's path to turn aside,
> —To spend his life for Rome, and deem his birth
> Not purposed for himself, but all the earth.
> His was a feast, to vanquish hunger's pain,
> A palace, if his roof withheld the rain.
> For costly garments, he was rich enough,
> Clothed in a Roman gown of homespun stuff.

[1] Mommsen, *Hist. of Rome* (E.T.) iv. p. 156.
[2] Cic. *ad Attic.* 2, 1; see Boissier, *Cicero and his Friends* (E.T.), 277 f.
[3] *Mur.* 31.

Creating sons, Desire was satisfied,
And Rome herself was Cato's child and bride.
Justice and Honour ruled his single mind,
Whose Good lay in the Good for all mankind ;
And in no deed of his might Pleasure dare
To steal an entrance or demand a share.[1]

After Pompey's death, the whole interest of the *Pharsalia* is transferred to Cato. This could be justified on purely military grounds, as Cato had at least an independent command in Africa, although he did not succeed to Pompey's position as *generalissimo*. But it is clear that Lucan cared much less about strategy than character, and Cato alone fulfilled his ideal of

A brave man struggling in the storms of fate,
And greatly falling, with a falling state.[2]

In the dangers of the Libyan desert, the Stoic leader receives a eulogy such as the most successful general might envy. He reminds his men that honour lies in the effort, not the event—*ire sat est*. He marches on foot, and, though parched with thirst, waits—like a Sidney—for the humblest camp-follower to drink before him. His route lies near a famous oracle, which his staff urge him to consult; but, though a Stoic did not officially deny the truth of oracles, a philosopher had no need of a refuge for weaker brethren.[3] Thinking of these, Lucan himself deplored the silence of the Delphic oracle as the greatest loss of his own age; but his Cato—satisfied with the " diviner " of his own heart—refuses to consult the shrine, in a speech of real dignity and even sublimity of thought:[4]

[1] *Phars.* 2, 380-391.

[2] W. C. Summers' view (*Silver Age of Lat. Lit.* p. 41) that there are three heroes—Pompey, Caesar, and Lucan himself—implies, I suppose, that Lucan read himself into Cato.

[3] Epict. *Diss.* 2, 7, 3; Cic. *Div.* 1, 5, 9; 6, 10. See Lucan 5, 111.

[4] 9, 564 f.

Within his heart the silent voice divine
Prompted an answer worthy of the shrine:
What should I ask? "Whether I choose to fall
Free to the end, or live a tyrant's thrall?"
Or, "Is life nothing, be it brief or long?"
"Can any violence work a good man wrong?"
"Is Fortune's threat on Virtue vainly spent?"
Or, "Does Success add nothing to the good intent?"
All this we *know;* Ammon can do no more
Than testify the truth we knew before.
God is about us; and, do what we will,
We do God's bidding, though his voice be still.
He needs no revelation, having shown
Once, at our birthtime, all that may be known.
Nor has he plunged the Truth in barren sand
For a few travellers in a desert land.
Wherever there is earth and sea and air,
Wherever Heaven and Virtue—God is there.
Shall we search further? Vainly shall we rove,
When every feeling, every sight, is Jove.
Doubters may fear, and seek prophetic aid;
I, being sure of death, am unafraid.
Death waits alike the coward and the bold:
—Thus hath God said; 'tis all we need be told.

Lucan's character of the Happy Warrior may challenge comparison with a more modern and more famous eulogy. Cato, with this "triumph" in the sands of Africa, had won a nobler victory than Pompey, who had thrice mounted the Capitol in his triumphal car. Such a man, to Lucan, seemed divine—indeed, if Rome were but free, she would have given him his apotheosis. The celebrated line

victrix causa deis placuit sed victa Catoni

has been called a bathos as well as a blasphemy. But in reality it is neither. As Lucan's uncle had said, we are all very near God—*prope est a te deus, tecum est, intus est;*[1] and

[1] Sen. *Ep.* 4, 12.

the Stoic was nearest of all. With due allowance for a flourish of rhetoric, the antithesis in the epigram is sound Stoicism.

The poet did not live to describe the last act in Cato's drama. That act would have crowned the play; for to a Stoic—as is well known—self-destruction was not a weakness to be blamed or at best condoned, but an example to be admired—a vindication of the right to show free will, by disobeying Fate without sin, if honour demanded. Lucan could sometimes be as sublime as he was often ridiculous; and, if he rose high in his panegyric on Pompey, he would surely have risen far higher in his final estimate of Cato. Nevertheless, for our purposes, his portrait is complete. Whatever we may think of the Stoic type in general, or of Lucan's Cato in particular, we must admit that the figure stands out in bold relief, as contrasted with the rather sketchy drawing of the other characters in the *Pharsalia*. We may not like his Cato, or admire his virtue overmuch. We may prefer Aeneas, who is not so immaculate. But we cannot deny that Cato has been drawn by a loving hand, so that he embodies, once for all, the type which the best Romans thought most worthy of imitation. To our minds, perhaps, the worst that can be said of the type is that it is so largely negative. It would not, indeed, be fair to condemn Lucan's Stoics, as Johnson condemned Addison's, with the sarcasm that the object of all the characters and the result of every situation seems to be, how not to act. On the contrary, the Stoics of the *Pharsalia*—whether a humble centurion like Volteius, or Cato himself—can act as well as talk; but it must be acknowledged that the typical Roman Stoic, though by no means a pacifist, is happiest in passive resistance. Addison—in the most celebrated passage of his tragedy—was here true to his original: Cato does not care to command success, provided that he deserves it.

There was good reason for the eighteenth century to admire a Cato, whether in Lucan or Addison. The ages of the two poets (from a literary point of view) had so much in common that a modern translator of Lucan instinctively turns to the Popian couplet, which alone seems to preserve the savour of Lucan's rhetoric. Both ages, moreover, sought only for the embodiment of the universal idea—the business of the poet was "to examine not the individual but the species; to remark general properties and large appearances. He does not number the streaks of the tulip, or describe the different shades in the verdure of the forest".[1]

It is easy enough, at the present day, to find fault with the Johnsonian theory, and to point out that the poet's real business is to handle the type in such a way as to give it individuality. The characters of Chaucer and Shakespeare have "general properties" and "large appearances"; but, none the less, the Wife of Bath and Hamlet have just those "streaks of the tulip" that give them a vivid and intense personality. The danger of the purely "typical" delineation of character lies in a temptation to force the note. A Miles Gloriosus or a Trimalchio, who had been created simply as the embodiment of a single characteristic —to be "conceit" or "snobbishness" personified—is bound to be exaggerated. Their creator cannot draw on individual peculiarities and personal mannerisms to vary the monotony of the *leit-motif.* The Epic heroes, although they were sketched boldly and, to some extent, in outline, were never merely typical, because they were first and foremost ***men.*** Achilles and Odysseus have each a dominant characteristic; but, though the one is "warlike" and the other "wily," neither is confined to a single Humour.[2] Both are complex, versatile, personal. In Latin epic, as we have just seen, Aeneas—if tending rather more to the type—is still

[1] Johnson, *Rasselas*, ch. 22. See Dennis, *Reflections upon a Late Rhapsody* (annotations).

[2] Macaulay's Review of Madame D'Arblay (1843) should perhaps have the credit of finally exploding the doctrine of Humours in literature.

essentially a Greek hero; a superman, but still a man. Lucan, however, whether consciously or unconsciously, pushed the Aristotelian theory of the Universal to an extreme from which Aristotle himself might well have recoiled. Aristotle's favourite character—the Oedipus of Sophocles—is much more than a typical hero; he is also an individual, with human failings as well as heroic excellence. But, the Roman poetic "character" deliberately shunned complexity. Here the poets were far behind the historians and biographers: the Hannibal of Livy has great virtues and "equal vices"; the Tiberius of Tacitus may be overdrawn, but (though suspicious and cruel) he is by no means a mere embodiment of Suspicion and Cruelty. Roman historians, in fact, were as realistic as the Roman sculptors, whose gallery of the Emperors reveals a deep psychological study of persons. The Roman poets, however, followed a different tradition, ultimately derived from Plautus and Terence, who, in their turn, had borrowed stock types of the New Comedy. If it is asked why Menander and Diphilus, in their Greek Comedy, were content with the stock types, the answer must be that they were the first to bring Comedy into touch with ordinary life; and drama cannot proceed *per saltum*, from the ideal flower to the streaks of the tulip. There must be an intermediate stage in which it is sufficient to note the general properties and large appearances. Greek comedy was arrested at this stage, and the Romans took over the typical slave, or the old miser, or young lover. The matter was, at its outset, mere literary tradition, for there is no reason to suppose that Plautus and Terence troubled themselves over Aristotelian theories; but tradition was afterwards supported by the usual misunderstanding of Aristotle. The Greek philosopher had bidden the poet to copy the Type, and his followers held that the Type must not be contaminated. Horace's advice:

> *respicere exemplar vitae morumque iubebo*
> *doctum imitatorem*

might well refer, in theory, to the actual imitation of life, as we know it, full of inconsistencies, vacillations, compromises; but in practice the Chremes must always be "angry," the Medea "ferocious". Here, at least, the neo-classics not unfairly interpreted the Romans: as John Dennis understands Horace: "When a Poet would draw the Character of a covetous or a revengeful person, he is not to draw after *Lucius* or *Caius;* but to consult the universal pattern within him, and there to behold what Revenge or Covetousness would do in such and such Natures, upon such and such Occasions"—for Lucius and Caius, he adds, are but imperfect copies of the Idea, and the poet, in copying them, must degenerate still further from the original.[1]

For modern appreciation, perhaps, the Cato of Lucan is an unfortunate example of the Roman theory. His hero is not merely a type, but something aesthetically worse—a type of Perfection. Ethically, the perfect Stoic was well worth drawing, not only for the Romans, who imagined no higher ideal than Stoicism, but for ourselves, who can still learn much from that noble philosophy. Artistically, however, Lucan's Cato is a failure. We miss the fault or weakness which Aristotle knew was needful for a hero's fall; we are merely dazzled by a blaze of light which leaves no shade; and we have learnt that no human being is a compendium of either virtues or vices.

So far—if this criticism is sound—the influence of the Stoics on Lucan's poetry was a doubtful blessing. But this inspiration did not end with portraiture. It is not too much to say that the whole conception of the *Pharsalia* would have been different, if Lucan had never heard of Stoicism. Commentators have strangely underrated the importance of philosophy as the chief—if not the only—cause of Lucan's complete break with Epic convention.[2] Virgil, it is true,

[1] *Reflections upon a Late Rhapsody* (annotations).

[2] Neither Heitland in his masterly Introduction nor Butler (*Post-Augustan Poetry*) suggests the view here stated.

had toned down the more savage or puerile aspects of the Olympian religion. He had rejected the crude theomachy of Homer; but his gods, if they no longer fought each other, at least took sides in the human conflict, and helped or hindered the fortunes of Aeneas. Lucan swept away the whole Homeric machinery. Beyond and above the human actors, there is only Fate or that *parens rerum*, a god who is indistinguishable from Fate, to order and direct events. Now, classical poetry is so wedded to tradition, Roman art so dependent on Greek, that only the very strongest motive could have caused this rebellion. It has been thought that the disappearance of the gods is simply due to the historical subject: they might well have intervened in the days of Aeneas, or even in the Punic war, but they could not directly prompt a Caesar or Pompey, in whose time—less than a century before Lucan—the gods no longer walked with men. But Lucan's contemporary, Petronius, disproves this theory. His chief criticism on the *Pharsalia*—for he had certainly that poem, or part of it, in mind—turns on this very question. A poet, he says, must not neglect the supernatural; he must make his characters move *per deorum ministeria;* and then Petronius shows how a poem on the Civil War should be written, using all the hackneyed resources of divine interference. Petronius, at least, saw nothing grotesque in the mythical convention applied to recent history; and, even in the age of Nero, there might have been many readers who would have accepted the *deorum ministeria* as no convention at all, but actual truth; just as in one battle, fresh to present memory, human heroism was thought by many to be more than human, and only to be explained by the theory of angelic aid. Anyhow, Petronius won, for all later Roman epic returned to the Myth. To Statius and Valerius Flaccus the first essential was to follow in Virgil's footsteps; even Silius—although we are told that he was a Stoic—allowed tradition to override philosophy; so that it must have required some courage for Lucan to break away from "the fair humanities of old religion," even if they no longer "lived in the path of reason."[1] Stoicism alone could have given him the courage. How might deities be ranged on this side and on that? God is not Many, but one God, and He is the minister of Fate—

Iuppiter est quodcunque vides, quodcunque moveris

—a line which, as Mr. Abercrombie well remarks, would certainly explode any supernatural machinery that could be invented.[2]

Lucan was therefore forced to follow the "historical" method, and so came under the censure of Petronius, who remarked that poetry could not compete with history—the historians could do the thing better. It is unfortunate that this critic's own version of the Civil War is flat and conventional enough; but negatively, at least, Petronius had a strong case. The *purely* historical method—such as we see, for example, in Lucan's actual account of the battle of Pharsalus—is not poetry at all. But Lucan, after all, was well aware that history is not poetry, that a particular action has no poetic meaning unless it can be translated into universal terms. The motives of human action are often as mysterious as the mystery of the physical Universe; and though a poet cannot explain the ultimate causes of existence, he must adopt some working hypothesis, assuming some power or agency to symbolize—if not to cause in any literal sense—the mainspring of events. Lucan himself was content with Fate; but Fate or Fortune or Chance is a shadowy, unsubstantial being, more suited to the scientific than the poetic mind. Poetry, as Wordsworth

[1] Coleridge after Schiller. Plessis (*la Poésie lat.* p. 560) wrongly attributes the absence of myth to the example of Ennius. That poet certainly used the Olympian machinery; see Serv. on *Aen.* 1, 20; 1, 254; 1, 281; 4,576 and other fragments.

[2] L. Abercrombie, *Epic*, p. 75.

saw, needs flesh and blood—in a word, personality. And hence every great poet has instinctively sought for some Person or Persons who should be responsible for human affairs, or, if not directly responsible, at least cognisant of their meaning. Poetically, the need is so strong that such a Person must be invented, if the poet does not believe him to exist. We have seen how Lucretius felt, and tried to solve the problem. A modern avatar of Lucretius offers a still more striking analogy. In the *Dynasts*, Mr. Hardy stands in precisely the same relation to Napoleon as Lucan stood to Caesar. Both poems were written about a century after the events, when some perspective could be attained, but when the action had not yet passed into ancient history, too remote to affect the life and interests of the reader. Both poets disbelieve in any interference with human doings by supernatural powers, the only difference being that, while Lucan's Fate is at least a sentient force, Mr. Hardy's "Immortal Will" is unconscious and unimpassioned, with clock-like laws—

> An automatic sense
> Unweeting why or whence.

It is interesting to observe how the two epic poets—for the *Dynasts*, though formally a drama, is really, of course, an epic—have evaded the pure historic method. Lucan might have taken for himself as a text the Virgilian line

> *Flectere si nequeo Superos, Acheronta movebo:*

the gods being ruled out, he has recourse to Hell, and loves to transplant his hearers from the historic (and prosaic) stage of reality to the mysterious world of the imagination, where a Thessalian witch may raise the unwilling spirit of a dead soldier, or the ghost of Cornelia may visit her husband before his final catastrophe. In Lucan, the half-gods at all events remain, when the gods have disappeared. But now that even witches have joined the twilight of the gods, one might have thought that an Epic poet would be hard pressed to find compensation for the loss of supernatural agency. Mr. Hardy has thought it necessary to suspend his disbelief. His Intelligences or Spirits, who comment on the human actors, are as indispensable to his poetry as they are unjustifiable to his philosophy. It is by means of this supernatural chorus, now mocking, now compassionate, that the English poet has given unity to his vast drama, and has pointed its significance.

Opinions may differ as to the success of Mr. Hardy's experiment. It has been held that his attempt to poeticize Schopenhauer's metaphysical theory of the World as Will is unconvincing. Yet the use of the supernatural in the *Dynasts*—even though there is only "a willing suspension of disbelief"—is one which Lucan might have welcomed, if it had not been outside the range of classical imagination. The machinery was ready to hand—no nation deified abstract qualities so profusely as the Romans, with their Justice, Shame, Faith, Honour, and a hundred more. All these "Personifications," as they are commonly and not very correctly called, might have played the part of Hardy's mocking or pitiful spirits. But the real obstacle was that the Romans never used these personifications as persons. They were too remote, too bloodless and abstract, to be of any value for a Roman poet, just as they are nearly always frigid and unsatisfactory in their eighteenth-century revival. Dr. Johnson was quite right in remarking that these "airy beings are suffered only to do their natural office and retire," though he was unfortunate in choosing Victory as an example, since that abstraction, at least, rose to the dignity of a real and personal goddess, round whose altar were fought the last desperate battles of dying paganism.[1]

No doubt the case against abstraction—strong as it is—may be pressed too far. To the Romans a personified Quality was not quite the unsubstantial shadow of neo-

[1] *Lives* (Milton), 256.

classic imitation. From time immemorial they had been accustomed to worship *indigitamenta*, unembodied spirits which presided over every action of life—Terminus, the spirit of boundaries, Domiducus, of the bride's journey to her husband's home, and the like—and this animism, though overlaid by personal Olympian deities, was always a potent force in popular religion. Several of these abstract Qualities (besides Victory) were raised to the status of an official cult, with temples and flamens, and the whole apparatus of organized worship. A people who thus personified Faith and Concord were prepared to find a poetic as well as a religious place for these so-called abstractions. Horace's *Virtus* or Virgil's *Fama* belonged to a sisterhood of Good or Evil Spirits, which, if not of human flesh and blood, could be visualized as concretely as the goddesses of Olympus. They may have had no mythology, but they had at least as much personality as some (though not all) of Milton's angels.

Even in modern times, the Personification has a use, despite Romantic disgust.[1] A living poet—after commenting on the usual frigidity of the Popian abstraction, acknowledges the success of Drayton's sonnet:

> —Now, at the last gasp of his latest breath,
> When, his pulse failing, Passion speechless lies,
> When Faith is kneeling by his bed of death,
> And Innocence is closing up his eyes. . . .[2]

Mr. Laurence Binyon might have added another poem—written no doubt with something of Drayton's inspiration—in which Rupert Brooke (otherwise no friend of the Absolute) spends all the resources of abstraction over the funeral of Youth. If Brooke could discover poetic value in what—

[1] Personification is not disowned by the modern painter or sculptor—a statue of Liberty has an emotional appeal (apart from its formal beauty) to those who have, or claim to have, liberty.

[2] L. Binyon in *Proceedings Brit. Acad.*, June, 1918 (*English Poetry in its Relation to Painting and the Other Arts*).

to us—is a mere personified quality, a Roman must have derived far more satisfaction from the same concept, which hovered on the borderline of divinity. Horace could speak of this very abstraction—Juventas, Youthfulness—as forming a pair with Mercury, one of the most human of gods. The little poem, in which he invokes Venus to enter Glycera's new shrine, may be quoted as an example of this easy transition from the abstract concept to the anthropomorphic god :[1]

Queen of Cyprus, hasten thence,
  Leave thy Grecian isles divine;
Take my lady's frankincense,
  Enter this fair-fashioned shrine.

With thee bring thy frolic Boy,
  Nymph and Grace in ungirt dress;
Mercury bring, and, strange to joy,
  If without thee, Youthfulness.

It may be objected that the word *Juventas*, which I have translated *Youthfulness*, is simply the Latin version of Hebe, who in Homer is a personal goddess. Surely, however, the Roman Juventas was far nearer to the class of Fides and Pax and Virtus, any one of whom might readily have taken her place in the poem, if the context had permitted. She belongs to the Indigitamenta rather than to the Pantheon.

Such Qualities, however—it must be confessed—are but poor substitutes for the humanized gods whose virtues—or vices—brought them into touch with men. To be worshipped, saints must have a golden legend, or at least some individual history. St George, even with his dragon, can never have the interest of Ste Jeanne d'Arc. Peace may have an altar; but, for all her good works, she cannot stir the emotions like even the most useless of the gods—a Proteus, rising from the sea, or a Triton, blowing his wreathèd horn.

[1] *Od.* I, 30.

Lucretius made one attempt to enlarge the magic circle: he tried to personify the sum-total of natural existence, Nature herself. But here even Lucretius faltered, and stopped short with the compromise—*if* Nature were given a voice, she would reproach the man who complained of her laws.[1] He must have felt that to personify the sum-total of atoms—to humanize a formula—was to place a heavy strain on Roman imagination. Later than Lucretius, a goddess Electricity was tried and found wanting. So, instead of a vague and unsubstantial abstraction, he was thrown back on the myths which his philosophy rejected, and the Prayer to Venus stands, as we have seen, a splendid monument to the eternal truth that Truth is not the same as Fact.

Lucan, more uncompromising than the great Epicurean, because he was a lesser poet, could neither find a poetic place for the gods, nor invent a convincing substitute. Like his own Cato, he was too thorough and—may one say?—too narrow to bow the knee, even though the god were not a Baal, but the beautiful goddess for whom Lucretius was willing to forgo his philosophy. It is something to trample superstition under foot, and Lucan, though in a less degree than Lucretius, is entitled to that honour. But a poet must be master not only of Superstition but of Philosophy itself; and Lucretius alone could show that, when Philosophy has done her best or worst, there still remains Poetry, who can bid the dead gods rise up and live again in her own kingdom.

V

It is perhaps in Satire—if that form of art is allowed to be poetical—that the closest alliance between Poetry and

[1] 3, 931. At a much later date, Claudian (*de laud. Stilich.* 2, 431) could do nothing more for Nature than make her portress at the door of the cave of the Years, who bows down before the Sun-god.

Philosophy might be expected. For satire deals with morals, with fact rather than imagination, and requires a standard by which to test the morality. This standard need not, of course, be philosophical: the great satirists of the world have for the most part been content with more or less elastic judgments of good taste, refinement, or moderation, and Roman satire was no exception. Horace, though in his "Satiric" period a mild Epicurean (with a strong distaste for Stoic arrogance), judges as a "gentleman" rather than as a philosopher. Juvenal has no philosophic bias at all: he may pay a vague compliment to Wisdom—*victrix fortunae sapientia*—but, as he takes care to add, Life is his only master; and Martial—a satirist in spirit, though not in form—owns precisely the same allegiance.[1] All the philosophy that Juvenal can claim—as in the Eighth Satire, on Virtue, or the noble conclusion of the Tenth—is the commonplace of the schools, such as had passed beyond the region of controversy into the stock of accepted Roman ethics. Indeed, it has recently been argued that, from Lucilius to Juvenal, the presentation of popular Stoic doctrine forms the essential basis of the whole satiric *genre*.[2] This is true, if we lay emphasis on the word "popular." None the less, as Satire was the most original and characteristic expression of Roman art, and as Stoicism was the predominant form of Roman thought, it was natural that the two should, at least once, come together, in Persius. The young contemporary of Lucan had more need of a Stoic training than either Horace or Juvenal, since he had far less knowledge of life. A youth "of the gentlest character, of virginal modesty, affectionate, frugal, and chaste"—so his biographer describes him—Persius was but slenderly equipped by experience to follow Horace. From a formal point of view, his originality lay only in substituting a crabbed, obscure, and

[1] Juv. *Sat.* 13, 20 f. and 120; Mart. 10, 4.
[2] C. W. Mendell in *Class. Phil.* xv. (1920), p. 138 f.

allusive style for the simple clarity of his model. But here imitation ends: the earnest pupil of the great teacher Cornutus owes no spiritual debt to a predecessor, whose code of the Golden Mean was so lenient that his satire served as a chronicle rather than a criticism of life. The fire and enthusiasm, the passionate love of virtue, which are the real and lasting distinction of Persius, are as far removed from the good-natured tolerance of Horace as from the indignation of Juvenal. For Persius never rouses the uneasy suspicion that Juvenal's *saeva indignatio* is a rhetorical pose. This is the more creditable, since—as we see from almost any page of Seneca—Stoicism was a forcing-house for rhetoric. To Seneca, the tyrant—in contrast to the Wise man, the only true "King"—evokes a plethora of invective;[1] Persius, with fine restraint and monumental brevity, can sum up the vices and sorrows of tyranny in a single line: "let tyrants see Virtue and pine for her loss:"

virtutem videant intabescantque relicta.[2]

The Stoicism which appealed to Persius was purely spiritual. There is no suggestion that the poet, like Lucan, took refuge in philosophy as a political creed. The reference to tyranny is common form, and need not imply an oblique criticism of the principate. Nor has Persius the least concern with the physical speculations which the Stoics had once shared with Epicureans. He invites his reader to learn "the causes of things," using the very words of Virgil's famous allusion to the physics of Lucretius; but these causes are final—"what we are, and what is the purpose of the life we are born to live."[3] Stoicism is now contracting its wide sphere of interest; it is shedding both metaphysics and science, in order to concentrate more nearly on morals; it is on its way to become the personal

[1] E.g. in the *Thyestes*. See generally F. L. Lucas, *Seneca*, p. 61 f.
[2] 3, 38. [3] 3, 66.

religion of Musonius, Epictetus, and Aurelius. This estimate of Persius may perhaps be questioned by some who, with his greatest editor, will see in him no anticipation of the last Stoic phase, and will prefer to class him with the earlier Stoics of the empire to whom he chronologically belongs. But it cannot be denied that the dominant note of their Stoicism was aggressive and political, whereas Persius cares only for the inner life. Military glory—to take a single point—means much to Lucan who, in spite of his fulminations against the "disgrace" of civil war, is at least an admirer of heroism, especially if the hero is a Stoic. Persius, when he speaks of the army at all, is frankly contemptuous: his centurion, a rough, "goat-smelling," uneducated boor, values a hundred Greek philosophers at a brass farthing: he has nothing in common with his brother officer in Lucan—the Volteius who, after fruitless bravery, could teach his men how Romans—and Stoics—should die.[1]

With Lucan and Persius, the direct influence of philosophy on the poets comes to an end, until the fourth century revival was almost spent. As far as philosophy was concerned, there were no doubt political reasons for its breakdown as a poetic stimulus. Lucan's death was not encouraging to the others, though Stoic opposition to the principate continued, and Vespasian (who seems to have been long-suffering) was compelled to execute Helvidius Priscus, the son-in-law of Thrasea, and to banish all philosophers, except Musonius, for conspiracy. Even Epictetus was driven from Rome in a later persecution by Domitian. The times were plainly unfavourable for any philosophic sympathies, though the "tyranny" of the empire may easily be exaggerated. Under the Flavians, Nero's acts, at all events, were always a subject for free speech, so that Statius, in one of his finest poems, could eulogize the author

[1] Lucan 4, 474 f.; Pers. 5, 189; cf. 3, 77.

of the *Pharsalia*, and Stoicism, as long as it kept to the ethical sphere, was always immune. After Domitian's death it had finally severed all connexion with politics; but the very fact that it had become a personal religion still further restricted its service for poetry. Stoicism grew too serious for amalgamation with the rhetoric which had now captured the Muses. It is significant that Aurelius, who had practised poetry and studied rhetoric in his youth, was grateful to his master Rusticus for having weaned him from both. On the side of poetry there were even stronger grounds for the divorce. Philosophy, as we have seen, was incompatible with the Myth, and the Flavian poets were desperately anxious to carry on the classical tradition, pouring out *Thebaids* or *Argonautica* or *Punica* on the well-worn lines of construction.[1] Lucan's poem may or may not have been a failure—the ancients themselves were divided on the question—but at all events he failed to create a school. Poets must imitate Virgil, but not the Virgil of the Sixth *Aeneid.* Ever since Boissier pointed out the "conspiracy of silence" which prevented allusion to Christianity in Ausonius and Claudian, it has become a commonplace to remark on the strong resistance of the old poetry to the new religion.[2] But it has not been so clearly observed that, long before the fourth century, the poets no less ignored the old philosophy. The point is not unimportant; for, if Christianity alone had been tabooed, the natural inference would be that the silence was due to religious hostility alone. There may have been such hostility, though Ausonius, at least, seems to have been quite indifferent—indeed, although nominally a Christian, he was essentially a pagan—but the fact that pagan philosophy shared the taboo points to the conclusion that the reasons were rather literary than intellectual. An

[1] Martial (4, 49; 10, 4) protested against this outworn mythology: so Juvenal (1, 1 f.).

[2] *Fin de Paganisme* 1, 5, ch. ii.

educated Roman certainly "believed" in some form of philosophy, whereas he could not have believed in Homeric or quasi-Homeric gods; but tradition demanded the presence of the gods, and, as philosophy could not be allowed to clip the angel's wings, it must go. A union which had been blessed by Lucretius and had lasted for a century was thus dissolved by mutual consent.

VI

The two partners were once more brought together, if only by misfortune. As long as Rome stood, the gods of Rome remained in control of poetry, and the myth sufficed for Claudian's stock-in-trade. But Alaric shattered the complacency of Roman literature as rudely as he had shaken the military prestige of Rome. War—as we know—even if successful, is apt to disturb the even tenour of poetry, and the most conservative of all traditions—the classical formula—felt so enormous a shock. The poem of Rutilius—a Gaul who, after holding the high office of prefect of Rome, returned to his native land soon after the disaster of 410 A.D.—has merits of its own; but it is chiefly interesting to us as a witness of the time. In form, the poem is purely "classical"; that is to say, Rutilius still recognizes the old gods of Rome, and—no less than Claudian or Ausonius—is a conspirator of silence, obstinately refusing to mention Christianity, although he finds occasion to abuse the life of the monks, and thereby seems indirectly to show his contempt for their religion.[1] His own paganism was centred in a passionate admiration for Rome, the "queen of the Universe," who had conquered the nations—

[1] As Christianity was now the official religion, no open criticism was permissible. His hatred of Judaism proves nothing, for the confusion between the two religions had long ceased; nor can his hatred of the monks be pressed—it was shared by Margaret of Navarre and many other Christians, not to lay stress on Henry VIII. But Rutilius was certainly a pagan at heart.

urbem fecisti quod prius orbis erat—and had won their love. But Rome herself now needed help and comfort; and the poet turns to Stoicism, which had at least a poetic history, and could take the place of a discredited Pantheon without too much incongruity. The whole poem breathes the spirit of the Porch: Rome has fallen, but she will rise again, as she rose after Allia and Cannae; for Providence rules the world and has ordained that Rome should be eternal, and meanwhile Virtue alone can prevail against the inconstancy of Fortune.

Rutilius sings a swan-song no less of pagan philosophy than of Rome. Both, in a sense, were imperishable; but, under their old form, they had done their work before Alaric battered on the Roman gates. Both, however, were to die hard; for a century later than Rutilius, philosophy was still linked with poetry, when Boethius wrote his *Consolation*. Long before the death of this great philosopher (in 524 A.D.) Christianity had so far triumphed that no professed opponent could have held high office. Boethius was therefore, at least nominally, a Christian; but the *Consolation* bears no trace of Christian dogma. Much has been written to explain the seeming difficulty; but there is really nothing very difficult to explain. To Boethius philosophy meant human reason; and he was trying to prove that reason, by itself, supported revelation—*ratio* and *fides* were in harmony.[1] This explanation is perhaps enough; but I think there is a further cause for the absence of a Christian colour. Boethius was too good a scholar to mix the Kinds. He had chosen a distinct classical form—the Menippean satire, with its admixture of prose and verse—and this form demanded a purely classical content. The shades of Menippus and Seneca and Petronius would have protested against contamination. It is true that Boethius put the

[1] See E. K. Rand in *Harvard Studies Class. Phil.* xv. (1904), p. 27, and *Boethius, ed.* H. F. Stewart and E. K. Rand, p. x.

form to a far nobler use than the others—Petronius in particular—but that was no excuse for outraging it with a theology which Seneca had never known.

But, if Philosophy was to make peace with Poetry, she demanded her own terms: the Myth must disappear, and Boethius expressly gives reason for its banishment. The *Consolation* opens with an elegy after the manner of Ovid's *Tristia*, under the auspices of the Latin Muses—"those meretricious Sirens who may accustom the sufferer to his disease, but cannot heal it." Then (Boethius adds) Philosophy appears and expels the Sirens with reproaches, bringing her own Muses to effect the cure; and for the rest of the work the Ovidian elegiacs make way for metres which, being for the most part based on Seneca, were more appropriate to philosophy.

Even with this purging it is surely a remarkable tribute to the vitality of Latin poetic tradition, that a philosopher, on the eve of his torture and death, could turn to the old conventional forms of verse, when his emotion grew too full to be expressed in prose. For, first and foremost, Boethius was a philosopher, a keen student of Plato—whose *Timaeus* he condenses into a single short poem [1]—not, however, a neoplatonist, but an eclectic, who tried to harmonize Plato with Aristotle, adding the best parts of Stoic morality to this blend of eclecticism. Starting as a philosopher, he seems to have felt that Poetry was not the foe but the ally of philosophy. As Symmachus, in another connexion, had said of Truth, so great a secret may be reached by more roads than one. From time to time the prose argument is interrupted, when colder reasoning gives way to prayer, or self-exhortation, or poetic summary. Neo-platonism, itself, gave little scope for poetry—a God, so infinitely removed from man, could scarcely appeal to the emotions, and here Boethius adds little to the very scanty fragments of Latin

[1] See Stewart and Rand (*op. cit.* p. 292).

verse which seem inspired by the latest of ancient creeds.[1] In the main, he borrows from Stoic morals, though he is so far from being a professed Stoic that he refutes the theory of the mind as a blank page at birth, maintaining the Platonic dogma of Recollection. This is a rare instance in which he allows argument to usurp a place in his verse. The great majority of his thirty-nine poems are ethical: on avarice, the vanity of life, the punishment of tyranny, the mastery of Fortune—all subjects familiar to a student of Seneca, but all made part of his own experience by a poet-philosopher who, for character and intellect alike, may fairly be thought superior to his model. In one poem, of real dignity, Boethius seems to pass through Stoicism and Neoplatonism to the essence of Christianity: the whole universe is ruled by the law of love—*cælo imperitans amor* —and love must therefore be the sanction for human morals.[2] But it is the Christianity which the Christians themselves acknowledged as shared by the heathen; and, indeed, the best comment on Boethius is to be found in the Cambridge Platonists, one of whom might be translating an ode of the *Consolation* when he wrote the noble verses:

Sing aloud! His praise rehearse
Who hath made the Universe;
He the boundless heavens has spread,
All the vital orbs has kned.

ending with the prayer:

Now myself I do resign;
Take me whole; I all am Thine.[3]

With the death of Boethius, six hundred years had passed since Lucretius had hurled the first thunderbolt of science against superstition, and had made good the claim of philosophy to carry on the splendid tradition of Empedocles.

[1] Tiberianus wrote a fine invocation to the Platonic God; see *Poet. Lat. Min.* 3, p. 267 (Garrod, *Oxf. Book*, No. 319).

[2] 2, 8; cf. 1, 6; 4, 6.

[3] H. More, *Philosophical Poems*, 1647.

As we have seen, the secular war with her bitter enemy, the Myth, was long waged with doubtful issue; but in the end, philosophy was victorious. Yet the Latin Sirens had their revenge; classical poetry—the poetry of Catullus and Virgil and Horace—had depended, for its very life, on the Myth, and perished with the stopping of its life-blood; while ancient philosophy, in the hour of its triumph, was already doomed to fall beneath the attacks of a younger and more powerful Religion. The two partners had been reunited only to die together in the *Consolation* of Boethius, who, whether as poet or philosopher, deserves the famous memorial that he was the last whom Cato and Tully would have acknowledged for their countryman.

Has the long connexion of the Roman philosophers and poets any bearing on present or future poetry? For the first time, since Empedocles, the ancient quarrel was composed by Lucretius; can it ever be fully composed again? Wordsworth, at least, thought that the two parties might join hands: "if a time should ever come when what is called science, thus familiarized to men, shall be ready to put on, as it were, a form of flesh and blood, the Poet will lend his divine aid to the transfiguration."[1] Wordsworth may be here a true prophet, even though more than a century has passed without the realization of his prophecy. It is obvious—as I have already said in discussing Lucretius—that no philosophic or scientific model of the Universe can be expected from a poet of to-day. Whatever the possibilities of the ancient atom, no second Lucretius could grapple with the modern electron as a subject for text-book teaching. The poet must begin where the text-book ends. Here—if the Man appears—the subject is not only ready but clamorous for presentment. For it is surely absurd to suppose that science should hinder idealism; on the contrary, the more it substitutes a new vision of the world for outworn

[1] *Preface to Lyrical Ballads*, 1800.

theories, the more it suggests new inspiration for the poet.[1] Indeed, it may be said that the best hope for modern poetry, on a grand scale, lies in a fresh interpretation of human life in the light of science. For this, the time may not yet be ripe; science is still busy with the rush of discoveries, and men are too nearly occupied with the marvels of a new world—the world of the modern chemist and physicist and electrician—to "recollect in tranquillity" the emotions that scientific wonders suggest. In recent years a whole element—the word itself sounds strangely out of date—has been added to human conquest, but the poetry of the air has yet to be written. In the end, the poet will surely deal with the new science, not didactically, like Lucretius as a teacher, but imaginatively, like Lucretius as a poet. He will leave to science her analysis, her research, her compilation of fact, her application of fact to practical life; but the abstract truth, the inner meaning of scientific fact—in a word, the philosophy of science—must always remain within the poet's province.

That the transfiguration has been so long delayed is due, not only to the newness of science, but to another cause, which—though in a very different manner—was of vital importance to Lucretius himself. The conflict of Religion and Science was undoubtedly a bar to the free development of scientific poetry throughout the greater part of the nineteenth century. Even before the century had started, Cowper, in the *Task*, complained of science for "playing tricks with Nature"; and a late addition to the *Pleasures of Hope* is instructive of Campbell's growing fear:

> Oh! star-eyed Science, hast thou wandered there,
> To waft us home the message of despair?

Later, in the great scientific outburst of the Victorian age, Tennyson tried to welcome the new message, which

[1] There are some good remarks on this point in E. C. Stedman's *Nature and Elements of Poetry* (1892), p. xiv f.

disclosed so many beauties in the world of sense. But his friendship was guarded and half-hearted, since Evolution gave no promise of the "larger hope," and mechanical science could only end—as he correctly prophesied—in "airy navies" adding horror to war. The other Victorians were even less sympathetic, whether, like Browning, they turned to the analysis of the human mind, or, like Morris, found a tower of ivory in ancient and medieval romance, or, like Arnold and Clough, took refuge in a vague Stoicism. Science seemed to be but a miserable comforter, a spectre at the feast rather than a form of flesh and blood.

There is now no need to protest with Lucretius against foul superstition. The nineteenth-century struggle with a narrow dogmatism has been succeeded by a peace, honourable to both sides, which has secured the result that Science and Religion should rather help than hinder one another. For Science, in the end, cannot do without the flesh and blood, and still waits for a Lucretius, at once religious—in the truest sense—and scientific, to transfigure her.

CHAPTER VI

LANGUAGE AND STYLE

I

THE art of classical poetry depends on a rigid observance of two principles: metre and poetic language. By common consent, the form must be more than simply rhythmical, although here, as we have already noticed, the Greek critics hesitate, and—at least in theory—refuse to dogmatize. In the same way, the Greeks accepted, in practice, the rule of a distinctive language, while, here again, there was nothing narrow-minded in their criticism. They recognized that the simplicity of Euripides was as "poetical" as the ornateness of Pindar or Aeschylus. Indeed, if comparisons were drawn, it was Aeschylus, rather than Euripides, who suffered.[1] Attic taste could tolerate defect in ornament more readily than excess. But even Euripides would have failed to satisfy the Wordsworthian canon. If he "reduced the swelling" of Aeschylus, his own diction cannot support the dogma that "there is no essential difference between the language of prose and metrical composition." Aristotle (who was quite orthodox about the distinction between the two styles)[2] remarked that, even when Euripides borrows from common life, he is really elevated although he creates the illusion of just talking; and Longinus believed that the secret lay in the arrangement of these common words, which lifted them above the commonplace.[3] This may not explain

[1] As in the *Frogs* of Aristophanes.
[2] *Rhet.* 3, 1, 8.
[3] Arist. *Rhet.* 3, 2, 5; Longin. 40, 2-4.

the whole secret—sublimity or elevation is not merely a matter of Order, as Longinus himself was well aware, when he defined it as the echo of a great soul—but, at least on the formal side, the explanation goes a long way. Between the ages of Aristotle and Longinus, the Greek critic Dionysius had shown the immense importance of arrangement, both in prose and verse.[1] He would have found no fault with the definition of poetry, as "the best words in the best order," by which Coleridge rebuked Wordsworth's own inconsistency for using the language of prose with frequent digressions from its normal arrangement. It may be argued that the order in languages like Greek and Latin is much less rigid than in English, so that a digression from the normal is less noticeable. But, after due allowance is made for the greater flexibility of the ancient languages, the fact remains that the poets far outran the prose writers in licence of order. When Ovid—to take an instance at random—wrote the couplet

hic ego qui iaceo tenerorum lusor amorum
ingenio perii Naso poeta meo

the order may, or may not be, the "best"—that is always a matter of opinion—but at any rate it is not the order of customary Latin speech. The point is the more important since—as will appear from the following pages—Latin never acquired a poetic vocabulary as copious and distinctive as Greek or English of the seventeenth century, though the French language has nearly always followed the example of its parent.[2]

But, while the order was recognized as essential, the actual words came first. If Greek criticism is largely verbal, the

[1] *de verb. comp.* See especially ch. 2, where he holds that arrangement or order (σύνθεσις) is even more important than the choice of words. The whole treatise deserves study in this connexion.

[2] Gray to West, 1742 (*ed.* Toynbee 2, p. 25: "The language of the age is never the language of poetry, except among the French, whose verse, when the thought or image does not support it, differs in nothing from prose." Brunetière (*Poésie lyrique en France*, p. 272) agrees.

explanation lies in an instinctive reverence for the Word—a conviction that there is a beauty in the Name corresponding to the beauty of the thing expressed; a belief summed up in the imperishable sentence of Longinus, that lovely words—*τὰ καλὰ ὀνόματα*—are in very truth the real light of the mind.[1] That the Roman ear could be as sensitive as the Greek, no reader of Catullus or Virgil will deny; indeed, the enormous pains which all Romans obviously spent on the choice and harmony of words is a proof that—whatever else might be wanted—the poet's first need was verbal felicity. Roman poetry must be reasonable; but this did not imply that its language was to be reduced to the level of commonsense.[2]

The poet "spoke another language." Not only were "plebeian" words excluded—and unfortunately we know too little of the plebeian dialect to judge the full effect of this exclusion—but poetic diction was itself a refinement of the refined speech heard in the Senate or Law-court. A poetry so near akin to rhetoric was bound to be based on the language of the orator; but the two styles were so far different that it is an orator himself who draws the distinction.[3] Cicero, in a famous passage, after noting the similarity of the two styles, concludes that the poet has less latitude in rhythm (which is of course obvious), that he is about equal to the orator in ornament (which means that the poet borrowed most of the rhetorical Figures), and that he has the advantage in licence of language.[4] It is with the last of these claims that we are now concerned, and we are confronted with a double question: firstly, was this true in Cicero's own time? and secondly, was it true in the Augustan age?

[1] 30, 1. So Dionysius *de comp.* 16.

[2] The heresy against which Coleridge and Hazlitt protested would have had no Roman support.

[3] Cic. *de orat.* 2, 61, *poetas omnino quasi alia quadam lingua locutos, non conor attingere.* (The orator is Antonius.)

[4] Cic. *de orat.* 1, 16, 70.

That it was not true, without reservation, for Cicero's own period is clear from his own contemporary Lucretius, who complained about the poverty of his native tongue for the expression of Greek philosophy in Latin verse. Here, however, the comparison is not between two forms of the Latin, but between Latin and Greek. Cicero himself was uncertain whether Latin prose could vie with the language of Lysias and Demosthenes; and even if he was on the whole convinced that the Romans had a medium for oratory not inferior to the Greeks, he knew, from his own experience, the difficulty of translating philosophical concepts into a language which was still new to abstract reasoning or ideal speculation.[1] In any case the real or supposed poverty of Lucretius in philosophical language proves very little for Latin poetry in general. The point is only important as showing the spirit of humility with which the Latin poets set about to form a style not unworthy of their Greek masters, and comparable with the ornate and abundant diction of Latin oratory.

The problem of verbal style could hardly have been clearly raised before the period of Cicero himself.[2] Ennius and the early poets were busy enough in adapting the metre, and made no great pretence at reproducing the delicacy of Greek language. Ennius is mainly "prosaic" in his vocabulary; and though Horace remarked that if you took his words—*belli ferratos postes*—to pieces, you would find *disiecti membra poetae*, the "limbs" were clearly the broken bits of the metaphor, and not the words in themselves, which are as ordinary as any Wordsworth could have wished. The pressing need for a poetic language was not felt until the first great wave of purely Roman poetry had been spent, and a younger school turned from the patriotic movement of the *Annals* to the fresh inspiration of Greece. It is

[1] See Cic. *Nat. deor.* 1, 4, 8; *Fin.* 1, 3, 10; *Tusc.* 2, 35.

[2] Lucilius (Book xxvi.) had made a start, satirizing the tragic diction of Pacuvius as *monstrificabile*.

unnecessary to discuss the history of this "neoteric" school; for our present purpose it is enough to bear in mind that its members—Laevius, Valerius Cato, and (a little later) Catullus, Calvus, Cinna, and others who are now mere names—were mainly concerned with Alexandrine poetry, whose distinctive character was verbal dexterity.[1] The problem for the neoterics was to reproduce this technical refinement—to suggest something of Greek delicacy and grace in a language which (as Quintilian long afterwards observed) had the advantage of strength, dignity, and fulness, but was deficient in the subtle charm, the finer *nuance* of the Greek.[2] This formal study of the Alexandrines was not confined to language—the neoteric innovations in metre are almost equally important—but, on the whole, the chief feature of the *poeticus decor* was the Word. In the selective process there was a double tendency—to discard as well as to innovate; and, though the two movements are of course intimately connected, their effect can best be judged if they are examined apart. Broadly speaking, we may say that the function of the neoterics was positive, of the Augustans, negative. It was the business of the older school to make all sorts of experiments with their own language, in order to widen the scope of the Ennian tradition, leaving to their successors the task of rejecting those metrical or verbal forms which failed to satisfy Augustan taste. To mention a single example in metre, it is well known that the neoterics tried to acclimatize the quadrisyllabic ending of the hexameter, that Cicero laughed at this spondaic affectation of the *cantores Euphorionis*, and that Lucretius (here anticipating the Augustans), after using the trick fairly often in his first five books, discarded it altogether in his last. In language, the process was the same. Laevius, Catullus, and, to a less

[1] Cato, the "Latin Siren," seems to have founded the school, though the honour has been claimed for Laevius, a generation earlier.

[2] Quint. 1, 5, 65-70; 12, 10, 27.

extent, Lucretius take all manner of liberties which Virgil and Horace either curtailed or entirely suppressed.

The most obvious and (to a Roman) the most natural experiment was to ascertain the limits within which Greek words could be Latinized. On general principles there was no objection to as free a borrowing from the Greek as that of Chaucer or Langland from the French, or of Milton from the Latin. From the earliest period of contact with Hellenic civilization, the Romans had been accustomed to loan-words, and the poets themselves might well remember that the very name for their own class was a Greek word (ποιητής), which even Virgil's influence could not eject in favour of the old Italian *vates*. Educated men were more or less bilingual, and Lucilius faithfully represented the fashion by interlarding his satire with Greek words—"mixing Chian and Falernian" to Horace's distaste.[1] Lucilius, however, as a satirist hardly comes within the range of "high" poetry: the question was, whether an admixture of foreign words was desirable or tolerable, in a really poetic diction. Both Lucretius and Catullus yielded to the charm of the Greek language, which even Augustan purism could not wholly banish; a century later Quintilian could still say that "Greek is so much pleasanter than Latin that our poets, whenever they wish their verses to be sweet, adorn them with Greek words".[2] In Lucretius, the large majority of loan-words are of course due to the subject—*homoeomeria* hardly adds to the sweetness of Latin—but the great poet does not confine himself to forced loans from philosophy. The remarkable line

ac musaea mele per chordas organici quae . . .

and its pair

et cycnaea mele Phoebeaque daedala chordis

are not merely a confession that Latin was then no language for the musician, but a test of its capacity to absorb the

[1] Hor. *Sat.* 1, 10, 20 f.

[2] Quint. 12, 10, 33.

greatest possible amount of a foreign element that Latin can assimilate, without ceasing to be Latin altogether. But Lucretius rarely makes these strange excursions, leaving such points of style to the neoterics, most or all whom were *graecissantes.*

Catullus has about sixty words borrowed from the Greek, and although many of them had long been familiar, their cumulative effect gives at least a touch of the exotic to his work.[1] As we see from Horace, the propriety of this licence was questioned in his day; and Virgil (who in his earliest work seems to have favoured the practice) finally decided against the Alexandrines.[2] The use of Greek words must not, of course, be confused with that of Greek inflections. Much of the subject-matter being drawn from Greece, it was inevitable that the question should arise whether Greek proper names should have Latin forms. Here, as in similar questions, there were two schools, in and after the time of Cicero. The matter was of wider interest than merely poetical usage—the genius of the Latin language was primarily the concern of the orators. Of these, the "Atticists", or purists, rejected Greek inflections: Caesar required *Calypsonem* on the analogy of *Iunonem*, and even Cicero, whose Atticism was tempered by Asianism, apologized for using *Piraeea* instead of *Piraeum.* This oratorical dispute was naturally passed on to the poets, and was still unsettled in the age of Augustus. Tibullus, both in language and metaphor, is far more "Attic" than Propertius. Technically, he is *elegans*, that is, simple and severe, a purist. Together with Lygdamus, he uses far fewer Greek inflections than either Propertius or Ovid.[3] Here at least there was

[1] Cf. Macrob. *Sat.* 6, 4, 22, *hac licentia largius usi sunt veteres, parcius Maro.* Virgil was criticized for such words as *lychnus*, *aethra*, *daedalus*.

[2] Hor. *A.P.* 52; see G. L. Hendrickson in *Class. Philology* xii. (1917), p. 77 f. and p. 328 f.

[3] See R. Bürger, *Beitr. zur Elegantia Tibulls* in Χάριτες (F. Leo), p. 388 f.; Sniehotta's and Zwiener's papers *de voc. graec. usu* in *Breslauer Phil. Abhandl.* 9 (1909). For *elegantia* as the translation of ἀττικισμός see Quint. 1, 8, 8.

room for legitimate variation of taste, and even the greatest champions of purism seem to have allowed that a foreign inflection might be proper to a foreign name. But, for other loan-words, the propriety of usage was more than doubtful, and Virgil's parsimony settled the practice for the future of Latin poetry. Patriotism gained the day, just as, in the sixteenth century, the English poets tried and condemned a host of Latin words which the Renascence had thrust on the language.

Apart from the introduction of Greek words the neoterics made various other attempts to give more grace, more warmth and colour, to the rigid and heavy tongue of Ennius. It is clear that the Augustans scrutinized all these innovations with some watchfulness—the dignity of Latin was at stake—and the failure of some very interesting experiments is noteworthy. In particular, the history of the compound word will illustrate the change in literary art between Catullus and Horace. This form—especially the compound adjective—has a very special place in poetic diction; and, among the languages which admit its free use, Greek is pre-eminent. Beautiful and expressive epithets—*ἰοστέφανος*, violet-crowned, *ἀργυρόπεζα*, silver-footed, *βαθύζωνος*, deep-girdled—these and hundreds more are Homeric models to which all later Greek poets could add their own contribution. For the form is capable of infinite extension, and no language that naturally admits the compound need become fixed or stereotyped. English is here served as fully as Greek. Since Chapman—directly influenced by Homer—restored the form, after a period of neglect, to its old place of honour in Early English, our own poets have never failed to recognize its pictorial and imaginative value. Shakespeare's "young-eyed" cherubins, Milton's "civil-suited" Morn, Shelley's "rainbow-skirted" shower, Keats' "azure-lidded"

Caesar had set the fashion of Atticism as against the Asian style, and this purism naturally spread from rhetoric to poetry.

sleep, Tennyson's "lily-cradled" bee, may challenge comparison with the most poetic fancy of Homer or Meleager.

Old Latin freely admitted the compound substantive and adjective, and certain specimens survived under religious protection, such as *ambarvalia*, *suovetaurilia*, *lectisternium*, *sacrosanctus*, or in titles of gods (Juno *domiduca*, *iterduca*, etc.). Latin poetry therefore started with no prejudice against the form, as we see from familiar lines like that of Pacuvius

repandirostrum incurvicervicum pecus

or

terrigenam, herbigradam, domiportam, sanguine cassam

in a translation by Lucilius or possibly Cicero himself, who quotes it.[1] There was thus good precedent for the neoterics in developing the use of the compound; and Laevius, in especial, delighted in forms like *tardigeniclus*, *pudoricolor*, and others still more striking (*trisaeclisenex*, *dulciorelocus*, *multigrumis*), which Gellius mentions with disapproval as "too poetic". Some of these formations strike our own ears as cumbrous, and we are not surprised that Quintilian felt *incurvicervicum* to be a poor substitute for the Greek κυρταυχένα.[2] But this criticism will hardly apply to many compounds in Catullus, who shows infinitely more taste than Laevius. In such lines as

ubi cerva silvicultrix, ubi aper nemorivagus

the epithets fall on the ear with a tone of haunting charm. No "single" adjectives, surely, could suggest, with such delicacy as well as force, the wild forest, peopled only with deer and boars, to which Attis, "the flower of the gymnasium," is condemned.

Yet these beautiful additions to the language of poetry

[1] Cic. *Div.* 2, 64, 113.

[2] Quint. 1, 5, 68; Gell. *N.A.* 19, 7, 13. See generally Cic. *de fin.* 3, 4, 15; Livy, 27, 11.

were allowed to drop. Of about seventy new compounds in Lucretius and Catullus very few survived in Augustan literature, and these only when formed after well-established models. In elegiac, the disuse was perhaps natural. The metre itself presents no difficulty—there is a wealth of compounds in the Greek Anthology—and Catullus could write

audit falsiparens Amphitryoniades,

but even Catullus is far more sparing of these forms in elegy than in other metres; and the later elegiac poets almost wholly renounce them. No doubt their stricter rules for the pentameter would exclude *Amphitryoniades*, but the real reason lay in their adoption of a language which rarely rose above the level of ordinary speech.[1]

In lyric, we might expect more licence; but here, again, we find the same disuse. Horace almost entirely avoids the double adjective in the *Odes*—a fact the more remarkable since, as a critic, he claimed the poet's right to add new words, with slight change, from the Greek.[2] The phrase, no doubt, is a little obscure, and might apply to any Greek word-formation; but it may, at least partly, refer to compounds formed on Greek analogy. If so, Horace belies the character which Pope gave him that

His precepts teach but what his works inspire.

A master of perfect language—*verbis felicissime audax*—Horace did not dare, or perhaps care, to add new words in compensation for the many which he rejected. His most striking compound (*tauriformis*) is innocuous enough; for the word is formed on the analogy of *multiformis*, which belongs to a class (*multi-*, *semi-*, *bi-*, *tri-*, etc.) where numerical notation hardly doubles the "simple" adjective. Even so, Horace seems to have had a special reason for his coinage: *tauriformis* belongs to an Ode in which the

[1] See below p. 249.

[2] *A.P.* 52 f.

poet is aiming at a dithyrambic effect, and the Greeks had recognized, both in theory and practice, that the more violent compounds were best fitted for the dithyramb.[1] But the "harper of a Roman lyre" was not often Dionysiac; in his normal mood he was content to express a Greek compound by a periphrasis, as when χαλκεοθώρηξ appears, in a Latin dress, as *tunica tectum adamantina.*[2]

The same economy is apparent in the other Augustans. Virgil does not object to familiar forms like *armipotens*, *horrisonus:* but these are all colourless, and call up no strong pictorial image—indeed, though philologically compounds, they are little more than simple adjectives with weak terminations, such as the forms in *-fer* and *-ger* which Ovid so freely employed. Here, as elsewhere, the post-Augustans followed the Augustan lead, except in certain fourth-century poets, who appear to have admired the school of Catullus. Tiberianus, for example, has one or two striking compounds (*auriflorus*, *flammifluus*, if the readings are correct), and Ausonius also indulges in a few neologisms like *floriparus*, *iricolor;* but Claudian, more classic than the Classics, refuses to coin words not justified by Virgilian use or analogy.

This rigid and deliberate rejection of a form, which—within limits—has real poetic value, forces us to conclude that the Augustans thought it bad Latin. The history of French literature confirms the conclusion: among other experiments the Pleiad attempted to naturalize the compound, and failed. It was said to be against the genius of the language, and it disappeared.[3] There is no wonder that modern French critics view the same disappearance in Latin poetry without a pang: their most elaborate and scholarly treatise on the subject takes no notice of the compound beyond a footnote in which it is said that these

[1] *Od.* 4, 4, 25; Arist. *Poet.* 22, 10; cf. *Rhet.* 3, 3, 1; Demetr. *on Style*, 91.
[2] *Od.* 1, 6, 13. Virgil's *per mille coloribus arcum* is another periphrasis.
[3] E.g. *deux-fois-né* (Ronsard), *terre-née*, *aime-chanson* (Belleau).

words—*longs et sans force!*—should be replaced by their simple constituents.[1] But Latin, after all, is not French; and some Anglo-Saxons, at least (tastes can here legitimately differ), may regret that later purism crushed the freedom of Catullus into the straight-jacket of Augustan correctness.

The "genius of the language" may have rightly excluded the compound; but that explanation will not account for the loss of another form—the diminutive. This, at least, as we see from Plautus, from Cicero's letters, and from Apuleius—to take three different periods—was good Latin. Diminutives (of substantives, adjectives, and even verbs) belonged, no doubt, to the popular language, but they were not vulgar—one cannot accuse Cicero of vulgarity—and the neoterics proved that the form was a literary asset of which any language might be proud. Here Laevius led the way, his amatory verse (the *Erotopaegnia*) giving full scope for terms of affection like *hirarula*, *tenellula;* and Catullus followed, with a wealth of diminutives which give his love-poems their peculiar note of tenderness as well as passion. We read

flendo turgiduli rubent ocelli

or

mitte brachiolum teres,
praetextate, puellulae;

we linger over the charm of *ore floridulo*, the pathos of *tui dulcis amiculi*; or—in another mood—we are astonished by the poisonous shafts of bitter irony in

ne laneum latusculum manusque mollicellas
inusta turpiter tibi flagella conscribillent;

and it astonishes us that later poets should have resigned an instrument so finely attuned to the expression of love—or hate. Yet, a generation after Catullus, the love-poets had

[1] Plessis, *la poésie latine*, p. 131.

almost wholly banned this idiom. As usual, Tibullus led the way in purism, Propertius being a little less rigid;[1] but, broadly, all the elegiac writers fall into line. Tibullus and Propertius (if not Ovid) were as ardent lovers as Catullus, but their passion was curbed by the Augustan bridle. Ovid writes *ocellus* once or twice—a grudging concession to metre—but otherwise he is strictly exclusive. He might have found *auricula* no less convenient; but, after Lucretius, that word disappeared from serious poetry, although—like many another diminutive—it took its revenge in the end, when *auricula* ousted *auris* as the parent of *oreille*. Ejected from its natural sphere, the diminutive had even less chance of survival in epic, unless its force had been forgotten or obscured, as in common forms like *capillus*, *lectulus*, *puella*, *tabella*, *tremulus*. Virgil, we know, was blamed for using *avunculus*;[2] and though its English equivalent "uncle" has (or once had) a humorous suggestion—even "aunt" is not beyond reproach—a Roman reader, who passed *socer* and *gener*, could have found no fault with the word except for its termination. For the same reason, *flosculus*, *rivulus*, and *hortulus*—all dear to modern composers of Latin verse—have little or no authority in Augustan models, however interesting they may be as evidence of modern taste unconsciously at variance with ancient practice. Virgil makes one exception in the *Aeneid*—a splendid proof of the rule. The pathos of the diminutive in

> *si quis mihi parvulus aula*
> *luderet Aeneas*

on the lips of Dido—a widow and childless—is one of the innumerable signs that Virgil puts Nature before the Rules.[3]

After the Augustans and Flavians, there was at least a temporary revulsion in favour of Republican poets, and the

[1] See Bürger, *l.c.* p. 371 f.

[2] Serv. on *Aen.* 3, 343, *quidam "avunculus" humiliter in heroico carmine dictum accipiunt.*

[3] This is noted by T. R. Glover, *Virgil*, p. 184.

diminutive was restored to fashion, no doubt owing to the growing popularity of Catullus.[1] In the Antonine age, Apuleius crowded his erotic verse with diminutives,[2] and Hadrian had already set the example in the celebrated poem which has so often invited and defied an English translation:

animula vagula blandula,
hospes comesque corporis,
quae nunc abibis in loca,
pallidula, rigida, nudula,
nec ut soles dabis iocos?

Ronsard, more fortunate than Pope or Byron, could keep up the whimsical, half-humorous, and wholly pathetic tenderness of the original by his adaptation:

Amelette Ronsardelette,
Mignonnelette, doucelette,
Tres-chère hostesse de mon corps,
Tu descens là bas faiblelette,
Pasle, maigrelette, seulette,
Dans le froid royaume des mors.[3]

Here, again, the dictators of French classicism were faithful to their Roman prototypes, and a form which Horace would have said "had too little splendour" was unsparingly condemned. But, in this respect, the English cannot cast a stone at Malherbe and Boileau, since Herrick's diminutives—"cherrylet," "shepardling," "youngling," and so forth—have no less failed to maintain themselves in poetry. In all such matters of taste, it is presumptuous for foreigners to criticize the judgment of natives—provided that the natives agree; but, as we have just seen, when Hadrian and Apuleius preferred Catullus, we have the right to doubt whether the Augustans were sole arbiters; and our doubts are confirmed by the later history of Latin and one, at least, of its daughters, Italian. Medieval Latin did not here stand

[1] See p. 61. [2] Baehrens, P.L.M. p. 114.
[3] The Pleiad were not the first to favour the diminutive; Jehannot de Lescurel had anticipated them in the XIVth century.

on its dignity; a poem of Godescalcus indulges in a perfect riot of diminutives, and that Saxon poet was no mean Latinist.[1] As for Italian, it is sufficient to note that, at the very time when French verse was under the heel of the classicists, Francesco Redi (1626-1698) could write

Venticelli et fresche aurette,
Dispiegando ali d'argento
Sull' azzurro pavimento,
Tesson danze amorosette,

while Carducchi, in modern verse, can supply as good examples.

The ban on the diminutive, as being popular or undignified, was part of a much wider taboo which rejected all vulgar or—as Dryden called them—"village" words. Horace's declaration—"I hate and spurn the crowd"—applied to the language of the people as well as to the people themselves. It became a text of artistic propriety.[2] Long before the Augustans, Lucilius had laughed at the "grand" habit of using Greek words for common objects like couch-legs and lamps.[3] Poetry could not be allowed to lower this standard of aristocracy; and Virgil is often obedient to the convention which we may cite as the "law of the excluded lamp". As Servius notes, he avoided this very word (*lucerna*), substituting its Greek equivalent.[4] In Epic, the rule could be observed without much difficulty; for, though Virgil prefers the "poetic" *ensis* to the technical *gladius*, terms for military equipment have a nobility as old as Homer; and the *Aeneid* is not much concerned with the

[1] *Mon. Germ. Hist. (Poet. Lat.)*, iii. p. 731, 6.

[2] See Hor. *Ep.* 2, 2, 111. Petron. 118, *refugiendum est ab omni verborum, ut ita dicam, vilitate, et sumendae voces a plebe semotae, ut fiat illud "odi profanum vulgus et arceo."*

[3] Lucil. in Baehrens. F.P.L. 34 = Macrob. 6, 4, 17, *porro clinopodas lichnosque ut dicimus σεμνῶς, ante "pedes lecti" atque "lucernas."*

[4] Serv. on *Aen.* 6, 726; see his notes on *Aen.* 1, 177, where he compares *Georg.* 1, 391.

"low" knives and blankets for which Dr. Johnson reproved the author of *Macbeth*.[1] The language of the *Georgics* was a severer test of style. Virgil had here to enumerate "agricultural implements," and though he found a more pleasing collective term in *arma*, there was hardly a poetic synonym for each separate tool. Luckily, the great principle of Imitation came to the rescue, overriding the negative of poetic diction. Hesiod, the acknowledged father of the *Georgics*, had followed the principle of calling a spade a spade, since it never occurred to that worthy farmer that a synonym was needed. Virgil was therefore free to compromise. His list—which includes (besides the "nobler" plough and waggon) the humble roller and hurdle, shows that he never shrank from the plain name. He has no equivalent for the "stercorarious heap", having—in addition to the strong Roman love of reality—a sense of humour. He selects his vocabulary with the consummate art which is its own justification, steering by supreme tact a straight course between the swelling whirlpool of the Turgid and the sunken shoals of the Flat.

As usual, the neo-classics exaggerated the classic purity of style. Dryden and Addison both admired Virgil for excluding "low phrases and terms of art"; they believed that "he writ not to mariners, soldiers, astronomers, gardeners, peasants, etc., but to all in general," and therefore avoided the cant of any profession.[2] But Virgil, as we have just seen, did not avoid the "cant" of agriculture. And we may feel sure that he would not have understood Dryden's objection to translating his *amaracus* by the "village" word "sweet-marjoram"—a word already consecrated by Spenser and Drayton, and worthy, one might think, to be welcomed with Kipling's

Basil, Rocket, Valerian, Rue,

[1] *Rambler*, 168.

[2] Dryden, *Dedication of the Aeneis*; see Addison on Virgil's *Georgics*.

and other excellent herbs that "almost sing themselves as they run."

We know, on Alfred de Vigny's authority, that it took ninety-eight years for the French Melpomene to pronounce *mouchoir*;[1] but Virgil and Horace were scarcely as sensitive as the students who hissed that fatal word in his translation of *Othello.* For the use of direct and simple words was by no means confined to the *Georgics*—it is the prevailing mark of all Augustan work, in spite of many excursions into elaborate and periphrastic speech. Virgil had another and a better model than Hesiod, in Lucretius, who—hardly touched by the neoteric movement—represented the direct line of Ennius. Lucretius was never afraid of the common word. At the time when poetic diction was still rampant in English verse, Bentley had noted his simplicity; and taking the splendid line

luna, dies et nox et noctis signa severa

he asked: Is not every word common? and is the total effect unpoetical?[2] For the answer we may turn to Coleridge, although even that great critic does not supply it in full. As a modern writer has well remarked, Coleridge "allows himself to be led by his German metaphysic into considering poetry as a *Ding an sich*, and deducing therefrom the proposition that poetry *must* employ a language different from that of prose."[3] At the present day we are shy of the Absolute, at all events in criticism. We prefer to construct our principles from facts rather than to force the facts into conformity with preconceived principles; and we find, in actual experience, that good poetry has been written in "poetic" language, never used in ordinary speech

[1] *Le More de Venise: Lettre à Lord. . . .*

[2] R. C. Jebb, *Bentley*, p. 69, quoted by Glover, *Virgil*, p. 63. The fact that Bentley was quibbling on the ambiguity of the word "common" does not concern us in this isolated sentence; he went to the root of the matter long before Wordsworth developed his views.

[3] J. M. Murry, *Aspects of Literature*, p. 192.

—the poetry of Homer and Aeschylus, of Spenser and Coleridge himself. But good poetry, again, has been written in the language of common life, and there have been infinite gradations between the two extremes. There is a well-known definition of poetry as "the sort of thing which poets write"; and if this is perhaps not altogether serious, we may be quite serious in adding that the language appropriate to poetry is the sort of language which poets use.

But Coleridge at least saw the essential truth. Wordsworth's real stumbling-block was (very rightly) the affected and stereotyped language which the eighteenth century mistook for poetic diction. His friend would have agreed that nothing is to be gained, and much to be lost, by calling a young woman a nymph. But the true objection to much of the eighteenth century verse lies in the spirit, not the letter—it was a translation of prose thoughts into poetic language. Coleridge's great service was to insist that poetry expresses more passion than prose, and for this reason demands a language of its own. That language might, on occasion, be composed of ordinary words; but such words, if used in their ordinary sense, could rarely give poetic pleasure.[1] Coleridge took Wordsworth's own lines—

> The silence that is in the starry sky,
> The sleep that is among the lonely hills—

and pertinently asked: "Are those words *in those places* (the italics are his) commonly employed in real life to express the same thought or outward thing?" Common words, in fact, will give poetic pleasure only if they bear some significance or suggestion which is not commonplace. If we apply this test to the Lucretian line, we see that,

[1] Wordsworth of course modified his original position; in the Preface of 1800 he attempted to discover how far pleasure may be given by "a selection of the real language of men in a state of vivid sensation." The emphasis on selection and vivid sensation is noteworthy.

although all the words are usual, the collocation *noctis signa severa* is no more commonplace than Keats' reminiscence *the earnest stars*. Possibly, however, our analysis must be extended; for it might be pointed out that the first half of the line consists of ordinary words used in their ordinary sense, without further suggestion. If we feel pleasure in the simplicity of *luna dies et nox* (apart from the beauty of the cadence), is it not due to the fact that really great things need, or admit, no adornment of language? As everyone knows, the Romans preferred *Phoebe* to *luna;* and what would now be considered a worn-out tag, was at least justified by a mythological association then comparatively fresh; but Lucretius, with his strong grasp of reality, knew that no ornament could improve Nature in her vastness and magnificence, just as Dante saw

delle cose belle che porta il Ciel,

and was content that the beauty of these heavenly things should speak for itself.

Horace, no less than Virgil, is indebted to Lucretius, or rather to the sense of fact, the need of plain speaking, which is not so much distinctively Lucretian as Roman. Lyric poetry—one might think—could have demanded a special vocabulary, if only to mark its derivation from Sappho and Alcaeus, whose language, though never florid, is certainly "poetical." But Horace, when he is most Roman and least subject to the spell of Greece, is quite straightforward. His patriotic odes—as distinguished from imitations of Greek fancy—are completely realistic. In the very poem which proclaims his superiority to the vulgar herd, he speaks without periphrasis of the builder and the canvassing politician.[1] The poet who could write *caementa demittit redemptor* and *descendat in campum petitor* was not one to lay stress on the law of the excluded lamp—a word which, by the way,

[1] *Od.* 3, 1.

Horace himself does not exclude.[1] Indeed there are whole odes containing no word that would not have passed muster in Ciceronian prose.[2]

If we sum up the general tendencies of the neoterics and contrast them with the Augustan fashion, we see that the earlier forward movement was checked by two principles which the later school applied to all poetry. Of course the application was not equally strict for all the Kinds. The Greek division of oratory into three " characters " had been transferred to Latin poetic criticism, and the language varied according as the style was *tenuis*, *moderatus*, or *validus*, Virgil using all the three in his three great works. Obviously, a style appropriate for Epic must be modified for Elegy and still more for Satire; but, apart from the distinctions of species, there was a recognized language for the whole genus.[3] This language must be dignified, and it must be established. Of these two principles perhaps the latter was more strictly observed; for dignity is more or less a matter of opinion, whereas there can be little dispute whether a word is " in use " or a neologism. The rule of *usus*, or *consuetudo*, was in fact the chief negative to the free expansion of poetic language. It springs, in part, from the belief in a " natural " connexion between word and thing—a subject of endless debate in ancient times. There were Romans who considered language as "conventional," and these might have had less regard, in the abstract, for the natural sanctity of the Word; but all Romans venerated their own language, and looked askance at innovation. It was as difficult for a new word to force its way into the close corporation of Latin literature as for a *novus homo* to enter the Roman senate.

[1] *Od.* I, 27, 5.

[2] E.g. 3, 6, where *Hesperia* for *Italia* is perhaps the sole poeticism. Horace is true to his theory (*A.P.* 243, *tantum de medio sumptis accedit honoris*).

[3] See Donat. *vit. Verg.* 255. Elegiac style was always rooted in the colloquial language, though elevated, to a greater or less extent, according to its subject; see A. L. Wheeler in *Proc. Class. Assoc.* xviii. (1921).

Julius Caesar, in a tract which he found time to write while crossing the Alps, warned an author to avoid new words like a rock at sea.[1] No doubt Caesar takes an extreme position as an analogist and Atticist. There were many who freely admitted unusual words in oratory, which, as we have seen set the standard for all forms of literature.[2] Others, like Quintilian, were on the whole conservative, but shrank from Caesar's stark and uncompromising Atticism. Horace no less avoids the extreme. He clings to *usus*, and his preference for the known word is shown by his precept as well as his own practice:

> *dixeris egregie, notum si callida verbum*
> *reddiderit iunctura novum*—

novelty depends, not on the word itself, but on its order or place—a view which is strikingly like the criticism of Longinus on Euripides. But Horace is no Caesarian; Caecilius and Plautus "had enriched the language," and why should a licence permitted to them be denied to Virgil and Varius? Only—the poet adds—the licence must be rare, and must never offend the final arbiter, usage.[3] In later times, even this tiny loophole was blocked by the watchfulness of critics like Gellius and Macrobius, who were painfully anxious to show that words, commonly thought to be Virgil's invention, were borrowed from some older source.[4] A poet could not be allowed to tamper with the language, when even an emperor—Tiberius—was warned that, though he might enfranchize a man, he could not give citizenship to a word.[5]

[1] Caes. *de analogia* in Gell. *N.A.* 1, 10, 4; cf. Macrob. *Sat.* 1, 5, 2.

[2] See Norden, *Kunstprosa*, p. 188. For Quintilian cf. 1, 5, 71. *usitatis (verbis) tutius utimur, nova non sine quodam periculo fingimus . . . audendum tamen*, and an admirable chapter on *consuetudo* as the *consensus eruditorum*, 1, 6, 43-45. See generally Cic. *de orat.* 3, 153 f.; *Orat.* 201.

[3] *A.P.* 48 f., 71 f.

[4] Gell. *N.A.* 1, 21, 5 on *amaror*; cf. Macrob. *Sat.* 6, 4, 16.

[5] Suet. *Gramm.* 22.

II

So far, we have dealt only with the process of pruning by which the Augustans shaped the overgrowth of the neoterics into classic proportions. But no poetry can live on negations—whether of form or ideas—least of all, a poetic art which was instinct with the vitality of a new age, and needed a medium worthy of the high purpose and brilliant hopes that were centred in the government of Augustus. On the positive side, it was the business of the poets to repair the losses inflicted on the language of Catullus by their own purism. They were determined to create a national poetry, and therefore rightly rejected the words and forms which could not be assimilated to the national language. But, if Greek words (and even inflexions) were denied, the expressive syntax of Greek poetry might perhaps be naturalized no less than its prosody and metre. The two languages were so nearly akin that the stiffness of prose construction could be softened by the more pliant and elastic grammar of the Greeks, without any damage to the "genius of the language". Some such licence was a necessity rather than a mere ornament, since—as every schoolboy who writes Latin verse is painfully aware—a metre based on quantity presents difficulties far greater than one in which only accent has to be considered. The influence of Greek grammar began, to some extent, with the influence of Greek poetry itself; but the movement was progressive, affecting Virgil more than Lucretius, Horace, more than Catullus. To give many details would be needless, especially as we are all familiar with editorial comments on "Greek constructions". Editors, however, have not always noted the value of an artifice, which may sometimes originate from metrical necessity, but may also have a real poetic use. For since the majority of Latin words were shared by prose and verse, it was the more important to give them distinction in verse; and one method of marking the difference is by variety in syntax. When Horace wrote *desine mollium querellarum*, or *uxor invicti Iovis esse nescis*, he used words not only common in themselves, but common in their context; but, by an unusual syntax, he raised the power of the expression above the values of prose speech.

Nevertheless, it may be doubted whether such an artifice is a permanent gain to poetry. Horace knew that Nature was not amenable to the pitchfork, and was himself cautious enough in tampering with the nature of a language. The evidence of history seems to prove that a foreign grammar is even more intractable than foreign words. In France, Ronsard and his school were as unfortunate in their Latin constructions as in their other experiments. In England, Spenser and Milton succeeded, for their own generations, in giving a distinctly classical cast to their poetic grammar; but, in the long run, their efforts failed, and—if we admire—we cannot now imitate such constructions as "knew not eating death," or

> Who, always vacant, always amiable.
> Hopes thee.

There remained one other source on which a Roman could draw. If he might not neologize, he was free to archaize. In oratory and formal conversation the limits, within which archaism was permitted, naturally varied according to varying fashion in the neglect or popularity of the pre-Augustans.[1] There was a distinct movement towards archaism in the age of Nero, when Seneca scoffed at a literary set who talked like the Twelve Tables.[2] Sallust had already set the example, and the pedantry of Tiberius was condemned by Augustus, whose own style is described as elegant and temperate.[3] The emperor's taste cannot have failed to affect

[1] See above p. 61.

[2] Seneca, *Ep.* 114, 13. The great archaizing movement was in the time of the Antonines, but Latin poetry was then negligible.

[3] Suet. *Gram.* 10; *Aug.* 86.

the court writers, both in prose and verse; and Augustan orators, at all events, seem to have gone no further than to choose—in Quintilian's often-quoted phrase—the oldest of new words and the newest of old.[1] The poets, however, had proverbially a licence; and though some Augustans, like Tibullus, were "elegant," there was a traditional right to archaize which Horace accepts: it is almost a duty to "recover beautiful words once spoken by Cato or Cethegus," and so to "endow Latium with a rich language."[2] His own poems owe not a little of their beauty to occasional archaism either in word or form—*adorea*, *Diespiter*, *duellum*, *Graius*, and the like.[3]

Archaism, of course, has other and deeper roots. It has a sentimental as much as a practical value, and the Romans, with their strong hold on tradition, were not likely to underrate continuity in language, as in religion and social life. The words of Macrobius—*vetustas quidem nobis semper*, *si sapimus*, *adoranda est*—are late, but a true motto of the Roman spirit at any period.[4]

For Lucretius to imitate Ennius, for Virgil to imitate both, was not merely the sincerest flattery; it was a claim to be in the succession—to wear the "crown of unfading leaf that Ennius first brought down from Helicon." It is with these words that Lucretius ranges himself in the line of poets, fitly using, here, as so often, the archaic words of Ennius—*poemata nostra clara cluebunt.*

No doubt Lucretius had special reason for his archaism, besides his link with Ennius. A true Epicurean, he held aloof from party dissensions, and only in a single passage betrayed a consciousness that his country was about to plunge into civil war. Otherwise, for all his humanity, he seems strangely detached from present fact. As a scholar

[1] Quint. 1, 6, 41. [2] *Ep.* 2, 2, 115; *A.P.* 70.

[3] See generally F. Ruckdeschel, *Archaismen u. Vulgarismen in der Sprache. des Horaz* (1911).

[4] *Sat.* 3, 14, 2.

and poet, he lives in the company of Empedocles and Euripides; as a Roman, he harks back to the great days of the good Ancus and the Scipios, two thunderbolts of war; as a philosopher, he advises his friends—according to the Epicurean ideal of "living unseen"—to avoid the struggle and ambition of politics. No wonder that, with such associations, Lucretius spoke a language as strange to the Forum as his own character was strange to the times. How far he reverted to the past can best be seen by comparing his poem with the slightly earlier verse of Cicero, who—though himself a warm admirer of Ennius—is far more modern in style. Some account must be taken of the difference in subject—Cicero was writing of recent history, to which archaisms were not appropriate—but, in any case, an orator, living in the full glare of public life, and only an amateur in poetry, could not use language like the quietistic Epicurean.

To turn from Lucretius to Virgil is to pass from Spenser to Shakespeare. In both pairs we are aware of a change of vocabulary, for which the difference of a decade or two can offer no explanation. Ben Jonson could not fairly have complained of Lucretius, as he complained of Spenser, that he "writ no language," but Lucretius certainly did not write the language of his own day. Virgil, like Shakespeare, borrows freely from the past, but the borrowed material is fused with current speech. He speaks to the Augustans in their own tongue, though he often reminds them that it was spoken by Ancus as well as by Augustus. The conscious, emphatic, deliberate archaism of Lucretius is replaced by delicate suggestion and subtle reminiscence.

Here, again, the springs of archaism are complex; but, without pretence of "fathoming a poet's mind," we may at least guess at certain lines of thought which seem to have influenced the Virgilian style. For the *Georgics*, at least, there is no difficulty in understanding the part played by archaism, though this is always restrained and occasional, rather than a marked or constant feature. Here the poet himself confesses his aim—*angustis hunc addere rebus honorem*[1]—and part of this honour could be given to a humble theme by the dignity of ancient words.[2]

In the *Aeneid*, the theme was not humble, but for that very reason the call of antiquity was far stronger. Both subject (ancient Italy) and style (the Epic tradition) suggested the words of Cato and Cethegus. Virgil's debt to Ennius is too well known to need more than a passing reference—a debt sometimes open and confessed, as in the old rhythms or formulae, like *divom pater atque hominum rex*, *Iupiter hac stat*, *restituit rem*, in which the younger poet carries on the succession. Much more often, however, the debt is repaid with interest, the archaic roughness being smoothed and adapted to Virgil's own cadence, as when the line

est locus, Hesperiam quem mortales perhibebant

is transformed into the Virgilian

est locus, Hesperiam Grai cognomine dicunt.[3]

Virgil, in fact, very rarely uses the old-fashioned diction that we might think appropriate to his epic subject. Neither Spenserian nor Romantic, he never cares to date his language. Hence, though he affects certain forms which have the ring of Ennius—*olle*, *ausim*, *faxo*, *fuat*, *iusso*, and others—his archaism is far less noticeable than that of Lucretius. He is sparing, for instance, in the use of the old genitive (*-ai*) and infinitive (*-ier*) which occur so often in the *De Rerum Natura*.

His language is thus the resultant of two opposite forces. The lure of Antiquity was counteracted by the belief in Progress. The fact deserves emphasis, for at the present day we are too apt to view the "classics" as representing a

[1] *Georg*. 3, 290.
[2] See Quint. 8, 3; cf. 1, 7, 18, *Vergilius amantissimus vetustatis*.
[3] Macrob. *Sat*. 6, 1 f.

static rather than a progressive ideal; and consequently we have no sympathy with the medieval conception of Virgil as a prophet. We think of him either as harking back to the past or as glorying in the present, not as a believer in future progress. It is true that all ancient conceptions of development or evolution were bounded by the Cyclic theory. No school of thought anticipated the modern notion of an increasing purpose, in the sense of a continuous movement towards some goal of greater perfection in material or moral well-being. The universal process was limited to fixed symmetrical periods, and at the completion of each period the wheel starts on a new revolution. None the less, it makes all the difference whether, at a given time, the circumference of the wheel is moving upward or downward. Lucretius had no doubt that the earth was aged and effete—she who had once borne the largest monsters could now scarcely bear the smallest insect—and the time of her dissolution into the original atoms must be drawing nigh. His creed has been called pessimistic, which is not strictly true, since it claimed to provide for a happy life, attainable at small cost by all who followed Epicurus; but hedonism, however temperate, cannot always satisfy its votaries, and the Atomic preacher had his darker moments. It is not without significance that one such moment should have occurred to Lucretius at the end of his Second Book, when his scientific doctrines are remorselessly pushed to their logical and inevitable conclusion:

> Further, the fruitful vine, the shining corn
> In the beginning sprang from mother earth
> Herself; spontaneously she brought to birth
> Sweet fruit and joyful crops, that now are born
> Stunted and feeble, though we strive and strain
> With sweat of panting oxen, with tired swain,
> With plough that ill persuades the barren soil
> To yield our husbandry a meagre gain.
> For now the farmer, spent in years of toil,

Shakes his grey head, comparing mournfully
Present and past—how blest his father's lot
Then, when a man served God in piety,
And lived far happier in a humble plot.
So, too, the dresser of the old, worn vine
Blames hurrying Time, and wearies Heaven, nor thinks
How step by step the world ages, and sinks
Down to the tomb, whereunto all decline.[1]

If, to Lucretius, the whole world was hastening to a general destruction, the ruin of his own microcosm, the Roman republic, was even more imminent; for the political troubles of the poet's lifetime were obviously tending to the final crash. Philosophy apart, Lucretius, like his aged farmer, had good reason to praise the past.

In 40 B.C. (when Virgil wrote the fourth *Eclogue*) there was still room enough for disquiet. The battle of Philippi (42 B.C.) was followed by the expropriation of lands to satisfy the discharged armies of the triumvirate, and Virgil was himself a sufferer. The decade between Philippi and Actium seemed to give little prospect of a Golden Age. Yet there was at least a temporary peace and promise of better things, so that a young poet could look to the future with hope. Virgil was just thirty—old enough to remember the horrors of civil war, young enough to welcome a new dispensation, guided by Octavian, who had now become, in effect, though not in theory, the autocrat of Rome. If it be true that the strongest and most binding of all emotions is felt, "when the poet's consciousness of this world is tinged with man's universal longing for a world more perfect,[2] there was ample reason for Virgil to be profoundly moved. Horace —still in his Epicurean stage—was touched by the new spirit, but could only hope for regeneration in a distant land;[3]

[1] 2, 1157 (Giussani's text).
[2] Sir H. Newbolt, *New Study*, p. 243. [3] *Epod.* 16.

Virgil, more optimistic, was the prophet of a new Italy.[1] In part, the prophecy miscarried—the Child (whether Julia or Gallus or another) decidedly failed as a Saviour, and the Roman Empire itself was a dubious return to the Golden Age—but we are here concerned with Virgil's belief, and not with the course of history after him. The fourth Eclogue is "common form" in general conception, and—if it may possibly owe something, at third or fourth hand, to Isaiah—it certainly lacks the supreme inspiration of the Hebrew prophecy.[2] But, though a poet of the first century could not have believed in the actual return of the Golden Age—even divested of grape-bearing brambles and scarlet sheep—Virgil really believed, and not without reason, that the wheel had come full circle. The world's great age had truly begun anew:—the arts of peace were now to flourish, and, not least, the art of poetry.

The Augustan Muse was to be worthy of her time:

si canimus silvas, silvae sint consule dignae.

If her feet rested on the sure foundations of the Roman past, her head must be lifted to the Julian star. A new vision demanded a new mode of expression, as well as reverence for the old. Virgil's archaism shews the reverence, but his normal diction belongs to his own age, of which the keynote was Refinement. The famous boast of Augustus that he found a Rome of brick and left it marble, was applied in metaphor by Johnson to Dryden. It would have been more appropriate to Virgil and his circle. Their business was to purge the language of all rough and "horrid" elements, to eliminate the last traces of the rude Saturnian

[1] R. S. Conway (*New Studies*, p. 34) agrees with Mackail (*Lat. Lit.* p. 95) that the scene of the fourth Eclogue is an idealized Italy.

[2] See generally *Virgil's Messianic Eclogue* by J. B. Mayor, W. Warde Fowler, and R. S. Conway, 1907, and T. F. Royds, *Virgil or Isaiah?* also Conway, *New Studies*, p. 33; Frank, *Vergil*, p. 134.

style, to polish and select words that were intended for the ears of Augustus himself.

In substance, therefore, the poets of the *Aeneid* and the *Odes* were restricted to a medium of expression in which quality counted for more than quantity. As we have seen, most of the attempts to widen the language had been found wanting. The Augustan canon was established. From the nature of the case, the vocabulary could not be copious—the words used by Shakespeare far outnumber those of Virgil and Horace together—but every word has passed a rigid scrutiny. And, if this test eliminates the exuberance of Shakespeare, it admits a horizon broad enough to range from Olympus to Hades, from the court of Dido to the farmyard and the plough.

To praise the language of the *Aeneid* is superfluous, since even Virgil's detractors, ancient or modern, have agreed in allowing its perfection. But here lay the danger. The very excellence of Augustan diction was one of the chief hindrances to any future development. After and because of Virgil, poetic language became fixed, and therefore crystallized. Hitherto, as we have seen, poetry had used at least a selection of the words current in educated speech; henceforward, it could no longer keep pace with the changes in the spoken language. Turning from Virgil to Livy, we feel that the verbal expression of verse and prose is essentially the same; whereas, if we compare Petronius with Lucan, or (later) Apuleius and Ammianus with Claudian, we find that poetry has been forced to neglect the evolution of spoken Latin. Horace had made some allowance for elasticity, but his successors failed to observe that a language which ceases to be fluid ceases to be vital;[1] and so they preferred to stop at the point reached by Horace himself, rather than to follow his advice by keeping in touch with the usage of their own day.

[1] V. Hugo, pref. to *Cromwell:* une langue ne se fixe pas . . . le jour où elles se fixent, c'est qu'elles meurent.

Unable to broaden the base of poetic expression, the post-Augustans were driven to contract it. They saw that the heritage of the Augustans was pure gold, but it might still be possible to gild the gold. Hence they carried the principle of selection to an absurd extreme, putting on their expurgatorial index words which had splendour enough for Virgil and Horace. Both of these had naturally used the noble word for a noble thing—*navis;* but, in the next century, the "ship" is superseded by its "poetic" equivalent—*ratis*, *carina*, *puppis*. Lucan's long description of a sea-fight is in many ways abominable stuff, but not least, perhaps, in respect of his misplaced exclusiveness. Here he outdoes even Dryden; for although the author of the *Annus Mirabilis* abjured, in theory, all technical words, he was blamed by Johnson (who did not like "okum" or "calking-iron") for inconsistency: "in the battle his terms seemed to have blown away; but he deals liberally with them in the dock."[1] Lucan does not follow the fleets to the dock, but his terms in the sea-fight have been so thoroughly blown away, that he excludes *navis* altogether, though its synonyms occur in over fifty places.[2] An eighteenth-century poet, with his bark on the billowy main, might have envied this record. It is true that Lucan and Statius do not often yield to the temptation of the synonym. For both, the old sense of the natural word survives. Indeed, when concerned with war or camp-life, Lucan flies to the other extreme, and becomes pedestrian. But, whether prosaic or poetic, the language of post-Augustan verse was atrophied. The nemesis of Virgil's unrivalled beauty lay in the disastrous fact that a poet like Statius, thinking to follow his master at a distance, was really treading on his

[1] *Life of Dryden*, 256.

[2] Lucan 3, 509-762. The point seems to have been missed by commentators. Statius (*Silv.* 3, 2) is another example, and the ban is carried on by Valerius Flaccus in the *Argonautica*.

heels. No less than the minor followers of Dryden and Pope, the post-Augustans brought a vehicle of expression, perfect for its own time, into a contempt which has reacted on the fame of those who used the vehicle with moderation and propriety.

CHAPTER VII

THE ORNAMENTS OF LATIN VERSE

POETRY, on its purely formal side, has often been defined as the art of making a pattern or design in words.[1] The metaphor must not be pressed, since the design of a carpet or wallpaper is regular throughout, whereas poetry admits—and, indeed, requires—some deviation from the type, to avoid monotony: the whole art of the verse-maker is to give variety within the limits imposed by the metre—to digress from the fixed rhythm so far, and only so far, that no other rhythm may be suggested by the variations. Bearing this difference in mind, we may accept the metaphor as a useful analogy, and may even develop it, by regarding the metre as the plan or design itself, and the words as threads, of varying colours, which are the material of the tracery. So far, we have been concerned only, or mainly, with the threads in bulk; it remains to examine the pattern in which they are arranged; or—to drop the metaphor—we have to view them, not as a mere vocabulary, but as composed, blended, and interwoven. Here, after all, is the real beginning of poetic art. The *Gradus* is not a poem. It might seem superfluous to mention this elementary truth; but, as a fact, both the practice and criticism of poetry have often suffered from the assumption that the Word is an end in itself. The eighteenth century was, no doubt, the greatest sinner; but in every generation (not least, in our own) there are words on which the minor poet

[1] See J. W. Mackail, *Lectures on Poetry*, p. 12.

seems to fasten, as if they were invested with some peculiar magic or virtue. Even great poets have been dazzled by this *aura* surrounding "beautiful words", as when Keats, in the loveliest of his lines, was reminded of a tolling bell by the word *forlorn;* and *perilous*, which he used in the same passage with such effect, has certainly become a danger to his followers. But, though Keats could load every rift with poetic ore, he knew that these words were counters for his imagination to marshal. The Greek critics, in laying stress on Arrangement, used the term in its widest sense, including not only logical synthesis but euphony. But the necessity of clearness—the *lucidus ordo* of Horace—was often taken for granted, and a critic like Dionysius lays perhaps more stress on euphony as the essential of composition.[1] That the Romans, too, with their love for intellectual poetry, were above all things concerned with lucid order, is so evident as to need no proof;[2] but, like the Greeks, they paid as much attention to the euphonic order. Although there are various ways of producing beauty by verbal juxtaposition, no method, perhaps, has been so widely used in European poetry as the devices of assonance and alliteration. Poetic melody is indeed attainable without the conscious use of either; but, in a greater or less degree, they are natural to poetry as forms of its repeated pattern.

In itself, Repetition is not especially poetic, since it is rooted in an association of ideas which is instinctive to the human mind. Just as one train of thought "suggests" another, so one word calls up another, by the likeness of sound as often as of sense. Indeed, the mind often seems to hanker after more repeated sound than the poet thinks it fit to supply. How, otherwise, can we account for the fact that Milton's "fresh woods" are so freely misquoted? The poet wanted no feeble synonym for pastures, but the alli-

[1] See Roberts on Dionys. *de comp. verb.* p. 27.

[2] The importance of this order in Horace is the keynote of Prof. Naylor's edition.

teration of "fresh fields" is too strong for the inaccurate to resist. Still, Repetition—in some form or other—is the basic expression of poetry, since all rhythm, whether of dance or song, is repetitive; and, although the sense of rhythm may be satisfied by metre alone, the employment of assonance and alliteration is at least a powerful help to the rhythm. Sometimes alliteration has been organic and structural, inseparably linked with the metre, as in English down to the time of Langland. At other times, the expectation which metre holds out has been gratified by rhyme, a development of assonance;[1] and rhyme may supersede alliteration, as in French poetry, which generally avoids any marked alliterative effect. There, rhyme seems to be a necessity, in order to mark an emphatic syllable at the end of a line consisting of syllables duly counted and pronounced with even stress; but the absence of a stress-accent makes a distinct alliteration far less tolerable than in English, with its strongly accented syllables. Besides this, the effect of French verse depends on more delicate sound-values, whereas English taste admits broader and more striking harmonies. In English itself, alliteration—after losing its structural function—was reintroduced as a luxury, which could be observed or neglected according to the changing fashion of different periods or the taste of individual poets. But English has nearly always found the artifice "apt", if not absolutely necessary; for, as Johnson noted, the language is "overstocked with consonants", and needs, far more than French, the euphony of liquids and nasals to smooth the harshness of its rougher sounds.[2]

Greek poetry had no need of alliteration. A quantitative metre is sufficiently marked without further aid—the progress of the line is clear from beginning to end, and

[1] On the function of rhyme see Th. Watts-Dunton, *Poetry and the Renascence of Wonder*, p. 61 f.; B. de Selincourt in *Essays and Studies* (English Assoc.), vii. p. 7 f.

[2] Johnson, *Life of Collins*, 17; *Rambler*, 88.

the syllables of each foot, being recognized as long or short, do not require alliteration to emphasize the stress. The rare instances of obvious alliteration seem to spring from a desire to express some particular effect, such as labour or anger or contempt.[1] On the other hand, the Greek had less reason to seek for assonance, because the wonderful range of their vowel-sounds provided it without search. The "roll", for which the Homeric hexameter is famous, seems due, not only to the majestic swing of the metre itself, but also to the vowels, whether they are arranged in harmonious contrast, or in assonance, as *ἀθάνατοι θεοὶ ἄλλοι*—an effect which we shall see was carefully avoided by Latin poets later than Catullus.

In both these forms of repetition, Latin poetry went its own way; imitation was confined to the metre—and even this was freely handled to suit the language—while, for verbal melody, the Romans depended on their own ears. If they had imitated, not only the spirit, but the "letter" of Greek, we should have missed many of the most characteristic—and musical—lines of Lucretius and Virgil. Their harmonies are so alien to the Greek that we must look elsewhere for their origin, and there can be no doubt that this was an Italian legacy.[2] Although the remains of Saturnian verse are so scanty, both alliteration and assonance can be traced as a feature of early Latin poetry. One, at least, of the Scipionic epitaphs is alliterative;[3] and an ancient "charm,"

terra pestem teneto
salus hic maneto,

suggests that Italian poetry, if left to develop by itself, might have anticipated the rhyming monkish verse. It is

[1] Good examples are Aesch. *Suppl.* 1006; Soph. *O.C.* 371; Eur. *Med.* 502 f. See Norden, *Kunstprosa*, p. 59 f.

[2] See E. Norden on *Aen.* 6, p. 405 f.

[3] Buechler, *Carm. Ep.* 9, beginning

magna sapientia multasque virtutes.

quite probable that Virgil was thinking of this or similar ritual lines in his incantation,

limus ut hic durescit, et haec ut cera liquescit.[1]

Such jingles are conspicuous in the early Graeco-Roman period. Ennius (who is fond of verbal plays like *urbe orba sum*) uses assonance in a passage of high pathos:

haec omnia vidi inflammari;
Priamo vi vitam evitari,
Iovis aram sanguine turpari

—lines, it may be noted, which called forth Cicero's admiring exclamation, *o poetam egregium.*[2] In Cicero's own age, the Roman knight Laberius could play (like John of Gaunt) on his own misfortune, in a line of passionate satire:

viri excellentis mente clemente edita;

and Ovid makes the deserted Ariadne reproach Theseus with the conceit:

verbera cum verbis mixta fuere meis.[3]

Assonance, as a regular feature of style, can only be prominent in verse which is founded on parallelism; for, as Norden has pointed out,[4] parallel lines are naturally emphasized by endings of similar sound, as in the three lines from Ennius, which have just been quoted. But there is little or no formal parallelism in classical verse, so that assonance is irregular and sporadic rather than systematic.[5] The nearest approach to its formal use is in the pentameter, whose parallel halves are so often marked by the rhyme of adjective and substantive. Lines like the first pentameter in Tibullus

et teneat culti iugera multa soli

(where the order in the first half is not determined by the metre) prove that here, at least, parallelism is not avoided.

[1] *Ecl.* 8, 80.
[2] *Tusc.* 3, 44. Such plays are frequent in the poems of Adam of St Victor.
[3] *Heroid.* 10, 38.
[4] Norden, *Kunstprosa*, p. 820 f.
[5] See below p. 261.

It was here, in a sense, the Roman equivalent for rhyme, which, whether we regard it as "satisfying expectation," or as linking a verse-system, has a real function.

Apart from this functional use, assonance always retained a kind of fascination for the Roman ear. Dr. Verrall noted that Horace, the most careful of poets, was pleased with the sound of *quae caret ora cruore nostro.*[1] We might add a still more famous line from Virgil:

tendebantque manus ripae ulterioris amore,

where, indeed, the term "jingle" is quite unworthy to describe the wonderful music of this haunting cadence. Such effects, it is clear, were sought after, rather than disliked, and their use can hardly be condemned by those of us who have not yet discarded rhyme.

What has been said of Latin vowel-assonance applies, with even greater force, to the alliteration of consonants. The Greeks, as we have seen, did not care to "hunt the letter," and the different taste of the Romans may be curiously seen in the fact that Cicero, translating a Greek poem, instinctively uses a strong alliteration which is quite absent in the original. We may instance his version from *Theseus* of Euripides:

nam qui haec auditu a docto meminissem viro
futuras mecum commentabar miserias,
aut mortem acerbam aut exili maestam fugam
aut aliquam semper molem meditabar mihi.[2]

A comparison with the Greek will show that Cicero is here meeting a purely Latin want, just as Swinburne, imitating a Greek tragedy, colours his *Atalanta* with English alliteration.

This Latin practice is, indeed, so insistent that a recent attempt has been made to prove that Latin verse is *essentially* alliterative. Professor Evans thinks that he can reduce

[1] *Companion to Latin Stud.* p. 605.

[2] Cic. *Tusc.* 3, 14. For the choice of the letter (*m*) see below p. 264.

this alliteration (including assonance) to a rule, which he formulates as follows:

"Subject to certain indulgences, *every ictic syllable must rhyme with some other ictic syllable in its own line*, meaning that at least one effective letter (consonant or vowel) in every ictic syllable must rhyme with a like letter in some other ictic syllable."[1] As normal instances he gives *múnere dónat:* (n, n), *cóllocáta puéllulám:* (*c, c, l, l*), *última coéna tuó sít precor ílla viró:* (*lt, o, o, t, l, o*). It would take too long to mention the "indulgences" which are needed in order to supplement the normal rule, nor can justice be done to Mr. Evans' far-reaching theory in a brief reference. The weak point in the theory is that the number of vowels and consonants is very limited, and—as reviewers of the book have suggested—what appears to be conventional law may really be an arithmetical necessity. There is the further difficulty that many lines prove too much: Mr. Evans allows that the minimum rarely satisfied the ear of the Latin versifier, who often aimed at meretricious embellishment. But the number and nature of these embellishments seem hard to reduce to any rule, being left to individual taste. Therefore, even if we grant the existence of the minimum, Latin verse plainly exhibits far more variety in alliteration than in old English, where *Piers the Plowman* has very strict rules. As is well known, the practice of early Latin poets differed widely from that of the later; and it is with these individual differences that we are here concerned.

From an historical point of view, the results are interesting. The theory of survival from Old Italian is certainly supported by the excessive use of alliteration in Ennius, whose grotesque line on Titus Tatius is only too familiar. This extravagance, however, is not often visible, and many of his longer fragments give some very pleasing

[1] W. J. Evans, *Alliteratio Latina* (1921).

harmonies. It is not surprising that Lucretius, carrying on the poetic torch of Ennius, should have revelled in alliteration. Besides innumerable doublets (*mari magno*) and triplets (*verbera ventorum vitare*), he has even quartets (*magna modis multis miranda*), and more intricate combinations such as:

denique cur homines tantos natura parare,
non potuit pedibus qui pontum per vada possent
transire, et magnos manibus divellere montes,
multaque vivendo mortalia vincere saecla? [1]

Here, and often in Lucretius, the "aid" of alliteration can scarcely be called "artful," if art should be concealed. A painful editor may warn us to "observe the alliteration," but the warning is quite unnecessary—the effect is sharp, instantaneous, and obtrusive, like hammer-strokes on the ringing anvil. No later Roman poet—except on occasion—made so much parade of an artifice which is generally acknowledged to be the most effective if latent, or at all events not too openly flaunted. A poet may be highly artificial, but may wish his readers to be unconscious of his artifice, with only a vague feeling of pleasure which they cannot put into words—or letters. Still more often, perhaps, the poet himself may be unaware, or only half aware, of his own mechanism. If he were consciously mechanical, he would cease to be a poet. A great artist in words remarked that "few writers are probably conscious of the length to which they push their melody of letters"; and he illustrated this remark by his own experience in discarding one monosyllable for another, without realizing, at the time, the reason for his preference. It was only by looking back on what he had already written that the mystery was solved; the second word contained an open A, and for nearly half a page he had been riding that vowel to the death.[2]

[1] I, 199 f.
[2] R. L. Stevenson, *Essays in the Art of Writing* (1905), p. 31.

This unconsciousness cannot be said to apply to Lucretius, who certainly parades his art. Nor, as we shall see, does it apply to many of his contemporaries and successors, who often follow the tradition with perfect lack of concealment. But, with Catullus, the problem becomes more complex. We can no longer feel confident that much of his alliteration was intended to be obvious. Sometimes it is there, but more or less concealed; sometimes the poet himself, like Stevenson, may have been unaware of his own preferences. To begin with, he is absolutely Lucretian in lines like:

dea magna, dea Cybelle, dea domina Dindymei,

or, in a longer passage:

sicine me patriis avectam, perfide, ab aris,
perfide, deserto liquisti in litore, Theseu?
sicine discedens neglecto numine divom
immemor, a, devota domum periuria portas?[1]

On the other hand, there is a marked difference of style in some of his finest work. Alliteration is inconspicuous or entirely wanting in the two poems on the Sparrow, or the first of his love-songs to Lesbia, or the poem on Spring (2, 3, 5, 46). All the four contain assonances—*deliciae meae puellae; nox est perpetua una dormienda; diversae variae viae*—and this may well be a substitute and compensation; but the absence of repeated consonants (except in the last quotation) brings this class of poem nearer to the Greek than to the Italian method. That Catullus should have gone to both extremes, in the use or avoidance of alliteration, is not wonderful; as a neoteric, he followed Greek fashion, but he was himself an Italian, with a native tradition which even the "newest" poet could not wholly ignore.

Between those two extremes, there should in theory be a mean. It is unlikely that a poet, such as Catullus—markedly alliterative in a large part of his work, and as markedly

[1] 64, 132; cf. 68B, where the repetition of *p* (17-20), of *c* (91-100), and *d* (103-106) is very insistent.

abstaining from the device in other parts—should not sometimes compromise. We expect to find a modern alliteration, more or less concealed, whether intentionally or not; and, as a fact, there are certain poems in which this *via media* can be traced. In none of them is the alliteration obtrusive or Lucretian; but it exists, and—which is more interesting—it has, I believe, a distinct significance in each poem.

There are at least four pieces in the collection of Catullus (30, 31, 45, 101) which are all so characteristic of his genius at its highest that no one of them could well be omitted from any Latin anthology. These poems are all short, and in each a single letter seems to give the dominant note. One (No. 45) differs from the other three in stressing an initial vowel instead of a consonant, so that the repetition is more likely to escape notice or to be thought purely accidental. The note is struck in the first word and sustained in the opening lines of the beautiful hendecasyllables:

Acmen Septimius suos amores
tenens in gremio, "mea", inquit, "Acme,
ni te perdite amo atque amare porro
omnes sum assidue paratus annos . . ."

It is continued in 8-9, 15-18, and swells to a triumphant climax in 20:

mutuis animis amant, amantur.

Catullus, like Stevenson, has "run the sound to death", but it is surely a noble death.

Is this reiteration a mere accident, due to the fact that the lady's name and the verb "to love" happen to begin with the same letter? "Coincidence" would be a simple—and ample—explanation, if the poem stood alone. But it does not. In No. 30, of which the first line is

Alfene, immemor atque unanimis false sodalibus,

the letter *f* is prominent in almost every one of the twelve verses. In the poem on Sirmio (31) the letter *l* is obviously haunting the poet's mind. Finally, there is the pathetic farewell to his dead brother (101), the alliteration of which may be adequately shown by an English rendering:

Through many a land I came, o'er many a wave,
  My brother, to thy grave,
That I might give the parting gift, and speak
  Mere words, and vainly seek
Answer from thy mute dust; for *thou* art gone,
  And *me* Fate leaves alone.
Yet, take the mournful rites our fathers paid,
  Last offerings, duly made,
Wet with the tears that of my misery tell:
And hail, for ever more, hail and farewell!

In the original, *m* runs through the whole threnody, with *f* as a subordinate attendant.

No careful reader will be likely to deny this predominance of a single letter, giving a kind of unity to each of these short poems. But was the choice of the letter immaterial and fortuitous, or did Catullus, consciously or unconsciously, search for a special letter to express a particular emotion? A reader mainly familiar with modern poetry might assume that no letter was particularly appropriate to the mood in which Catullus wrote these poems. Such a reader knows, of course, that certain letters fitly express certain emotions—that, when Tennyson, for example, wrote the lines, so often quoted in this connexion,

The moan of doves in immemorial elms
And murmur of innumerable bees,

these consonants and vowels are "onomatopoetic." But a vast number of alliterations—notably in Swinburne—seem to resist all such analysis. They appear to be quite without significance, except for their purely musical value. Is it not possible—it may be asked—that Catullus was solely guided by the music, and that the key-letter in each of these poems has no special bearing on the content of that poem?

I do not think that the letter was fortuitous. On the contrary, in all these poems, the poet's mood or subject seems to demand the key-letter, and no other. *Acme* and *amor*—the two suggest each other, and a poem in the key of A results; *Alfene*, *false*—the whole theme in F is the contrast between fact and falsehood; Sirmio, on the lovely lake—the L, as Plato knew, was itself "liquid," and the pleasure of the laughing waves, of

Lake water lapping with low sounds by the shore,

leads on to the pleasure of the poet's lakeland home (*libenter*, *laetus*, *lar*) in contrast with the labour of foreign travel. Finally, the recurrent M in the elegy is due to the twin ideas of *miseria* and *mors*, which attract so many kindred words to be a μίμημα or "mimicry" of overmastering sorrow.

We need not suppose that Catullus deliberately sat down to compose a poem "in the key" of A or F, though I do not see why it should be ridiculous for a poet to treat the letter as a musician treats its (partial) analogy, the note. But I feel convinced that he was aiming at a definite effect—in other words, that the letter was deliberately chosen. If this explanation seems far-fetched and superfluous, it must be remembered that the relation of word and thing was far closer to the ancients than it seems to ourselves. Plato had analysed the letters on the theory that they were imitative, and the Stoics had developed this theory, holding that a word expressed the sound which the notion conveyed to the mind—*voluptas* was "smooth," *crux*, harsh, because sound must agree with meaning.[1] In particular, the initial letter of a word was significant: thus *v* (in spite of *voluptas*) was "violent"—an idea probably suggested by *vis* and its real or supposed cognates. Since the time when Lucilius spoke of the life-force

—vis est vita, vides: vis nos facere omnia cogit—

[1] See [Augustine] *Principia dialecticae*, Migne, 32, 1409; Origen, *c. Cels.* 1, p. 18; F. Muller, *de vet. imprimis Romanorum stud. etym.*, p. 54.

scores of passages in Lucretius and Virgil express the idea of power, virility, or vitality by this alliteration. So *m* was a "moaning" letter,[1] as many poets ancient and modern have realized. Even if Swinburne's alliteration—as suggested above—is largely "musical," he must have felt that the letter was significant in the lines

> Seeing these mine own slain by mine own, and me
> Made miserable above all miseries made.

Lucretius, like Cicero, needed this letter to express the pathos of sorrow and death; and his wonderful description of Iphigenia's sacrifice is densely packed with *maesta*, *muta metu*, *mactatu*—all summed up in the burning climax of *malorum*.

That Catullus, too, felt this significance of *m* is clear from another poem (38) which may be placed side by side with the lament for his brother. It is very short (only eight lines), but the letter of the key-word (*male*) is repeated no less than seven times, until it dies away, with a sob, in the *maestius* of the concluding line:

> More and more, each day and hour, dejection,
> Cornificius, falls on your Catullus:
> —Heaven knows—a melancholy burden!
> Speech is easy, no great thing to give me;
> But what word of comfort have you uttered?
> This the meed of friendship? I am angered.
> Send some message—as mournful as the the saddest
> Simonidean tears of consolation![2]

It is hardly necessary to add that no letter was wholly or even mainly associated with a single motion. If *m*—to take the last example—is often used for sorrow or death, that

[1] Quint. 12, 10, 31, *quasi mugiente litera*.

[2] The versions of Catullus were written before the appearance of Mr. W. J. Evans' *Alliteratio Latina*, in which he lays stress on observing the Latin alliteration in an English rendering (p. xxix).

letter is equally common, in Latin as in English, to suggest murmuring or magnitude, the two ideas being combined in the *murmura magna minarum* of Lucretius, or the *magno cum murmure montis* of Virgil. It may even stand for the most opposite notions, as when Ennius can put a wealth of softness and affection into the tender line

mater optuma, tu multo mulier melior mulierum;

while, in the same passage, he can express, in *mari magno* the vastness and majesty of the sea. And there are, of course, countless examples, in Latin as in English, of alliteration as purely melodious, an appeal to the ear rather than to the intellect. The letter *p* may be contemptuous, since the lip-sound is a "natural" expression of disgust; but when Holofernes affected the letter, his playful princess only "argued facility."

Nevertheless, there seems good reason to hold that the Romans were far more impressed with the natural associations of particular letters than the moderns. Since Catullus is acknowledged to be, above all things, an artist, we cannot, I think, refuse him an artistry in the letter as well as the word; and, when we find a single sound predominating in a short poem, we may feel sure that the poet was perfectly conscious of his own choice, though he may not have intended his reader to be equally conscious. When the poem is longer, or when more than one train of thought is involved, there may still be alliteration, but its psychology is different. The repetition of a single sound would be monotonous, and so the harmony becomes complex. To take only one instance from Catullus, the hymn to Diana (34) opens with an intricate alliteration of *d* and *p*, which have no "natural" significance, but have been obviously suggested by *Dianae* and *puellae et pueri*. This combination, running through the first two stanzas, is interwoven in the second stanza with a new motive in *m* followed by *s*, which latter is accentuated by the marked assonance of the striking lines

silvarumque virentium
saltuumque reconditorum
amniumque sonantum.

The fourth stanza returns to the sequence *dd pp d*, with the appearance of the softer labial (*Lucina*, *lumine*, *Luna*) already announced by *Latonia* in line 5; and the poem concludes on the strong note of the sibilant, which fills the last stanza with words of good omen and religious faith, *sancta* and *sospites*.

From Catullus it is natural to turn to Horace, who—in spite of a marked aloofness—had certainly studied his predecessor, and betrays his influence. The Horatian hymn (I, 21) clearly owes its general conception to the hymn of Catullus, and possibly its alliteration is part of the debt. But Horace does not seem to search for the curious, intricate harmonies which pleased Catullus, nor does he appear to lay much stress on the "natural" letter, though in this hymn he ends with a prayer, or rather an imprecation—

pestemque a populo et principe Caesare in
Persas atque Britannos—

where the sound is well suited to the sense. One or two of his shorter poems have a single letter predominant (e.g. *o fons Bandusiae*, where *f* is insistent), but his alliteration, in general, seems to be less significant, and certainly more restrained, than its use by Catullus.[1] Here, as elsewhere, it was the business of the Augustans to curb the freedom and prune the luxuriance of the neoterics; and both assonance and alliteration were severely disciplined before they were allowed their place in the Court poetry.

[1] Horace is fond of *p*; cf. 1, 4, 13; 2, 8, 6 f.; 2, 13, 25 f.; 2, 14, 25 f.; (with *c*); 3, 8, 25 (with *l*, *n*); so *d*, 4, 5, 12; 4, 6, 25 f.; t l, 3, 23 f. The *carmen saeculare* is remarkable for its alliteration; cf. especially 60-72 (*a*), with the concluding stanza (*d*).

Assonance—as we have just seen—still continued to retain its hold on poetic favour; witness the line of Virgil:

te veniente die te decedente canebat;

or of Tibullus:

et teneam moriens deficiente manu;

but it was fenced by rigorous limitations. Thus, all the Augustans rejected ὁμοιόπτωτα (ὁμοιοτέλευτα)—strong vowels in juxtaposition; and Servius, though so little concerned with the beauties of style, is always ready to note Virgil's care in this matter.[1] So the scheme of *deliciae meae puellae* had to go; such assonance must be avoided at all costs, whether by separation of the words or by alternative forms, as when Virgil preferred *cuium pecus* to *cuius* (even at the risk of doubtful Latinity) and *equi biiuges* to *biiugi*.

In the same way, the extravagance of the consonant was checked, and the majority of Augustan poets were either careless of its effect, or at least successfully concealed their art. Ovid, in the *Metamorphoses*, seems as anxious to avoid it as any eighteenth-century poet. Besides Horace, whom we have already glanced at, Virgil alone continued to observe the Italian tradition, sometimes with all its frank excess. He is Lucretian, if not Ennian, in

neu patriae validas in viscera vertite vires

and

se causam clamat crimenque caputque malorum

and

mitteret in magnum imperium, metuensque moneret.

But in general his alliteration is far more subtle and elusive. As in Milton, it is nearly always present, but rarely prominent. In its more accentuated form, it appears chiefly in scenic descriptions, such as that of the storm in the *Georgics*, or the Elysian fields and Jupiter's council, in

[1] Occasional ὁμοιόπτωτα have a special effect as in *Aen.* 2, 721; 4, 376. In 7, 812 (a careful passage) the assonance seems to be an archaism.

the *Aeneid.*[1] Like Spenser, Virgil knew that verbal music —except for special effects—must depend on the interweaving of sounds far more than on the iteration of a single note. His typical method may be illustrated by a modern application of the *sortes Vergilianae.* In a copy of the *Aeneid*, opened at random, the eye was caught by the paragraph :

nox erat, et placidum carpebant fessa soporem
corpora per terras, silvaeque et saeva quierant
aequora: cum medio volvuntur sidera lapsu,
cum tacet omnis ager, pecudes, pictaeque volucres,
quaeque lacus late liquidos, quaeque aspera dumis
rura tenent, somno positae sub nocte silenti
lenibant curas et corda oblita laborum.[2]

Here there happens to be " significant " alliteration in the *l* and *s* (of silent sleep) ; but the whole effect, with the interwoven *p*, *c*, *v*, is a harmony which is its own justification. As far as there is any special reason—beyond the music—it may be said that Virgil uses assonance and alliteration to give unity to the period or paragraph—just as Catullus had unified the short poem—either linking clause to clause, in a single paragraph,[3] or joining one paragraph to another by some form of musical repetition. Virgil thus employs alliteration as Dante regularly employs its cognate, rhyme, not as a mere ornament, but a structural device.[4]

In Post-Augustan verse, two influences kept alive the alliterative tradition. Manilius, in writing such lines as

perpetuo populi privato in limine praetor[5]

is evidently conscious of his enemy Lucretius ; but it was naturally Virgil who set the seal to the fashion. The

[1] *Georg.* 1, 325-330 ; *Aen.* 6, 637-644, 10 ; 96-103. [2] *Aen.* 4, 522.

[3] E.g. *Aen.* 5, 124-128 (a single period) ; *Georg.* 1, 326-330 (where two periods are linked by the letter *f*).

[4] On Virgil's assonance and alliteration see C. E. S. Headlam in *Class. Rev.* xxxv. Feb.-March (1920) and May-June (1921), p. 61.

[5] 4, 212 ; cf. 1, 913 ; 2, 67 f. 201-2 ; 4, 180-182, 273-6 ; 5, 223 f.

Flavians, in spite of deference to the greatest of their poets, were Ovidian rather than Virgilian in most matters of technique, and had little taste (or, perhaps, little ear) for subtle harmonies of the letter. But there was a distinct revival of the artifice in the fourth century, and here the agreement of Ausonius, Claudian, and Rutilius proves that there is no question of individual caprice, though the same motives may not have influenced the three poets in the same degree. Ausonius, a student of early Latin, may have wished to archaize; but, in the main, he was a close follower of Virgil, and the alliteration of the *Mosella* is plainly Virgilian.[1] In Claudian, again, the device is more rhetorical; and it has been suggested that the repetition of a letter serves as a link to connect the various parts of a metrical period. Thus, a remarkable passage of seven lines, in which *m* is conspicuous, leads up to a climax of "monstrosities":

omnia cesserunt eunucho consule monstra.[2]

Rutilius goes even further than the other two, so that Vessereau, his French editor, feels constrained to apologize for a habit so uncongenial to his countrymen, though he remarks that Rutilius has the countenance of Gallo-Roman poets down to the seventh century.[3] It is quite possible that both Ausonius and Rutilius were here following native taste; but, more probably, the growing habit of alliteration is the result of the widening chasm between popular speech and "classical" Latin, as well as the breakdown of the feeling for quantity. For quantitative metre was more and more ceasing to be recognised as rhythmical; in Latin, as in contemporary Greek, accent was becoming supreme. The same phenomenon that we see beginning in Nonnus

[1] Cf. e.g. *Mos.* 60 f.

[2] *Eutr.* 1, 1 f. I owe this explanation to an unpublished paper on Claudian by Mr. H. R. Carter.

[3] Vessereau, p. 379 f., who quotes Ranniger, *über die Allit. bei den Gallo-lat.*, Lindau, 1895.

and Musaeus appears in the stress-accent of Commodian, which is struggling with quantity. Rutilius may well have felt that some other harmony was wanted to supplement the failing lure of classical scansion; and he only foreshadowed, by a few centuries, the logical development of alliteration as the key of *Piers the Plowman.*

THE REFRAIN

It has been pointed out that, in assonance and alliteration, the classical poets are using one form of the natural rhythmic impulse which is the base of poetic expression. They used these devices, however, as mere occasional ornaments, since quantitative metre was sufficient to supply the need of rhythm. For the same reason, it was unnecessary for them to lay stress on other phases of Repetition which have often played a great part in moulding poetic form. Parallelism of Form and Sense (the essential feature of Hebrew verse) is of course quite foreign to Graeco-Roman tradition;[1] and the burden or refrain, which the Hebrews also employed with such splendid effect, was almost equally neglected. This neglect might be quoted as a proof—if proof were necessary—that the Greeks had moved very far from "primitive" poetry; for it may be held, with some probability, that the origin of the Refrain goes back to a very early—perhaps the earliest—use of poetry as part of sacred ritual, in which the song is a magic incantation, with repetitions corresponding to the recurring rhythm of the dance. At first, indeed, what afterwards became the refrain of a poem was the whole prayer.[2] Such prayers existed in Greece, sometimes never developed into poems, as in the Eleusinian incantation, ὕε κύε; sometimes forming the basis of a lyric, as in a hymn to Dionysus

[1] Parallelism of *form* may be traced, as a survival, in Greek folk poetry (see Norden, *Kunstprosa*, p. 822 f.); but, as stated above, it has left little trace in classical literature, while parallelism of *sense* (as in the Hebrew psalms) is still more alien to classical modes.

[2] See R. G. Moulton, *Modern Study of Literature*, p. 38.

with the refrain ἄξιε ταῦρε, "honoured Bull". Ritual repetition has left other traces in Greek literature, notably in the tragic chorus. Aeschylus seems as Hebraic as Hellenic in the splendid chorus of the *Agamemnon* with its repeated prayer

αἴλινον αἴλινον εἰπέ· τὸ δ' εὖ νικάτω.

But in tragedy the refrain had hardly passed beyond its original limit as an incantation; for the rest, choral verse was content with the metrical correspondence of strophe and antistrophe, without verbal responses. Outside the tragedy, we find a refrain in the song of Harmodius and Aristogeiton—ἐν μύρτου κλαδὶ τὸ ξίφος φορήσω—and it was a regular feature of the paean and the marriage-song in the incantation to Hymen. But these songs are of course religious, or semi-religious; in such Greek poetry as we may fairly call secular, the refrain established itself in one class alone, and this belonging to the latest period of great Hellenic literature. Theocritus made the bucolic refrain a mark of pastoral poetry which has always survived as a character of the style. The poet no doubt derived his idea from earlier and ruder songs of Greek shepherds; but there is no evidence that the secular songs of these shepherds employed the refrain. It is much more likely that the refrains which Theocritus heard were ritual, and it is as ritual that they occur in Theocritus himself. "Begin, dear Muses, begin the bucolic song," "My magic wheel, draw back my lover home"—these and other burdens are simply prayers—the "vain" repetitions which poetry has borrowed from religion.

But Greek poetry, although in one sense so instinct with religion, owes very little to religious forms. The lovely fragments of lyric, in particular, shew hardly any traces of the refrain. Yet it is in lyric that the value of a repeated line, or phrase, or idea, is most evident in modern poetry. A song must be the expression of a single mood or theme,

[1] *Ag.* 121 f.; cf. *Pers.* 657 f.

and the poem itself has often been suggested by a few words, or even a single word, giving the key-note of the whole composition. In Mme de Stael's words, *il faut un premier mot;* and we are reminded that Poe gave the credit for his best-known poem to the word *nevermore.* The phrase or word becomes a "*text*" to which the thought perpetually turns and returns. Its function is to unify the composition, and to prevent the details from obscuring the theme. Or, again, it may act as a chorus to explain the motive; or, in an impassioned lyric, it may relieve a strain which would be unbearable without the help of calm and simple words, whose mere repetition—apart from their sense—is soothing. If poetry is emotion recollected in tranquillity, we might well explain the burden as the special mark of the tranquillizing process. From the burdens of twelfth-century Provence, or the rondel of Charles d'Orleans—

> Le temps a laissié son manteau—

to Hugo's *Gastibelza*—

> Le vent qui vient à travers la montagne
> Me rendra fou,

or from Wyatt's *Forget not yet* and Carew's *Ask me no more* to the rebirth of this last phrase in Tennyson, the course of French and English poetry—to take no other languages—is marked by a long sequence of songs which owe their beauty and often their very being to the magic of the repeated word.[1]

It is in this respect that Greek lyric differs—at least technically—from the modern; and, as the Greeks employed the burden in prayer, the conjecture may be hazarded that one reason, at least, for its neglect in secular poetry lay in the fact that its suggestions were too ritualistic. If we turn

[1] Yet the burden does not belong to the origins of our own poetry. It was practically unknown to Old English, though an example is quoted, not earlier than the eleventh century, which may have been suggested by the Latin ecclesiastical chants. See Guest, *Hist. of Engl. Rhythms*, p. 604.

to the earliest Latin poetry, we find exactly the same phenomenon; although, no doubt, the later disuse of the burden was due to imitation of Greek practice rather than to any Roman theory as to its religious significance. This pre-Hellenic poetry must have been largely a matter of ritual, since there is good evidence that it was mainly connected with religion, and Roman religion was little more than a due observance of rite. One such song has been preserved—the well-known hymn of the Arval Brothers, with its threefold *enos*, *Lases*, *iuvate*, and other thrice-repeated lines. But, although this particular hymn survived, with meaning more than half-forgotten, the great mass of indigenous poetry, whether sacred or secular, was swept away by the flood of Hellenic literature, which was to prescribe, once for all, the scope and technique of the Latin lyric. Catullus could not here go beyond his Greek warrant. On the authority of the Greek hendecasyllabic *skolia*, he introduced the refrain, as the first and last lines of two or three poems in hendecasyllables, and his follower Martial used the same device, generally in the same metre.[1] But neither Catullus nor Horace employed it in pure lyric; for the hendecasyllable, though often lyrical in feeling, belongs to that border-line of metre which is as appropriate to satire and invective as to love or pathos. There remained the Marriage Song and the Bucolic, where Catullus and Virgil were safe; in all the other "kinds", repetition was eyed askance. It is true that Ovid more than once returns to an expressive line, in

tempora noctis eunt: excute poste seram

and

impia quid dubitas, Deianira, mori.[2]

In both instances, however, this repetition is at irregular intervals, and neither affects the pattern of the verse, nor is

[1] Cat. 16, 36, 57; Mart. 2, 6; 4, 64; 4, 89; 7, 26. In some other epigrams of Martial there is a slight variation, as in 2, 41.

[2] *Amor.* 1, 6; *Heroid.* 9.

the keynote of the poem. Ovid's artifice, in fact, is not poetical but merely rhetorical. In much the same way, he experiments, in one or two places, with another form of repetition, the first half of the hexameter becoming the second half of pentameter:

militat omnis amans, et habet sua castra Cupido;
Attice, crede mihi militat omnis amans [1]

This, again, is sheer rhetoric, with no bearing on poetic form; but it happened to suggest the development of a *genre*, which attained an ill-deserved vogue in later verse. By the time of Martial whole poems (*versus echoici*), constructed on this pattern, had become fashionable; and Martial himself wrote an epigram—he must have felt that one was enough—with the echo *rumpitur invidia.* The same misplaced ingenuity gave birth to *versus recurrentes* or *reciproci*, in which the first couplet was reversed, so as to form the next. Martial himself was too good an artist to waste time on these and similar eccentricities, which he only mentions with the scathing remark,

turpe est difficiles habere nugas,
et stultus labor est ineptiarum.[2]

But his warning was lost on Ausonius, who loved such *ineptiae* as centos and acrostics and "poems" with monosyllabic endings. In default of good literature, these crazes persisted till the time of Apollinaris Sidonius in the fifth century, and indeed through the middle ages. Their only interest is that they represent, not the true classical tradition, but a vain attempt to break away into some novelty of expression. An original age might have turned the refrain or echo to some poetic use; and at least one poet of the

[1] *Amor.* 1, 9, 1; so 3, 6, 61, *Ilia pone metus; Rem. Am.* 385, *Thais in arte mea; Heriod.* 5, 117, *Graia invenca venit.* The late poem *Epist. Didonis* (P.L.M. 4, 271) has repetitions in this Ovidian manner, but as a more regular refrain.

[2] 2, 86.

decadence came very near to the discovery. For the unknown author of the *Pervigilium Veneris*—who may have lived at any time between the Antonines and the fifth century—was divinely inspired in the splendid line,

cras amet, qui numquam amavit, quique amavit, cras amet,

which gives the keynote of that wonderful poem. According to Pater's fancy, the writer seems to have caught up the words of some mystic hymn, sung by a chorus in honour of Isis, as personifying the vital principle of spring. However, this may be, he certainly "sought"—and found—"the word" in a sense which no other classical poet had imagined. In itself this formulaic line is, of course, nothing new, being plainly suggested by the bucolic refrain. What *is* new, is the unity which it gives to the poem in a measure beyond the repeated line of the *Eclogues*. In these, the refrain is often well chosen, striking the right note, as in the *Pharmaceutria*—

ducite ab urbe domum, mea carmina, ducite Daphnin,

where the incantation really sums up the motive of the poem. Sometimes, however, the note is by no means so obvious. There is nothing inevitable or unifying in

incipe Maenalios mecum, mea tibia, versus.

So far from holding the threads together, this line simply cuts them. It has nothing whatever to do with the theme. But even when Virgil is here successful, it can hardly be contended that his refrain is essential to the poem, except perhaps in the *Pharmaceutria* and its famous original by Theocritus. But the burden of the *Pervigilium* is not merely the theme; it is the whole germ from which the rest of the poem has grown. Accustomed as we are to this artistic form, we may easily fail to recognize that we meet it here at the very moment of its birth in Western literature. Yet, as far as Latin poetry was concerned, it died at birth;

for the *Pervigilium*—whatever its precise date—was the child of a dying Rome. The poet himself, in his last lines, seems conscious that he is singing a swan-song not only for himself:

quando fiam uti chelidon, ut tacere desinam?

He feels the deepening shades of that Amyclaean silence which were soon to overwhelm the whole world of Roman poetry. But the refrain survived, to grow with full vigour and vitality in a new environment, strangely remote from the old, and yet strangely akin. For it reappears, in its oldest and most natural form, as the prayer. There is a long distance of time and thought between Aeschylus and Godescalcus, in the ninth century;[1] but in the noble hymn, of which every stanza begins with

o deus miseri
miserere servi

and ends with

heu, quid evenit mihi,

the double refrain seems to recall, in a new spirit and a new theology, the haunting cry of the chorus in the *Agamemnon.*

[1] *Mon. Germ. Hist.* (*poet. Lat.*), iii. p. 729. The burden is found of course much earlier in hymns, e.g. in the baptismal hymn attributed to Fortunatus (6th century).

INDEX